AMERICAN SLAVERY AS IT IS

Selections from the Testimony of a Thousand Witnesses

DOVER THRIFT EDITIONS

Edited by
Theodore Dwight Weld

DOVER PUBLICATIONS, INC.
MINEOLA, NEW YORK

DOVER THRIFT EDITIONS

GENERAL EDITOR: SUSAN L. RATTINER
EDITOR OF THIS VOLUME: TERRI ANN GEUS

Bibliographical Note

This Dover edition, first published in 2017, contains a selection of personal narratives from *American Slavery As It Is: Testimony of a Thousand Witnesses*, published by the American Anti-Slavery Society, New York, in 1839. The selections in this book are being reprinted exactly as they were previously published in an effort to preserve the consistency of the original documents and their historical context, which may include archaic terminology and spelling.

Library of Congress Cataloging-in-Publication Data

Names: Weld, Theodore Dwight, 1803–1895, compiler. | American Anti-Slavery
   Society, issuing body.
Title: American slavery as it is: selections from the testimony of a
   thousand witnesses / edited by Theodore Dwight Weld.
Description: Dover thrift editions. | Mineola, New York: Dover Publications,
   Inc., [2017] | "This Dover edition, first published in 2017, contains a
   selection of personal narratives from American Slavery As It Is: Testimony
   of a Thousand Witnesses, published by the American Anti-Slavery Society,
   New York, in 1839."
Identifiers: LCCN 2017016526 | ISBN 9780486819266 | ISBN 0486819264
Subjects: LCSH: Slaves—United States—Social conditions. | Slave
   narratives—United States.
Classification: LCC E449 .W4422 2017 | DDC 306.3/62092—dc23
LC record available at https://lccn.loc.gov/2017016526

Manufactured in the United States by LSC Communications
81926401   2017
www.doverpublications.com

Introduction

READER, YOU ARE empannelled as a juror to try a plain case and bring
in an honest verdict. The question at issue is not one of law, but of
fact—"What is the actual condition of the slaves in the United States?"
A plainer case never went to a jury. Look at it. TWENTY-SEVEN
HUNDRED THOUSAND PERSONS in this country, men, women, and
children, are in SLAVERY. Is slavery, as a condition for human beings,
good, bad, or indifferent? We submit the question without argument.
You have common sense, and conscience, and a human heart;—pro-
nounce upon it. You have a wife, or a husband, a child, a father, a
mother, a brother or a sister—make the case your own, make it
theirs, and bring in your verdict. The case of Human Rights against
Slavery has been adjudicated in the court of conscience times innumerable. The same verdict has always been rendered—"Guilty"; the
same sentence has always been pronounced, "Let it be accursed";
and human nature, with her million echoes, has rung it round the
world in every language under heaven, "Let it be accursed. Let it be
accursed." His heart is false to human nature, who will not say
"Amen." There is not a man on earth who does not believe that
slavery is a curse. Human beings may be inconsistent, but human
nature is true to herself. She has uttered her testimony against slavery
with a shriek ever since the monster was begotten; and till it perishes
amidst the execrations of the universe, she will traverse the world
on its track, dealing her bolts upon its head, and dashing against it
her condemning brand. We repeat it, every man knows that slavery
is a curse. Whoever denies this, his lips libel his heart. Try him; clank
the chains in his ears, and tell him they are for *him*. Give him an hour
to prepare his wife and children for a life of slavery. Bid him make
haste and get ready their necks for the yoke, and their wrists for the

coffle chains, then look at his pale lips and trembling knees, and you have *nature's* testimony against slavery.

Two million seven hundred thousand persons in these States are in this condition. They were made slaves and are held such by force, and by being put in fear, and this for no crime! Reader, what have you to say of such treatment? Is it right, just, benevolent? Suppose I should seize you, rob you of your liberty, drive you into the field, and make you work without pay as long as you live, would that be justice and kindness, or monstrous injustice and cruelty? Now, every body knows that the slaveholders do these things to the slaves every day, and yet it is stoutly affirmed that they treat them well and kindly, and that their tender regard for their slaves restrains the masters from inflicting cruelties upon them. We shall go into no metaphysics to show the absurdity of this pretence. The man who *robs* you every day, is, forsooth, quite too tenderhearted ever to cuff or kick you! True, he can snatch your money, but he does it gently lest he should hurt you. He can empty your pockets without qualms, but if your *stomach* is empty, it cuts him to the quick. He can make you work a life time without pay, but loves you too well to let you go hungry. He fleeces you of your *rights* with a relish, but is shocked if you work bareheaded in summer, or in winter without warm stockings. He can make you go without your *liberty,* but never without a shirt. He can crush, in you, all hope of bettering your condition, by vowing that you shall die his slave, but though he can coolly torture your feelings, he is too compassionate to lacerate your back—he can break your heart, but he is very tender of your skin. He can strip you of all protection and thus expose you to all outrages, but if you are exposed to the *weather,* half clad and half sheltered, how yearn his tender bowels! What! slaveholders talk of treating men well, and yet not only rob them of all they get, and as fast as they get it, but rob them of *themselves,* also; their very hands and feet, all their muscles, and limbs, and senses, their bodies and minds, their time and liberty and earnings, their free speech and rights of conscience, their right to acquire knowledge, and property, and reputation;—and yet they, who plunder them of all these, would fain make us believe that their soft hearts ooze out so lovingly toward their slaves that they always keep them well housed and well clad, never push them too hard in the field, never make their dear backs smart, nor let their dear stomachs get empty.

But there is no end to these absurdities. Are slaveholders dunces, or do they take all the rest of the world to be, that they think to bandage our eyes with such thin gauzes? Protesting their kind regard for those whom they hourly plunder of all they have and all they get! What! when they have seized their victims, and annihilated all their *rights,* still claim to be the special guardians of their *happiness!* Plunderers of their liberty, yet the careful suppliers of their wants? Robbers of their earnings, yet watchful sentinels round their interests, and kind providers of their comforts? Filching all their time, yet granting generous donations for rest and sleep? Stealing the use of their muscles, yet thoughtful of their ease? Putting them under *drivers,* yet careful that they are not hard-pushed? Too humane forsooth to stint the stomachs of their slaves, yet force their *minds* to starve, and brandish over them pains and penalties, if they dare to reach forth for the smallest crumb of knowledge, even a letter of the alphabet!

It is no marvel that slaveholders are always talking of their *kind treatment* of their slaves. The only marvel is, that men of sense can be gulled by such professions. Despots always insist that they are merciful. The greatest tyrants that ever dripped with blood have assumed the titles of "most gracious," "most clement," "most merciful," &c., and have ordered their crouching vassals to accost them thus. When did not vice lay claim to those virtues which are the opposites of its habitual crimes? The guilty, according to their own showing, are always innocent, and cowards brave, and drunkards sober, and harlots chaste, and pickpockets honest to a fault. Every body understands this. When a man's tongue grows thick, and he begins to hiccough and walk cross-legged, we expect him, as a matter of course, to protest that he is not drunk; so when a man is always singing the praises of his own honesty, we instinctively watch his movements and look out for our pocket-books. Whoever is simple enough to be hoaxed by such professions, should never be trusted in the streets without somebody to take care of him. Human nature works out in slaveholders just as it does in other men, and in American slaveholders just as in English, French, Turkish, Algerine, Roman and Grecian. The Spartans boasted of their kindness to their slaves, while they whipped them to death by thousands at the altars of their gods. The Romans lauded their own mild treatment of their bondmen, while they branded their names on their flesh with hot irons, and when old, threw them into their fish ponds, or like Cato "the Just," starved them to death. It is the boast of the Turks that they treat their slaves as though they were their children, yet their common name for them is "dogs," and for the merest trifles, their feet are bastinadoed to a jelly, or their heads clipped off with the scimetar. The Portuguese pride themselves on their gentle bearing toward their slaves, yet the streets of Rio de Janeiro are filled with naked men and women yoked in pairs to carts and wagons, and whipped by drivers like beasts of burden.

Slaveholders, the world over, have sung the praises of their tender mercies towards their slaves. Even the wretches that plied the African slave trade, tried to rebut Clarkson's proofs of their cruelties, by speeches, affidavits, and published pamphlets, setting forth the accommodations of the "middle passage," and their kind attentions to the comfort of those whom they had stolen from their homes, and kept stowed away under hatches, during a voyage of four thousand miles. So, according to the testimony of the autocrat of the Russias, he exercises great clemency towards the Poles, though he exiles them by thousands to the snows of Siberia, and tramples them down by millions, at home. Who discredits the atrocities perpetrated by Ovando in Hispaniola, Pizarro in Peru, and Cortez in Mexico,— because they filled the ears of the Spanish Court with protestations of their benignant rule? While they were yoking the enslaved natives like beasts to the draught, working them to death by thousands in their mines, hunting them with bloodhounds, torturing them on racks, and broiling them on beds of coals, their representations to the mother country teemed with eulogies of their parental sway! The bloody atrocities of Philip II., in the expulsion of his Moorish subjects, are matters of imperishable history. Who disbelieves or doubts them? And yet his courtiers magnified his virtues and chanted his clemency and his mercy, while the wail of a million victims, smitten down by a tempest of fire and slaughter let loose at his bidding, rose above the *Te Deums* that thundered from all Spain's cathedrals. When Louis XIV. revoked the edict of Nantz, and proclaimed two millions of his subjects free plunder for persecution,— when from the English channel to the Pyrennees the mangled bodies of the Protestants were dragged on reeking hurdles by a shouting populace, he claimed to be "the father of his people," and wrote himself "His most *Christian* Majesty."

But we will not anticipate topics, the full discussion of which more naturally follows than precedes the inquiry into the actual condition and treatment of slaves in the United States.

As slaveholders and their apologists are volunteer witnesses in their own cause, and are flooding the world with testimony that their slaves are kindly treated; that they are well fed, well clothed, well housed, well lodged, moderately worked, and bountifully provided with all things needful for their comfort, we propose—first, to disprove their assertions by the testimony of a multitude of impartial witnesses, and then to put slaveholders themselves through a course of cross-questioning which shall draw their condemnation out of their own mouths. We will prove that the slaves in the United States are treated with barbarous inhumanity; that they are overworked, underfed, wretchedly clad and lodged, and have insufficient sleep; that they are often made to wear round their necks iron collars armed with prongs, to drag heavy chains and weights at their feet while working in the field, and to wear yokes, and bells, and iron horns; that they are often kept confined in the stocks day and night for weeks together, made to wear gags in their mouths for hours or days, have some of their front teeth torn out or broken off, that they may be easily detected when they run away; that they are frequently flogged with terrible severity, have red pepper rubbed into their lacerated flesh, and hot brine, spirits of turpentine, &c., poured over the gashes to increase the torture; that they are often stripped naked, their backs and limbs cut with knives, bruised and mangled by scores and hundreds of blows with the paddle, and terribly torn by the claws of cats, drawn over them by their tormentors; that they are often hunted with bloodhounds and shot down like beasts, or torn in pieces by dogs; that they are often suspended by the arms and whipped and beaten till they faint, and when revived by restoratives, beaten again till they faint, and sometimes till they die; that their ears are often cut off, their eyes knocked out, their bones broken, their flesh branded with red hot irons; that they are maimed, mutilated and burned to death over slow fires. All these things, and more, and worse, we shall *prove*. Reader, we know whereof we affirm, we have weighed it well; *more and worse* WE WILL PROVE. Mark these words, and read on; we will establish all these facts by the testimony of scores and hundreds of eye witnesses, by the testimony of *slaveholders* in all parts of the slave states, by slaveholding members of Congress and of state legislatures, by ambassadors to foreign courts, by judges, by doctors of divinity, and clergy men of all denominations, by merchants, mechanics, lawyers and physicians, by presidents and professors in colleges and *professional* seminaries, by planters, overseers and drivers. We shall show, not merely that such deeds are committed, but that they are frequent; not done in corners, but before the sun; not in one of the slave states, but in all of them; not perpetrated by brutal overseers and drivers merely, but by magistrates, by legislators, by professors of religion, by preachers of the gospel, by governors of states, by "gentlemen of property and standing," and by delicate females moving in the "highest circles of society." We know, full well, the outcry that will be made by multitudes, at these declarations; the multiform cavils, the flat denials, the charges of "exaggeration" and "falsehood" so often bandied, the sneers of affected contempt at the credulity that can believe such things, and the rage and imprecations against those who give them currency. We know, too, the threadbare sophistries by which slaveholders and their apologists seek to evade such testimony. If they admit that such deeds are committed, they tell us that they are exceedingly rare, and therefore furnish no grounds for judging of the general treatment of slaves; that occasionally a brutal wretch in the *free* states barbarously butchers his wife, but that no one thinks of inferring from that, the general treatment of wives at the North and West.

They tell us, also, that the slaveholders of the South are proverbially hospitable, kind, and generous, and it is incredible that they can perpetrate such enormities upon human beings; further, that it is absurd to suppose that they would thus injure their own property, that self-interest would prompt them to treat their slaves with kindness, as none but fools and madmen wantonly destroy their own property; further, that Northern visitors at the South come back testifying to the kind treatment of the slaves, and that the slaves themselves corroborate such representations. All these pleas, and scores of others, are bruited in every corner of the free States; and who that hath eyes to see, has not sickened at the blindness that saw not, at the palsy of heart that felt not, or at the cowardice and sycophancy that dared not expose such shallow fallacies. We are not to be turned from our purpose by such vapid babblings. In their appropriate places, we propose to consider these objections and various others, and to show their emptiness and folly.

The foregoing declarations touching the inflictions upon slaves, are not haphazard assertions, nor the exaggerations of fiction conjured up to carry a point; nor are they the rhapsodies of enthusiasm, nor crude conclusions, jumped at by hasty and imperfect investigation, nor the aimless outpourings either of sympathy or poetry; but they are proclamations of deliberate, well-weighed convictions, produced by accumulations of proof, by affirmations and affidavits, by written testimonies and statements of a cloud of witnesses who speak what they know and testify what they have seen, and all these impregnably fortified by proofs innumerable, in the relation of the slaveholder to his slave, the nature of arbitrary power, and the nature and history of man.

Of the witnesses whose testimony is embodied in the following pages, a majority are slaveholders, many of the remainder have been slaveholders, but now reside in free States.

Another class whose testimony will be given, consists of those who have furnished the results of their own observation during periods of residence and travel in the slave States.

We will first present the reader with a few PERSONAL NARRATIVES furnished by individuals, natives of slave states and others, embodying, in the main, the results of their own observation in the midst of slavery—facts and scenes of which they were eye-witnesses.

In the next place, to give the reader as clear and definite a view of the actual condition of slaves as possible, we propose to make specific points, to pass in review the various particulars in the slave's condition, simply presenting sufficient testimony under each head to settle the question in every candid mind. The examination will be conducted by stating distinct propositions, and in the following order of topics.

1. THE FOOD OF THE SLAVES, THE KINDS, QUALITY AND QUANTITY, ALSO, THE NUMBER AND TIME OF MEALS EACH DAY, &C.
2. THEIR HOURS OF LABOR AND REST.
3. THEIR CLOTHING.
4. THEIR DWELLINGS.
5. THEIR PRIVATIONS AND INFLICTIONS.
6. *In conclusion*, a variety of OBJECTIONS and ARGUMENTS will be considered which are used by the advocates of slavery to set aside the force of testimony, and to show that the slaves are kindly treated.

Between the larger divisions of the work, brief personal narratives will be inserted, containing a mass of facts and testimony, both general and specific.

PERSONAL NARRATIVES

MR. NEHEMIAH CAULKINS, of Waterford, New London Co., Connecticut, has furnished the Executive Committee of the American Anti-Slavery Society, with the following statements relative to the condition and treatment of slaves, in the south eastern part of North Carolina. Most of the facts related by Mr. Caulkins fell under his personal observation. The air of candor and honesty that pervades the narrative, the manner in which Mr. C. has drawn it up, the good sense, just views, conscience and heart which it exhibits, are sufficient of themselves to commend it to all who have ears to hear.

The Committee have no personal acquaintance with Mr. Caulkins, but they have ample testimonials from the most respectable sources; all of which represent him to be a man whose long established character for sterling integrity, sound moral principle and piety, have secured for him the uniform respect and confidence of those who know him.

Without further preface the following testimonials are submitted to the reader.

"This may certify, that we the subscribers have lived for a number of years past in the neighborhood with Mr. Nehemiah Caulkins, and have no hesitation in stating that we consider him a man of high respectability and that his character for truth and veracity is unimpeachable.

PETER COMSTOCK.	D. G. OTIS.
A. F. PERKINS, M.D.	PHILIP MORGAN.
ISAAC BEEBE.	JAMES ROGERS, M. D."
LODOWÍCK BEEBE.	

Waterford, Ct., Jan. 16th, 1839.

Mr. Comstock is a Justice of the Peace. Mr. L. Beebe is the Town Clerk of Waterford. Mr. I. Beebe is a member of the Baptist Church.

Mr. Otis is a member of the Congregational Church. Mr. Morgan is a Justice of the Peace, and Messrs. Perkins and Rogers are designated by their titles. All those gentlemen are citizens of Waterford, Connecticut.

"To whom it may concern. This may certify that Mr. Nehemiah Caulkins, of Waterford, in New London County, is a near neighbor to the subscriber, and has been for many years. I do consider him a man of *unquestionable veracity* and certify that he is so considered by people to whom he is personally known.   EDWARD R. WARREN."
Jan. 15*th*, 1839.

Mr. Warren is a Commissioner (Associate Judge) of the County Court, for New London County.

"This may certify that Mr. Nehemiah Caulkins, of the town of Waterford, County of New London, and State of Connecticut, is a member of the first Baptist Church in said Waterford, is in good standing, and is esteemed by us a man of truth and veracity.
                          FRANCIS DARROW, Pastor of said Church."
Waterford, Jan. 16*th*, 1839.

"This may certify that Nehemiah Caulkins, of Waterford, lives near me, and I always esteemed him, and believe him to be a man of truth and veracity.
                                          ELISHA BECKWITH."
Jan. 16*th*, 1839.

Mr. Beckwith is a Justice of the Peace, a Post Master, and a Deacon of the Baptist Church.

Mr. Dwight P. Janes, a member of the Second Congregational Church in the city of New London, in a recent letter, says:

"Mr. Caulkins is a member of the Baptist Church in Waterford, and in every respect a very worthy citizen. I have labored with him in the Sabbath School, and know him to be a man of active piety. The most *entire confidence* may be placed in the truth of his statements. Where he is known, no one will call them in question."

We close these testimonials with an extract, of a letter from William Bolles, Esq., a well known and respected citizen of New London, Ct.

"Mr. Nehemiah Caulkins resides in the town of Waterford, about six miles from this City. His opportunities to acquire exact knowledge in relation to Slavery, in that section of our country, to which his narrative is confined, have been very great. He is a carpenter, and was employed principally on the plantations, working at his trade, being thus almost constantly in the company of the slaves as well as of their masters. His full heart readily responded to the call, [for information relative to slavery,] for, as he expressed it, he had long desired that others might know what he had seen, being confident that a general knowledge of facts as they exist, would greatly promote the overthrow of the system. He is a man of undoubted character; and where known, his statements need no corroboration.

Yours, &c. WILLIAM BOLLES."

NARRATIVE OF MR. CAULKINS

I feel it my duty to tell some things that I know about slavery, in order, if possible, to awaken more feeling at the North in behalf of the slave. The treatment of the slaves on the plantations where I had the greatest opportunity of getting knowledge, *was not so bad* as that on some neighboring estates, where the owners were noted for their cruelty. There were, however, other estates in the vicinity, where the treatment was better; the slaves were better clothed and fed, were not worked so hard, and more attention was paid to their quarters.

The scenes that I have witnessed are enough to harrow up the soul; but could the slave be permitted to tell the story of his sufferings, which no white man, not linked with slavery, *is allowed to know*, the land would vomit out the horrible system, slaveholders and all, if they would not unclinch their grasp upon their defenceless victims.

I spent eleven winters, between the years 1824 and 1835, in the state of North Carolina, mostly in the vicinity of Wilmington; and four out of the eleven on the estate of Mr. John Swan, five or six miles from that place. There were on his plantation about seventy slaves, male and female: some were married, and others lived together as man and wife, without even a mock ceremony. With their owners generally, it is a matter of indifference; the marriage of slaves not being recognized by the slave code. The slaves, however, think much of being married by a clergyman.

The cabins or huts of the slaves were small, and were built principally by the slaves themselves, as they could find time on Sundays and moonlight nights; they went into the swamps, cut the logs, backed or *hauled* them to the quarters, and put up their cabins.

When I first knew Mr. Swan's plantation, his overseer was a man who had been a Methodist minister. He treated the slaves with great cruelty. His reason for leaving the ministry and becoming an overseer, as I was informed, was this: his wife died, at which providence he was so enraged, that he swore he would not preach for the Lord another day. This man continued on the plantation about three years; at the close of which, on settlement of accounts, Mr. Swan owed him about $400, for which he turned him out a negro woman, and about twenty acres of land. He built a log hut, and took the woman to live with him; since which, I have been at his hut, and seen four or five mulatto children. He has been appointed a *justice of the peace,* and his place as overseer was afterwards occupied by a Mr. Galloway.

It is customary in that part of the country, to let the hogs run in the woods. On one occasion a slave caught a pig about two months old, which he carried to his quarters. The overseer, getting information of the fact, went to the field where he was at work, and ordered him to come to him. The slave at once suspected it was something about the pig, and fearing punishment, dropped his hoe and ran for the woods. He had got but a few rods, when the overseer raised his gun, loaded with duck shot, and brought him down. It is a common practice for overseers to go into the field armed with a gun or pistols, and sometimes both. He was taken up by the slaves and carried to the plantation hospital, and the physician sent for. A physician was employed by the year to take care of the sick or wounded slaves. In about six weeks this slave got better, and was able to come out of the hospital. He came to the mill where I was at work, and asked me to examine his body, which I did, and counted twenty-six duck shot still remaining in his flesh, though the doctor had removed a number while he was laid up.

There was a slave on Mr. Swan's plantation, by the name of Harry, who, during the absence of his master, ran away and secreted himself in the woods. This the slaves sometimes do, when the master is absent for several weeks, to escape the cruel treatment of the overseer. It is common for them to make preparations, by secreting a mortar, a hatchet, some cooking utensils, and whatever things they can get that will enable them to live while they are in the woods or swamps. Harry staid about three months, and lived by robbing the rice grounds, and by such other means as came in his way. The slaves generally know where the runaway is secreted, and visit him at night and on

Sundays. On the return of his master, some of the slaves were sent for Harry. When he came home he was seized and confined in the stocks. The stocks were built in the barn, and consisted of two heavy pieces of timber, ten or more feet in length, and about seven inches wide; the lower one, on the floor, has a number of holes or places cut in it, for the ancles; the upper piece, being of the same dimensions, is fastened at one end by a hinge, and is brought down after the ancles are placed in the holes, and secured by a clasp and padlock at the other end. In this manner the person is left to sit on the floor. Harry was kept in the stocks *day and night for a week*, and flogged *every morning*. After this, he was taken out one morning, a log chain fastened around his neck, the two ends dragging on the ground, and he sent to the field, to do his task with the other slaves. At night he was again put in the stocks, in the morning he was sent to the field in the same manner, and thus dragged out another week.

The overseer was a very miserly fellow, and restricted his wife in what are considered the comforts of life—such as tea, sugar, &c. To make up for this, she set her wits to work, and, by the help of a slave, named Joe, used to take from the plantation whatever she could conveniently, and watch her opportunity during her husband's absence, and send Joe to sell them and buy for her such things as she directed. Once when her husband was away, she told Joe to kill and dress one of the pigs, sell it, and get her some tea, sugar, &c. Joe did as he was bid, and she gave him the offal for his services. When Galloway returned, not suspecting his wife, he asked her if she knew what had become of his pig. She told him she suspected one of the slaves, naming him, had stolen it, for she had heard a pig squeal the evening before. The overseer called the slave up, and charged him with the theft. He denied it, and said he knew nothing about it. The overseer still charged him with it, and told him he would give him one week to think of it, and if he did not confess the theft, or find out who did steal the pig, he would flog every negro on the plantation; before the week was up it was ascertained that Joe had killed the pig. He was called up and questioned, and admitted that he had done so, and told the overseer that he did it by the order of Mrs. Galloway, and that she directed him to buy some sugar, &c. with the money. Mrs. Galloway gave Joe the lie; and he was terribly flogged. Joe told me he had been several times to the smoke-house with Mrs. G, and taken hams and sold them, which her husband told me he supposed were stolen by the negroes on a neighboring plantation. Mr. Swan, hearing of the circumstance, told me he believed

Joe's story, but that his statement would not be taken as proof; and if every slave on the plantation told the same story it could not be received as evidence against a white person.

To show the manner in which old and worn-out slaves are some-times treated, I will state a fact Galloway owned a man about seventy years of age. The old man was sick and went to his hut; laid himself down on some straw with his feet to the fire, covered by a piece of an old blanket, and there lay four or five days, groaning in great distress, without any attention being paid him by his master, until death ended his miseries; he was then taken out and buried with as little ceremony and respect as would be paid to a brute.

There is a practice prevalent among the planters, of letting a negro off from severe and long-continued punishment on account of the intercession of some white person, who pleads in his behalf, that he believes the negro will behave better; that he promises well, and he believes he will keep his promise, &c. The planters sometimes get tired of punishing a negro, and, wanting his services in the field, they get some white person to come, and, in the presence of the slave, intercede for him. At one time a negro, named Charles, was confined in the stocks in the building where I was at work, and had been severely whipped several times. He begged me to intercede for him and try to get him released. I told him I would; and when his master came in to whip him again, I went up to him and told him I had been talking with Charles, and he had promised to behave better, &c., and requested him not to punish him any more, but to let him go. He then said to Charles, "As Mr. Caulkins has been pleading for you, I will let you go on his account"; and accordingly released him.

Women are generally shown some little indulgence for three or four weeks previous to childbirth; they are at such times not often punished if they do not finish the task assigned them; it is, in some cases, passed over with a severe reprimand, and sometimes without any notice being taken of it. They are generally allowed four weeks after the birth of a child, before they are compelled to go into the field, they then take the child with them, attended sometimes by a little girl or boy, from the age of four to six, to take care of it while the mother is at work. When there is no child that can be spared, or not young enough for this service, the mother, after nursing, lays it under a tree, or by the side of a fence, and goes to her task, return-ing at stated intervals to nurse it. While I was on this plantation, a little negro girl, six years of age, destroyed the life of a child about two months old, which was left in her care. It seems this little nurse, so called, got tired of her charge and the labor of carrying it to the quarters at night, the mother being obliged to work as long as she could see. One evening she nursed the infant at sunset as usual, and sent it to the quarters. The little girl, on her way home, had to cross a run, or brook, which led down into the swamp; when she came to the brook she followed it into the swamp, then took the infant and plunged it head foremost into the water and mud, where it stuck fast; she there left it and went to the negro quarters. When the mother came in from the field, she asked the girl where the child was; she told her she had brought it home, but did not know where it was; the overseer was immediately informed, search was made, and it was found as above stated, and dead. The little girl was shut up in the barn, and confined there two or three weeks, when a speculator came along and bought her for two hundred dollars.

The slaves are obliged to work from daylight till dark, as long as they can see. When they have tasks assigned, which is often the case, a few of the strongest and most expert, sometimes finish them before sunset; others will be obliged to work till eight or nine o'clock in the evening. All must finish their tasks or take a flogging. The whip and gun, or pistol, are companions of the overseer; the former he uses very frequently upon the negroes, during their hours of labor, without regard to age or sex. Scarcely a day passed while I was on the plantation, in which some of the slaves were not whipped; I do not mean that they were *struck a few blows* merely, but had a *set flogging*. The same labor is commonly assigned to men and women,— such as digging ditches in the rice marshes, clearing up land, chopping cord-wood, threshing, &c. I have known the women go into the barn as soon as they could see in the morning, and work as late as they could see at night, threshing rice with the flail, (they now have a threshing machine), and when they could see to thresh no longer, they had to gather up the rice, carry it up stairs, and deposit it in the granary.

The allowance of clothing on this plantation to each slave, was given out at Christmas for the year, and consisted of one pair of coarse shoes, and enough coarse cloth to make a jacket and trowsers. If the man has a wife she makes it up; if not, it is made up in the house. The slaves on this plantation, being near Wilmington, procured themselves extra clothing by working Sundays and moon-light nights, cutting cord-wood in the swamps, which they had to back about a quarter of a mile to the river; they would then get a permit from their master, and taking the wood in their canoes, carry it to Wilmington, and sell it to the vessels, or dispose of it as they best could, and with the money buy an old jacket of the sailors, some coarse cloth for a shirt, &c. They sometimes gather the moss from the trees, which they cleanse and take to market. The women receive their allowance of the same kind of cloth which the men have. This they make into a frock; if they have any under garments *they must procure them for themselves*. When the slaves get a permit to leave the plantation, they sometimes make all ring again by singing the following significant ditty, which shows that after all there is a flow of spirits in the human breast which for a while, at least, enables them to forget their wretchedness.*

> Hurra, for good ole Massa,
> He giv me de pass to go to de city
> Hurra, for good ole Missis,
> She bile de pot, and giv me de licker.
> Hurra, I'm goin to de city.

Every Saturday night the slaves receive their allowance of provisions, which must last them till the next Saturday night. "Potato time," as it is called, begins about the middle of July. The slave may measure for himself, the overseer being present, half a bushel of sweet potatoes, and heap the measure as long as they will lie on; I have, however, seen the overseer, if he think the negro is getting too many, kick the measure; and if any fall off, tell him he has got his measure. No salt is furnished them to eat with their potatoes. When rice or corn is given, they give them a little salt; sometimes half a pint of molasses is given, but not often. The quantity of rice, which is of the small, broken, unsaleable kind, is one peck. When corn is given them, their allowance is the same, and if they get it ground, (Mr. Swan had a mill on his plantation), they must give one quart for grinding, thus reducing their weekly allowance to seven quarts. When fish (mullet) were plenty, they were allowed, in addition, one fish. As to meat, they seldom had any. I do not

---

* Slaves sometimes sing, and so do convicts in jails under sentence, and both for the same reason. Their singing proves that they *want* to be happy not that they *are* so. It is the *means* that they use to make themselves happy, not the evidence that they are so already. Sometimes, doubtless, the excitement of song whelms their misery in momentary oblivion. He who argues from this that they have no conscious misery to forget, knows as little of human nature as of slavery.— EDITOR.

think they had an allowance of meat oftener than once in two or three months, and then the quantity was very small. When they went into the field to work, they took some of the meal or rice and a pot with them; the pots were given to an old woman, who placed two poles parallel, set the pots on them, and kindled a fire underneath for cooking; she took salt with her and seasoned the messes as she thought proper. When their breakfast was ready, which was generally about ten or eleven o'clock, they were called from labor, ate, and returned to work; in the afternoon, dinner was prepared in the same way. They had but two meals a day while in the field; if they wanted more, they cooked for themselves after they returned to their quarters at night. At the time of killing hogs on the plantation, the pluck, entrails, and blood were given to the slaves.

When I first went upon Mr. Swan's plantation, I saw a slave in shackles or fetters, which were fastened around each ankle and firmly riveted, connected together by a chain. To the middle of this chain he had fastened a string, so as in a manner to suspend them and keep them from galling his ankles. This slave, whose name was Frank, was an intelligent, good looking man, and a very good mechanic. There was nothing vicious in his character, but he was one of those high-spirited and daring men, that whips, chains, fetters, and all the means of cruelty in the power of slavery, could not subdue. Mr. S. had employed a Mr. Beckwith to repair a boat, and told him Frank was a good mechanic, and he might have his services. Frank was sent for, his *shackles still on*. Mr. Beckwith set him to work making *trunnels,* &c. I was employed in putting up a building, and after Mr. Beckwith had done with Frank, he was sent for to assist me. Mr. Swan sent him to a blacksmith's shop and had his shackles cut off with a cold chisel. Frank was afterwards sold to a cotton planter.

I will relate one circumstance, which shows the little regard that is paid to the feelings of the slave. During the time that Mr. Isaiah Rogers was superintending the building of a rice machine, one of the slaves complained of a severe toothache. Swan asked Mr. Rogers to take his hammer and *knock out the tooth*.

There was a slave on the plantation named Ben, a waiting man. I occupied a room in the same hut, and had frequent conversations with him. Ben was a kind-hearted man, and, I believe, a Christian; he would always ask a blessing before he sat down to eat, and was in the constant practice of praying morning and night.—One day when I was at the hut, Ben was sent for to go to the house. Ben sighed deeply and went. He soon returned with a girl about seventeen years of age, whom one of Mr. Swan's daughters had ordered him to flog. He brought her into the room where I was, and told her to stand there while he went into the next room: I heard him groan again as he went. While there I heard his voice, and he was engaged in prayer. After a few minutes he returned with a large cowhide, and stood before the girl, without saying a word. I concluded he wished me to leave the hut, which I did; and immediately after I heard the girl scream. At every blow she would shriek, "Do, Ben! oh do, Ben!" This is a common expression of the slaves to the person whipping them: "Do, Massa!" or, "Do, Missus!"

After she had gone, I asked Ben what she was whipped for: he told me she had done something to displease her young missus; and in boxing her ears, and otherwise beating her, she had scratched her finger by a pin in the girl's dress, for which she sent her to be flogged. I asked him if he stripped her before flogging; he said, yes; he did not like to do this, but was *obliged* to: he said he was once ordered to whip a woman, which he did without stripping her: on her return to the house, her mistress examined her back; and not seeing any marks, he was sent for, and asked why he had not whipped her: he replied that he had; she said she saw no marks, and asked him if he had made her pull her clothes off; he said, No. She then told him, that when he whipped any more of the women, he must make them strip off their clothes, as well as the men, and flog them on their bare backs, or he should be flogged himself.

Ben often appeared very gloomy and sad: I have frequently heard him, when in his room, mourning over his condition, and exclaim, "Poor African slave! Poor African slave!" Whipping was so common an occurrence on this plantation, that it would be too great a repetition to state the *many* and *severe* floggings I have seen inflicted on the slaves. They were flogged for not performing their tasks, for being careless, slow, or not in time, for going to the fire to warm, &c. &c.; and it often seemed as if occasions were sought as an excuse for punishing them.

On one occasion, I heard the overseer charge the hands to be at a certain place the next morning at sun-rise. I was present in the morning, in company with my brother, when the hands arrived. Joe, the slave already spoken of, came running, all out of breath, about five minutes behind the time, when, without asking any questions, the overseer told him to take off his jacket. Joe took off his jacket. He had on a piece of a shirt; he told him to take it off: Joe took it off: he then whipped him with a heavy cow-hide full six feet long.

At every stroke Joe would spring from the ground, and scream, "O my God! Do, Massa Galloway!" My brother was so exasperated, that he turned to me and said, "If I were Joe, I would kill the overseer if I knew I should be shot the next minute."

In the winter the horn blew at about four in the morning, and all the threshers were required to be at the threshing floor in fifteen minutes after. They had to go about a quarter of a mile from their quarters. Galloway would stand near the entrance, and all who did not come in time would get a blow over the back or head as heavy as he could strike. I have seen him, at such times, follow after them, striking furiously a number of blows, and every one followed by their screams. I have seen the women go to their work after such a flogging, crying and taking on most piteously.

It is almost impossible to believe that human nature can endure such hardships and sufferings as the slaves have to go through: I have seen them driven into a ditch in a rice swamp to bail out the water, in order to put down a flood-gate, when they had to break the ice, and there stand in the water among the ice until it was bailed out. I have *often* known the hands to be taken from the field, sent down the river in flats or boats to Wilmington, absent from twenty-four to thirty hours, *without any thing to eat,* no provision being made for these occasions.

Galloway kept medicine on hand, that in case any of the slaves were sick, he could give it to them without sending for the physician; but he always kept a good look out that they did not sham sickness. When any of them excited his suspicions, he would make them take the medicine in his presence, and would give them a rap on the top of the head, to make them swallow it. A man once came to him, of whom he said he was suspicious: he gave him two potions of salts, and fastened him in the stocks for the night. His medicine soon began to operate; and *there he lay in all his filth till he was taken out the next day.*

One day, Mr. Swan beat a slave severely, for alleged carelessness in letting a boat get adrift. The slave was told to secure the boat: whether he took sufficient means for this purpose I do not know; he was not allowed to make any defence. Mr. Swan called him up, and asked why he did not secure the boat: he pulled off his hat and began to tell his story. Swan told him he was a damned liar, and commenced beating him over the head with a hickory cane, and the slave retreated backwards; Swan followed him about two rods, threshing him over the head with the hickory as he went.

As I was one day standing near some slaves who were threshing, the driver, thinking one of the women did not use her flail quick enough, struck her over the head: the end of the whip hit her in the eye. I thought at the time he had put it out; but, after poulticing and doctoring for some days, she recovered. Speaking to him about it, he said that he once struck a slave so as to put one of her eyes entirely out.

A patrol is kept upon each estate, and every slave found off the plantation without a pass is whipped on the spot. I knew a slave who started without a pass, one night, for a neighboring plantation, to see his wife: he was caught, tied to a tree, and flogged. He stated his business to the patrol, who was well acquainted with him, but all to no purpose. I spoke to the patrol about it afterwards: he said he knew the negro, that he was a very clever fellow, but he had to whip him; for, if he let him pass, he must another, &c. He stated that he had sometimes caught and flogged four in a night.

In conversation with Mr. Swan about runaway slaves, he stated to me the following fact:—A slave, by the name of Luke, was owned in Wilmington; he was sold to a speculator and carried to Georgia. After an absence of about two months the slave returned; he watched an opportunity to enter his old master's house when the family were absent, no one being at home but a young waiting man. Luke went to the room where his master kept his arms; took his gun, with some ammunition, and went into the woods. On the return of his master, the waiting man told him what had been done: this threw him into a violent passion; he swore he would kill Luke, or lose his own life. He loaded another gun, took two men, and made search, but could not find him: he then advertised him, offering a large reward if delivered to him or lodged in jail. His neighbors, however, advised him to offer a reward of two hundred dollars for him *dead or alive,* which he did. Nothing however was heard of him for some months. Mr. Swan said, one of his slaves ran away, and was gone eight or ten weeks; on his return he said he had found Luke, and that he had a rifle, two pistols, and a sword.

I left the plantation in the spring, and returned to the north; when I went out again, the next fall, I asked Mr. Swan if any thing had been heard of Luke; he said he was *shot,* and related to me the manner of his death, as follows:—Luke went to one of the plantations, and entered a hut for something to eat. Being fatigued, he sat down and fell asleep. There was only a woman in the hut at the time: as soon as she found he was asleep, she ran and told her master, who took his rifle, and called two white men on another plantation: the three, with their rifles, then went to the hut, and posted themselves in different positions, so that they could watch the door. When Luke waked up he went to the door to look out, and saw them with their rifles, he stepped back and raised his gun to his face. They called to him to surrender; and stated that they had him in their power, and said he had better give up. He said he would not; and if they tried to take him, he would kill one of them; for, if he gave up, he knew they would kill him, and he was determined to sell his life as dear as he could. They told him, if he should shoot one of them, the other two would certainly kill him: he replied, he was determined not to give up, and kept his gun moving from one to the other; and while his rifle was turned toward one, another, standing in a different direction, shot him through the head, and he fell lifeless to the ground.

There was another slave shot while I was there; this man had run away, and had been living in the woods a long time, and it was not known where he was, till one day he was discovered by two men, who went on the large island near Belvidere to hunt turkeys; they shot him and carried his head home.

It is common to keep dogs on the plantations, to pursue and catch runaway slaves. I was once bitten by one of them. I went to the overseer's house, the dog lay in the piazza, as soon as I put my foot upon the floor, he sprang and bit me just above the knee, but not severely; he tore my pantaloons badly. The overseer apologized for his dog, saying he never knew him to bite a *white* man before. He said he once had a dog, when he lived on another plantation, that was very useful to him in hunting runaway negroes. He said that a slave on the plantation once ran away; as soon as he found the course he took, he put the dog on the track, and he soon came so close upon him that the man had to climb a tree, he followed with his gun, and brought the slave home.

The slaves have a great dread of being sold and carried south. It is generally said, and I have no doubt of its truth, that they are much worse treated farther south.

The following are a few among the many facts related to me while I lived among the slaveholder. The names of the planters and plantations, I shall not give, *as they did not come under my own observation*. I however place the fullest confidence in their truth.

A planter not far from Mr. Swan's employed an overseer to whom he paid $400 a year; he became dissatisfied with him, because he did not drive the slaves hard enough, and get more work out of them.

He therefore sent to South Carolina, or Georgia, and got a man to whom he paid I believe $800 a year. He proved to be a cruel fellow, and drove the slaves almost to death. There was a slave on this plantation, who had repeatedly run away, and had been severely flogged every time. The last time he was caught, a hole was dug in the ground, and he buried up to the chin, his arms being secured down by his sides. He was kept in this situation four or five days.

The following was told me by an intimate friend; it took place on a plantation containing about one hundred slaves. One day the owner ordered the women into the barn, he then went in among them, whip in hand, and told them he meant to flog them all to death; they began immediately to cry out "What have I done Massa? What have I done Massa?" He replied; "D—n you, I will let you know what you have done, you don't breed, I haven't had a young one from one of you for several months." They told him they could not breed while they had to work in the rice ditches. (The rice grounds are low and marshy, and have to be drained, and while digging or clearing the ditches, the women had to work in mud and water from one to two feet in depth; they were obliged to draw up and secure their frocks about their waist, to keep them out of the water, in this manner they frequently had to work from daylight in the morning till it was so dark they could see no longer.) After swearing and threatening for some time, he told them to tell the overseer's wife, when they got in that way, and he would put them upon the land to work.

This same planter had a female slave who was a member of the Methodist Church; for a slave she was intelligent and conscientious. He proposed a criminal intercourse with her. She would not comply. He left her and sent for the overseer, and told him to have her flogged. It was done. Not long after, he renewed his proposal. She again refused. She was again whipped. He then told her why she had been twice flogged, and told her he intended to whip her till she should yield. The girl, seeing that her case was hopeless, her back smarting with the scourging she had received, and dreading a repetition, gave herself up to be the victim of his brutal lusts.

One of the slaves on another plantation, gave birth to a child which lived but two or three weeks. After its death the planter called the woman to him, and asked her how she came to let the child die; said it was all owing to her carelessness, and that he meant to flog her for it. She told him, with all the feeling of a mother, the circumstances of its death. But her story availed her nothing against the savage brutality of her master. She was severely whipped. A healthy child four months old was then considered worth $100 in North Carolina.

The foregoing facts were related to me by white persons of character and respectability. The following fact was related to me on a plantation where I have spent considerable time and where the punishment was inflicted. I have no doubt of its truth. A slave ran away from his master, and got as far as Newbern. He took provisions that lasted him a week; but having eaten all, he went to a house to get something to satisfy his hunger. A white man suspecting him to be a runaway, demanded his pass: as he had none he was seized and put in Newbern jail. He was there advertised, his description given, &c. His master saw the advertisement and sent for him; when he was brought back, his wrists were tied together and drawn over his knees. A stick was then passed over his arms and under his knees, and he secured in this manner, his trowsers were then stripped down, and he turned over on his side, and severely beaten with the paddle, then turned over and severely beaten on the other side, and then turned back again, and tortured by another bruising and beating. He was afterwards kept in the stocks a week, and whipped every morning.

To show the disgusting pollutions of slavery, and how it covers with moral filth every thing it touches, I will state two or three facts, which I have on such evidence I cannot doubt their truth. A planter offered a white man of my acquaintance twenty dollars for every one of his female slaves whom he would get in the family way. This offer was no doubt made for the purpose of improving the stock, on the same principle that farmers endeavor to improve their cattle by crossing the breed.

Slaves belonging to merchants and others in the city, often hire their own time, for which they pay various prices per week or month, according to the capacity of the slave. The females who thus hire their time, pursue various modes to procure the money; their masters making no inquiry how they get it, provided the money comes. If it is not regularly paid they are flogged. Some take in washing, some cook on board vessels, pick oakum, sell peanuts, &c., while others, younger and more comely, often resort to the vilest pursuits. I knew a man from the north who, though married to a respectable southern woman, kept two of these mulatto girls in an upper room at his store; his wife told some of her friends that he had not lodged at home for two weeks together. I have seen these two *kept misses*, as they are there called, at his store; he was afterwards stabbed in an attempt to arrest a runaway slave, and died in about ten days.

The clergy at the north cringe beneath the corrupting influence of slavery, and their moral courage is borne down by it. Not the hypocritical and unprincipled alone, but even such as can hardly be supposed to be destitute of sincerity.

Going one morning to the Baptist Sunday school, in Wilmington, in which I was engaged, I fell in with the Rev. Thomas P. Hunt, who was going to the Presbyterian school. I asked him how he could bear to see the little negro children beating their hoops, hallooing, and running about the streets, as we then saw them, their moral condition entirely neglected, while the whites were so carefully gathered into the schools. His reply was substantially this:—"I can't bear it, Mr. Caulkins. I feel as deeply as any one can on this subject, but what can I do? MY HANDS ARE TIED."

Now, if Mr. Hunt was guilty of neglecting his duty, as a servant of HIM who never failed to rebuke sin in high places, what shall be said of those clergymen at the north, where the power that closed his mouth is comparatively unfelt, who refuse to tell their people how God abhors oppression, and who seldom open their mouths on this subject, but to denounce the friends of emancipation, thus giving the strongest support to the accursed system of slavery. I believe Mr. Hunt has since become an agent of the Temperance Society.

In stating the foregoing facts, my object has been to show the practical workings of the system of slavery, and if possible to correct the misapprehension on this subject, so common at the north. In doing this I am not at war with slaveholders. No, my soul is moved for them as well as for the poor slaves. May God send them repentance to the acknowledgment of the truth! Principle, on a subject of this nature, is dearer to me than the applause of men, and should not be sacrificed on any subject, even though the ties of friendship may be broken. We have too long been silent on this subject, the slave has been too much considered, by our northern states, as being kept by necessity in his present condition.—Were we to ask, in the language of Pilate, "what evil have they done"—we may search their history, we cannot find that they have taken up arms against our government, nor insulted us as a nation—that they are thus compelled to drag out a life in chains! subjected to the most terrible inflictions if in any way they manifest a wish to be released.—Let us reverse the question. What evil has been done to them by those who call themselves masters? First let us look at their persons, "neither clothed nor naked"—I have seen instances where this phrase would not apply to boys and girls, and that too in winter. I knew one young man seventeen years of age, by the name of Dave, on Mr. J. Swan's plantation, who worked day after day in the rice machine as naked as when he was born. The reason of his being so, his master said in my hearing, was, that he could not keep clothes on him—he would get into the fire and burn them off.

Follow them next to their huts; some with and some without floors:—Go at night, view their means of lodging, see them lying on benches, some on the floor or ground, some sitting on stools, dozing away the night;—others, of younger age, with a bare blanket wrapped about them; and one or two lying in the ashes. These things *I have often seen with my own eyes.*

Examine their means of subsistence, which consists generally of seven quarts of meal or eight quarts of small rice for one week; then follow them to their work, with driver and overseer pushing them to the utmost of their strength, by threatening and whipping.

If they are sick from fatigue and exposure, go to their huts, as I have often been, and see them groaning under a burning fever or pleurisy, lying on some straw, their feet to the fire with barely a blanket to cover them; or on some boards nailed together in form of a bedstead.

And after seeing all this, and hearing them tell of their sufferings, need I ask, is there any evil connected with their condition? and if so; upon whom is it to be charged? I answer for myself, and the reader can do the same. Our government stands first chargeable for allowing slavery to exist, under its own jurisdiction. Second, the states for enacting laws to secure their victim. Third, the slaveholder for carrying out such enactments, in horrid form enough to chill the blood. Fourth, every person who knows what slavery is, and does not raise his voice against this crying sin, but by silence gives consent to its continuance, is chargeable with guilt in the sight of God. "The blood of Zacharias who was slain between the temple and altar," says Christ, "WILL I REQUIRE OF THIS GENERATION."

Look at the slave, his condition but little, if at all, better than that of the brute; chained down by the law, and the will of his master; and every avenue closed against relief; and the names of those who plead for him, cast out as evil;—must not humanity let its voice be heard, and tell Israel their transgressions and Judah their sins?

May God look upon their afflictions, and deliver them from their cruel task-masters! I verily believe he will, if there be any efficacy in prayer. I have been to their prayer meetings and with them offered prayer in their behalf. I have heard some of them in their huts before day-light praying in their simple broken language, telling their heavenly Father of their trials in the following and similar language.

"Fader in heaven, look upon de poor slave, dat have to work all de day long, dat cant have de time to pray only in de night, and den massa mus not know it.* Fader, have mercy on massa and missus. Fader, when shall poor slave get through the world! when will death come, and de poor slave go to heaven"; and in their meetings they frequently add, "Fader, bless de white man dat come to hear de slave pray, bless his family," and so on. They uniformly begin their meetings by singing the following—

> "And are we yet alive
> To see each other's face," &c.

Is the ear of the Most High deaf to the prayer of the slave? I do firmly believe that their deliverance will come, and that the prayer of this poor afflicted people will be answered.

Emancipation would be safe. I have had eleven winters to learn the disposition of the slaves, and am satisfied that they would peaceably and cheerfully work for pay. Give them education, equal and just laws, and they will become a most interesting people. Oh, let a cry be raised which shall awaken the conscience of this guilty nation, to demand for the slaves immediate and unconditional emancipation.

NEHEMIAH CAULKINS.

NARRATIVE AND TESTIMONY OF
REV. HORACE MOULTON

MR. MOULTON is an esteemed minister of the Methodist Episcopal Church, in Marlborough, Mass. He spent five years in Georgia, between 1817 and 1824. The following communication has been recently received from him.

MARLBOROUGH, MASS., Feb. 18, 1839.

DEAR BROTHER—

Yours of Feb. 2d, requesting me to write out a few facts on the subject of slavery, as it exists at the south, has come to hand. I hasten

---

* At this time there was some fear of insurrection and the slaves were forbidden
 ~~~ld meetings.

to comply with your request. Were it not, however, for the claims of those "who are drawn unto death," and the responsibility resting upon me, in consequence of this request, I should forever hold my peace. For I well know that I shall bring upon myself a flood of persecution, for attempting to speak out for the dumb. But I am willing to be set at nought by men, if I can be the means of promoting the welfare of the oppressed of our land. I shall not relate many particular cases of cruelty, though I might a great number; but shall give some general information as to their mode of treatment, their food, clothing, dwellings, deprivations, &c.

Let me say, in the first place, that I spent nearly five years in Savannah, Georgia, and in its vicinity, between the years 1817 and 1824. My object in going to the south, was to engage in making and burning brick; but not immediately succeeding, I engaged in no business of much profit until late in the winter, when I took charge of a set of hands and went to work. During my leisure, however, I was an observer, at the auctions, upon the plantations, and in almost every department of business. The next year, during the cold months, I had several two-horse teams under my care, with which we used to haul brick, boards, and other articles from the wharf into the city, and cotton, rice, corn, and wood from the country. This gave me an extensive acquaintance with merchants, mechanics and planters. I had slaves under my control some portions of every year when at the south. All the brick-yards, except one, on which I was engaged, were connected either with a corn field, potato patch, rice field, cotton field, tan-works, or with a wood lot. My business, usually, was to take charge of the brick-making department. At those jobs I have sometimes taken in charge both the field and brick-yard hands. I have been on the plantations in South Carolina, but have never been an overseer of slaves in that state, as has been said in the public papers.

I think the above facts and explanations are necessary to be connected with the account I may give of slavery, that the reader may have some knowledge of my acquaintance with *practical* slavery: for many mechanics and merchants who go to the South, and stay there for years, know but little of the dark side of slavery. My account of slavery will apply to *field hands,* who compose much the largest portion of the black population, (probably nine-tenths), and not to those who are kept for kitchen maids, nurses, waiters, &c., about the houses of the planters and public hotels, where persons from the north obtain most of their knowledge of the evils of slavery. I will now proceed to take up specific points.

I. THE LABOR OF THE SLAVES

Males and females work together promiscuously on all the plantations. On many plantations *tasks* are given them. The best working
hands can have some leisure time; but the feeble and unskilful ones,
together with slender females, have indeed a hard time of it, and
very often answer for non-performance of tasks at the *whipping-posts*.
None who worked with me had tasks at any time. The rule was to
work them from sun to sun. But when I was burning brick, they
were obliged to take turns, and *sit up all night* about every other
night, and work all day. On one plantation, where I spent a few
weeks, the slaves were called up to work long before daylight, when
business pressed, and worked until late at night; and sometimes
some of them *all night*. A large portion of the slaves are owned by
masters who keep them on purpose to hire out—and they usually
let them to those who will give the highest wages for them, irre-
spective of their mode of treatment; and those who hire them, will
of course try to get the greatest possible amount of work performed,
with the least possible expense. Women are seen bringing their
infants into the field to their work, and leading others who are not
old enough to stay at the cabins with safety. When they get there,
they must set them down in the dirt, and go to work. Sometimes
they are left to cry until they fall alseep. Others are left at home,
shut up in their huts. Now, is it not barbarous, that the mother,
with her child or children around her, half starved, must be whipped
at night if she does not perform her task? But so it is. Some who
have very young ones, fix a little sack, and place the infants on their
backs, and work. One reason, I presume is, that they will not cry
so much when they can hear their mother's voice. Another is, the
mothers fear that the poisonous vipers and snakes will bite them.
Truly, I never knew any place where the land is so infested with
all kinds of the most venomous snakes, as in the low lands round
about Savannah. The moccasin snakes, so called, and water rattle-
snakes—the bites of both of which are as poisonous as our upland
rattle-snakes at the north,—are found in myriads about the stagnant
waters and swamps of the South. The females, in order to secure
their infants from these poisonous snakes, do, as I have said, often
work with their infants on their backs. Females are sometimes called
to take the hardest part of the work. On some brick yards where I
have been, the women have been selected as the *moulders* of brick,
instead of the men.

II. THE FOOD OF THE SLAVES

It was a general custom, wherever I have been, for the masters to give each of his slaves, male and female, *one peck of corn per week* for their food. This at fifty cents per bushel, which was all that it was worth when I was there, would amount to twelve and a half cents per week for board per head.

It cost me upon an average, when at the south, one dollar per day for board. The price of fourteen bushels of corn per week. This would make my board equal in amount to the board of *forty-six slaves*! This is all that good or bad masters allow their slaves round about Savannah on the plantations. One peck of gourd-seed corn is to be measured out to each slave once every week. One man with whom I labored, however, being desirous to get all the work out of his hands he could, before I left, (about fifty in number), bought for them every week, or twice a week, a beef's head from market. With this, they made a soup in a large iron kettle, around which the hands came at meal-time, and dipping out the soup, would mix it with their hommony, and eat it as though it were a feast. This man permitted his slaves to eat twice a day while I was doing a job for him. He promised me a beaver hat and as good a suit of clothes as could be bought in the city, if I would accomplish so much for him before I returned to the north; giving me the entire control over his slaves. Thus you may see the temptations overseers sometimes have, to get all the work they can out of the poor slaves. The above is an exception to the general rule of feeding. For in all other places where I worked and visited, the slaves had *nothing from their masters but the corn,* or its equivalent in potatoes or rice, and to this, they were not permitted to come but *once a day.* The custom was to blow the horn early in the morning, as a signal for the hands to rise and go to work, when commenced; they continued work until about eleven o'clock, A. M., when, at the signal, all hands left off, and went into their huts, made their fires, made their corn-meal into hommony or cake, ate it, and went to work again at the signal of the horn, and worked until night, or until their tasks were done. Some cooked their breakfast in the field while at work. Each slave must grind his own corn in a hand-mill after he has done his work at night. There is generally one hand-mill on every plantation for the use of the slaves.

Some of the planters have no corn, others often get out. The substitute for it is, the equivalent of one peck of corn either in rice or sweet potatoes; neither of which is as good for the slaves as corn.

They complain more of being faint, when fed on rice or potatoes, than when fed on corn. I was with one man a few weeks who gave me his hands to do a job of work, and to save time one cooked for all the rest. The following course was taken,—Two crotched sticks were driven down at one end of the yard, and a small pole being laid on the crotches, they swung a large iron kettle on the middle of the pole; then made up a fire under the kettle and boiled the hommony; when ready, the hands were called around this kettle with their wooden plates and spoons. They dipped out and ate standing around the kettle, or sitting upon the ground, as best suited their convenience. When they had potatoes they took them out with their hands, and ate them. As soon as it was thought they had had sufficient time to swallow their food they were called to their work again. *This was the only meal they ate through the day.* Now think of the little, almost naked and half-starved children, nibbling upon a piece of cold Indian cake, or a potato! Think of the poor female, just ready to be confined, without any thing that can be called convenient or comfortable! Think of the old toil-worn father and mother, without any thing to eat but the coarsest of food, and not half enough of that! then think of *home*. When sick, their physicians are their masters and overseers, in most cases, whose skill consists in bleeding and in administering large potions of Epsom salts, when the whip and *cursing* will not start them from their cabins.

III. HOUSES

The huts of the slaves are mostly of the poorest kind. They are not as good as those temporary shanties which are thrown up beside railroads. They are erected with posts and crotches, with but little or no frame-work about them. They have no stoves or chimneys; some of them have something like a fireplace at one end, and a board or two off at that side, or on the roof, to let off the smoke. Others have nothing like a fireplace in them; in these the fire is sometimes made in the middle of the hut. These buildings have but one apartment in them; the places where they pass in and out, serve both for doors and windows; the sides and roofs are covered with coarse, and in many instances with refuse boards. In warm weather, especially in the spring, the slaves keep up a smoke, or fire and smoke, all night, to drive away the gnats and musketoes, which are very troublesome in all the low country of the south; so much so that the whites sleep under frames with nets over them, knit so fine that the musketoes cannot fly through them.

Some of the slaves have rugs to cover them in the coldest weather, but I should think *more have not*. During driving storms they frequently have to run from one hut to another for shelter. In the coldest weather, where they can get wood or stumps, they keep up fires all night in their huts, and lay around them, with their feet towards the blaze. Men, women and children all lie down together, in most instances. There may be exceptions to the above statements in regard to their houses, but so far as my observations have extended, I have given a fair description, and I have been on a large number of plantations in Georgia and South Carolina up and down the Savannah river. Their huts are generally built compactly on the plantations, forming villages of huts, their size proportioned to the number of slaves on them. In these miserable huts the poor blacks are herded at night like swine, *without any conveniences of bedsteads, tables or chairs*. O misery to the full! to see the aged sire beating off the swarms of gnats and muske-toes in the warm weather, and shivering in the straw, or bending over a few coals in the winter, clothed in rags. I should think males and females, both lie down at night with their working clothes on them. God alone knows how much the poor slaves suffer for the want of convenient houses to secure them from the piercing winds and howling storms of winter, especially the aged, sick and dying. Although it is much warmer there than here, yet I suffered for a number of weeks in the winter, almost as much in Georgia as I do in Massachusetts.

IV. CLOTHING

The masters [in Georgia] make a practice of getting two suits of clothes for each slave per year, a thick suit for winter, and a thin one for summer. They provide also one pair of northern made sale shoes for each slave in *winter*. These shoes usually begin to rip in a few weeks. The negroes' mode of mending them is, to *wire* them together, in many instances. Do our northern shoemakers know that they are augmenting the sufferings of the poor slaves with their almost good for nothing sale shoes? Inasmuch as it is done unto one of those poor sufferers it is done unto our Saviour. The above practice of clothing the slave is customary to some extent. How many, however, fail of this, God only knows. The children and old slaves are, I should think, *exceptions* to the above rule. The males and females have their suits from the same cloth for their winter dresses. These winter garments appear to be made of a mixture of cotton and wool, very coarse and *sleazy*. The whole suit for the men consists of a pair of pantaloons and a short sailor-jacket, *without shirt, vest, hat, stockings, or any kind of loose garments*! These, if worn steadily when at work, would not probably last more than one or two months; therefore, for the sake of saving them, many of them work, especially in the summer, with no clothing on them except a cloth tied round their waist, and *almost all* with nothing more on them than pantaloons, and these frequently so torn that they do not serve the purposes of common decency. The women have for clothing a short petticoat, and a short loose gown, something like the male's sailor-jacket, *without any under garment, stockings, bonnets, hoods, caps, or any kind of over-clothes*. When at work in warm weather, they usually strip off the loose gown, and have nothing on but a short petticoat with some kind of covering over their breasts. Many children may be seen in the summer months *as naked as they came into the world*. I think, as a whole, they suffer more for the want of comfortable bed-clothes, than they do for wearing apparel. It is true, that some by begging or buying, have more clothes than above described, but the *masters provide them with no more*. They are miserable objects of pity. It may be said of many of them, "I was *naked* and ye clothed me not." It is enough to melt the hardest heart to see the ragged mothers nursing their almost naked children, with but a morsel of the coarsest food to eat. The Southern horses and dogs have enough to eat and good care taken of them, but Southern negroes, who can describe their misery?

V. PUNISHMENTS

The ordinary mode of punishing the slaves is both cruel and barbarous. The masters seldom, if ever, try to govern their slaves by moral influence, but by whipping, kicking, beating, starving, branding, *cat-hauling,* loading with irons, imprisoning, or by some other cruel mode of torturing. They often boast of having invented some new mode of torture, by which they have "tamed the rascals." What is called a moderate flogging at the south is horribly cruel. Should we whip our horses for any offence as they whip their slaves for small offences, we should expose ourselves to the penalty of the law. The masters whip for the smallest offences, such as not performing their tasks, being caught by the guard or patrol by night, or for taking any thing from the master's yard without leave. For these, and the like crimes, the slaves are whipped thirty-nine lashes, and sometimes seventy or a hundred, on the bare back. One slave, who was under my care, was whipped, I think one hundred lashes, for getting a small handful of wood from his master's yard without leave. I heard an overseer boasting to this same master that he gave one of the boys seventy lashes, for not doing a job of work just as he thought it ought to be done. The owner of the slave appeared to be pleased that the overseer had been so faithful. The apology they make for whipping so cruelly is, that it is to frighten the rest of the gang. The masters say, that what we call an ordinary flogging will not subdue the slaves; hence the most cruel and barbarous scourgings ever witnessed by man are daily and *hourly* inflicted upon the naked bodies of these miserable bondmen; not by masters and negro-drivers only, but by the constables in the common markets and jailors in their yards.

When the slaves are whipped, either in public or private, they have their hands fastened by the wrists, with a rope or cord prepared for the purpose: this being thrown over a beam, a limb of a tree, or something else, the culprit is drawn up and stretched by the arms as high as possible, without raising his feet from the ground or floor: and sometimes they are made to stand on tip-toe; then the feet are made fast to something prepared for them. In this distorted posture the monster flies at them, sometimes in great rage, with his imple- ments of torture, and cuts on with all his might, over the shoulders, under the arms, and sometimes over the head and ears, or on parts of the body where he can inflict the greatest torment. Occasionally the whipper, especially if his victim does not beg enough to suit him, while under the lash, will fly into a passion, uttering the most horrid oaths; while the victim of his rage is crying, at every stroke, "Lord have mercy! Lord have mercy!" The scenes exhibited at the whip- ping post are awfully terrific and frightful to one whose heart has not turned to stone; I never could look on but a moment. While under the lash, the bleeding victim writhes in agony, convulsed with torture. Thirty-nine lashes on the bare back, which tear the skin at almost every stroke, is what the South calls a very *moderate punishment!* Many masters whip until they are tired—until the back is a gore of blood— then rest upon it: after a short cessation, get up and go at it again; and after having satiated their revenge in the blood of their victims, they sometimes *leave them tied, for hours together, bleeding at every wound.*—Sometimes, after being whipped, they are bathed with a brine of salt and water. Now and then a master, but more frequently a mistress who has no husband, will send them to jail a few days, giving orders to have them whipped, so many lashes, once or twice a day. Sometimes, after being whipped, some have been shut up in a dark place and deprived of food, in order to increase their torments: and I have heard of some who have, in such circumstances, died of their wounds and starvation.

Such scenes of horror as above described are so common in Georgia that they attract no attention. To threaten them with death, with breaking in their teeth or jaws, or cracking their heads, is *common talk,* when scolding at the slaves.—Those who run away from their masters and are caught again generally fare the worst. They are generally lodged in jail, with instructions from the owner to have them cruelly whipped. Some order the constables to whip them publicly in the market. Constables at the south are generally savage, brutal men. They have become so accustomed to catching and whipping negroes, that they are as fierce as tigers. Slaves who are absent from their yards, or plantations, after eight o'clock P. M., and are taken by the guard in the cities, or by the patrols in the country, are, if not called for before nine o'clock A. M. the next day, secured in prisons; and hardly ever escape, until their backs are torn up by the cow-hide. On plantations, the *evenings* usually present scenes of horror. Those slaves against whom charges are preferred for not having performed their tasks, and for various faults, must, after work-hours at night, undergo their torments. I have often heard the sound of the lash, the curses of the whipper, and the cries of the poor negro rending the air, late in the evening, and long before day-light in the morning.

It is very common for masters to say to the overseers or drivers, "put it on to them," "don't spare that fellow," "give that scoundrel one hundred lashes," &c. Whipping the women when in delicate circumstances, as they sometimes do, without any regard to their entreaties or the entreaties of their nearest friends, is truly barbarous. If negroes could testify, they would tell you of instances of women being whipped until they have miscarried at the whipping-post. I heard of such things at the south—they are undoubtedly facts. Children are whipped unmercifully for the smallest offences, and that before their mothers. A large proportion of the blacks have their shoulders, backs, and arms all scarred up, and not a few of them have had their heads laid open with clubs, stones, and brick-bats, and with the butt-end of whips and canes—some have had their jaws broken, others their teeth knocked in or out; while others have had their ears cropped and the sides of their cheeks gashed out. Some of the poor creatures have lost the sight of one of their eyes by the careless blows of the whipper, or by some other violence.

But punishing of slaves as above described, is not the only mode of torture. Some tie them up in a very uneasy posture, where they must stand *all night*, and they will then work them hard all day—that is, work them hard all day and torment them all night. Others punish by fastening them down on a log, or something else, and strike them on the bare skin with a board paddle full of holes. This breaks the skin, I should presume, at every hole where it comes in contact with it. Others, when other modes of punishment will not subdue them, *cat-haul* them—that is, take a cat by the nape of the neck and tail, or by the hind legs, and drag the claws across the back until satisfied. This kind of punishment poisons the flesh much worse than the whip, and is more dreaded by the slave. Some are branded by a hot iron, others have their flesh cut out in large gashes, to mark them. Some who are prone to run away, have iron fetters riveted around their ancles, sometimes they are put only on one foot, and are dragged on the ground. Others have on large iron collars or yokes upon their necks, or clogs riveted upon their wrists or ancles. Some have bells put upon them, hung upon a sort of frame to an iron collar. Some masters fly into a rage at trifles and knock down their negroes with their fists, or with the first thing that they can get hold of. The whip-lash-knots, or rawhide, have sometimes by a reckless stroke reached round to the front of the body and cut through to the bowels. One slaveholder with whom I lived, whipped one of his slaves one day, as many, I should think, as one hundred lashes, and then turned the *butt-end* and went to beating him over the head and ears, and truly I was amazed that the slave was not killed on the spot. Not a few slaveholders whip their slaves to death, and then say that they died under a "moderate correction." I wonder that ten are not killed where one is! Were they not much hardier than the whites many more of them must die than do. One young mulatto man, with whom I was well acquainted, was killed by his master in his yard with *impunity*. I boarded at the same time near the place where this glaring murder was committed, and knew the master well. He had a plantation, on which he enacted, almost daily, cruel barbarities, some of them, I was informed, more terrific, if possible, than death itself. Little notice was taken of this murder, and it all passed off without any action being taken against the murderer. The masters used to try to make me whip their negroes. They said I could not get along with them without flogging them—but I found I could get along better with them by coaxing and encouraging them than by beating and flogging them. I had not a heart to beat and kick about those beings; although I had not grace in my heart the three first years I was there, yet I sympathised with the slaves. I never was guilty of having but one whipped, and he was whipped but eight or nine blows. The circumstances were as follows: Several negroes were put under my care, one spring, *who were fresh from Congo and Guinea.* I could not understand them, neither could they me, in one word I spoke. I therefore pointed to them to go to work; all obeyed me willingly but one—he refused. I told the driver that he must tie him up and whip him. After he had tied him, by the help of some others, we struck him eight or nine blows, and he yielded. I told the driver not to strike him another blow. We untied him, and he went to work, and continued faithful all the time he was with me. This one was not a sample, however—many of them have such exalted views of freedom that it is hard work for the masters to whip them into brutes, that is to subdue their noble spirits. The negroes being put under my care, did not prevent the masters from whipping them when they pleased. But they never whipped much in my presence. This work was usually left until I had dismissed the hands. On the plantations, the masters chose to have the slaves whipped in the presence of all the hands, to strike them with terror.

VI. RUNAWAYS

Numbers of poor slaves run away from their masters; some of whom doubtless perish in the swamps and other secret places, rather than return back again to their masters; others stay away until they almost famish with hunger, and then return home rather than die, while others who abscond are caught by the negro-hunters, in various ways. Sometimes the master will hire some of his most trusty negroes to secure any stray negroes, who come on to their plantations, for many come at night to beg food of their friends on the plantations. The slaves assist one another usually when they can, and not be found out in it. The master can now and then, however, get some of his hands to betray the runaways. Some obtain their living in hunting after lost slaves. The most common way is to train up young dogs to follow them. This can easily be done by obliging a slave to go out into the woods, and climb a tree, and then put the young dog on his track, and with a little assistance he can be taught to follow him to the tree, and when found, of course the dog would bark at such game as a poor negro on a tree. There was a man living in Savannah when I was there, who kept a large number of dogs for no other purpose than to hunt runaway negroes. And he always had enough of this work to do, for hundreds of runaways are never found, but could he get news soon after one had fled, he was almost sure to catch him. And this fear of the dogs restrains multitudes from running off.

When he went out on a hunting excursion, to be gone several days, he took several persons with him, armed generally with rifles and followed by the dogs. The dogs were as true to the track of a negro, if one had passed recently, as a hound is to the track of a fox when he has found it. When the dogs draw near to their game, the slave must turn and fight them or climb a tree. If the latter, the dogs will stay and bark until the pursuers come. The blacks frequently deceive the dogs by crossing and recrossing the creeks. Should the hunters who have no dogs, start a slave from his hiding place, and the slave not stop at the hunter's call, he will shoot at him, as soon as he would at a deer. Some masters advertise so much for a runaway slave, dead or alive. It undoubtedly gives much more satisfaction to know that their property is dead, than to know that it is alive without being able to get it. Some slaves run away who never mean to be taken alive. I will mention one. He ran off and was pursued by the dogs, but having a weapon with him he succeeded in killing two or three of the dogs; but was afterwards shot. He had declared, that he never would be taken alive. The people rejoiced at the death of the slave, but lamented the death of the dogs, they were such ravenous hunters. Poor fellow, he fought for life and liberty like a hero; but the bullets brought him down. A negro can hardly walk unmolested at the south.—Every colored stranger that walks the streets is suspected of being a runaway slave, hence he must be interrogated by every negro hater whom he meets, and should he not have a pass, he must be arrested and hurried off to jail. Some masters boast that their slaves would not be free if they could. How little they know of their slaves! They are all sighing and groaning for freedom. May God hasten the time!

VII. CONFINEMENT AT NIGHT

When the slaves have done their day's work, they must be herded together like sheep in their yards, or on their plantations. They have not as much liberty as northern men have, who are sent to jail for debt, for they have liberty to walk a larger yard than the slaves have. The slaves must all be at their homes precisely at eight o'clock, P.M. At this hour the drums beat in the cities, as a signal for every slave to be in his den. In the country, the signal is given by firing guns, or some other way by which they may know the hour when to be at home. After this hour, the guard in the cities, and patrols in the country, being well armed, are on duty until daylight in the morning. If they catch any negroes during the night without a pass, they are immediately seized and hurried away to the guard-house, or if in the country to some place of confinement, where they are kept until nine o'clock, A. M., the next day, if not called for by that time, they are hurried off to jail, and there remain until called for by their master and his jail and guard house fees paid. The guards and patrols receive one dollar extra for every one they can catch, who has not a pass from his master, or overseer, but few masters will give their slaves passes to be out at night unless on some special business; notwithstanding, many venture out, watching every step they take for the guard or patrol, the consequence is, some are caught almost every night, and some nights many are taken; some, fleeing after being hailed by the watch, are shot down in attempting their escape, others are crippled for life. I find I shall not be able to write out more at present. My ministerial duties are pressing, and if I delay this till the next mail, I fear it will not be in season. Your brother for those who are in bonds,

HORACE MOULTON.

NARRATIVE AND TESTIMONY OF
SARAH M. GRIMKÉ

Miss Grimké is a daughter of the late Judge Grimké, of the Supreme Court of South Carolina, and sister of the late Hon. Thomas S. Grimké.

As I left my native state on account of slavery, and deserted the home of my fathers to escape the sound of the lash and the shrieks of tortured victims, I would gladly bury in oblivion the recollection of those scenes with which I have been familiar; but this may not, cannot be; they come over my memory like gory spectres, and implore me with resistless power, in the name of a God of mercy, in the name of a crucified Savior, in the name of humanity; for the sake of the slaveholder, as well as the slave, to bear witness to the horrors of the southern prison house. I feel impelled by a sacred sense of duty, by my obligations to my country, by sympathy for the bleeding victims of tyranny and lust, to give my testimony respecting the system of American slavery,—to detail a few facts, most of which came under my *personal observation.* And here I may premise, that the actors in these tragedies were all men and women of the highest respectability, and of the first families in South Carolina, and, with one exception, citizens of Charleston; and that their cruelties did not in the slightest degree affect their standing in society.

A handsome mulatto woman, about 18 or 20 years of age, whose independent spirit could not brook the degradation of slavery, was in the habit of running away: for this offence she had been repeatedly sent by her master and mistress to be whipped by the keeper of the Charleston work-house. This had been done with such inhuman severity, as to lacerate her back in a most shocking manner; a finger could not be laid between the cuts. But the love of liberty was too strong to be annihilated by torture; and, as a last resort, she was whipped at several different times, and kept a close prisoner. A heavy iron collar, with three long prongs projecting from it, was placed round her neck, and a strong and sound front tooth was extracted, to serve as a mark to describe her, in case of escape. Her sufferings at this time were agonizing; she could lie in no position but on her back, which was sore from scourgings, as I can testify, from personal inspection, and her only place of rest was the floor, on a blanket. These outrages were committed in a family where the mistress daily read the scriptures, and assembled her children for family worship. She was accounted, and was really, so far as alms-giving was concerned, a charitable woman, and tender hearted to the poor; and yet this suffering slave, who was the seamstress of the family, was continually in her presence, sitting in her chamber to sew, or engaged in her other household work, with her lacerated and bleeding back, her mutilated mouth, and heavy iron collar, without, so far as appeared, exciting any feelings of compassion.

A highly intelligent slave, who panted after freedom with ceaseless longings, made many attempts to get possession of himself. For every offence he was punished with extreme severity. At one time he was tied up by his hands to a tree, and whipped until his back was one gore of blood. To this terrible infliction he was subjected at intervals for several weeks, and kept heavily ironed while at his work. His master one day accused him of a fault, in the usual terms dictated by passion and arbitrary power; the man protested his innocence, but was not credited. He again repelled the charge with honest indignation. His master's temper rose almost to frenzy; and seizing a fork, he made a deadly plunge at the breast of the slave. The man being far his superior in strength, caught his arm, and dashed the weapon on the floor. His master grasped at his throat, but the slave disengaged himself, and rushed from the apartment. Having made his escape, he fled to the woods; and after wandering about for many months, living on roots and berries, and enduring every hardship, he was arrested and committed to jail. Here he lay for a considerable time, allowed scarcely food enough to sustain life, whipped in the most shocking manner, and confined in a cell so loathsome, that when his master visited him, he said the stench was enough to knock a man down. The filth had never been removed from the apartment since the poor creature had been immured in it. Although a black man, such had been the effect of starvation and suffering, that his master declared he hardly recognized him—his complexion was so yellow, and his hair, naturally thick and black, had become red and scanty; an infallible sign of long continued living on bad and insufficient food. Stripes, imprisonment, and the gnawings of hunger, had broken his lofty spirit for a season; and, to use his master's own exulting expression, he was "as humble as a dog." After a time he made another attempt to escape, and was absent so long, that a reward was offered for him, *dead or alive*. He eluded every attempt to take him, and his master, despairing of ever getting him again, offered to pardon him if he would return home. It is always understood that such intelligence will reach the runaway; and accordingly, at the entreaties of his wife and mother, the fugitive once more consented to return to his bitter bondage. I believe this was the last effort to obtain his liberty. His heart became touched with the power of the gospel; and the spirit which no inflictions could subdue, bowed at the cross of Jesus, and with the language on his lips—"the cup that my father hath given me, shall I not drink it?" submitted to the yoke of the oppressor, and wore his chains in unmurmuring patience till death released him. The master who perpetrated these wrongs upon his slave, was one of the most influential and honored citizens of South Carolina, and to his equals was bland, and courteous, and benevolent even to a proverb.

A slave who had been separated from his wife, because it best suited the convenience of his owner, ran away. He was taken up on the plantation where his wife, to whom he was tenderly attached, then lived. His only object in running away was to return to her—no other fault was attributed to him. For this offence he was confined in the stocks *six weeks*, in a miserable hovel, not weather-tight. He received fifty lashes weekly during that time, was allowed food barely sufficient to sustain him, and when released from confinement, was not permitted to return to his wife. His master, although himself a husband and a father, was unmoved by the touching appeals of the slave, who entreated that he might only remain with his wife, promising to discharge his duties faithfully; his master continued inexorable, and he was torn from his wife and family. The owner of this slave was a professing Christian, in full membership with the church, and this circumstance occurred when he was confined to his chamber during his last illness.

A punishment dreaded more by the slaves than whipping, unless it is unusually severe, is one which was invented by a female acquaintance of mine in Charleston—I heard her say so with much satisfaction. It is standing on one foot and holding the other in the hand. Afterwards it was improved upon, and a strap was contrived to fasten around the ankle and pass around the neck; so that the least weight of the foot resting on the strap would choke the person. The pain occasioned by this unnatural position was great; and when continued, as it sometimes was, for an hour or more, produced intense agony. I heard this same woman say, that she had the ears of her waiting maid *slit* for some petty theft. This she told me in the presence of the girl, who was standing in the room. She often had the helpless victims of her cruelty severely whipped, not scrupling herself to wield the instrument of torture, and with her own hands inflict severe chastisement. Her husband was less inhuman than his wife, but he was often goaded on by her to acts of great severity. In his last illness I was sent for, and watched beside his death couch. The girl on whom he had so often inflicted punishment, haunted his dying hours; and when at length the king of terrors approached, he shrieked in utter agony of spirit, "Oh, the blackness of darkness, the black imps, I can see them all around me—take them away!" and amid such exclamations he expired. These persons were of one of the first families in Charleston.

A friend of mine, in whose veracity I have entire confidence, told me that about two years ago, a woman in Charleston with whom I was well acquainted, had starved a female slave to death. She was confined in a solitary apartment, kept constantly tied, and condemned to the slow and horrible death of starvation. This woman was notoriously cruel. To those who have read the narrative of James Williams I need only say, that the character of young Larrimore's wife is an exact description of this female tyrant, whose countenance was ever dressed in smiles when in the presence of strangers, but whose heart was as the nether millstone toward her slaves.

As I was traveling in the lower country in South Carolina, a number of years since, my attention was suddenly arrested by an exclamation of horror from the coachman, who called out, "Look there, Miss Sarah, don't you see?"—I looked in the direction he pointed, and saw a human head stuck up on a high pole. On inquiry, I found that a runaway slave, who was outlawed, had been shot there, his head severed from his body, and put upon the public highway, as a terror to deter slaves from running away.

On a plantation in North Carolina, where I was visiting, I happened one day, in my rambles, to step into a negro cabin; my compassion was instantly called forth by the object which presented itself. A slave, whose head was white with age, was lying in one corner of the hovel; he had under his head a few filthy rags, but the boards were his only bed, it was the depth of winter, and the wind whistled through every part of the dilapidated building—he opened his languid eyes when I spoke, and in reply to my question, "What is the matter?" he said, "I am dying of a cancer in my side."—As he removed the rags which covered the sore, I found that it extended half round the body, and was shockingly neglected. I inquired if he had any nurse. "No, missey," was his answer, "but de people (the slaves) very kind to me, dey often steal time to run and see me and fetch me some ting to eat; if dey did not, I might starve." The master and mistress of this man, who had been worn out in their service, were remarkable for their intelligence, and their hospitality knew no bounds towards those who were of their own grade in society: the master had for some time held the highest military office in North Carolina, and not long previous to the time of which I speak, was the Governor of the State.

On a plantation in South Carolina, I witnessed a similar case of suffering—an aged woman suffering under an incurable disease in the same miserably neglected situation. The "owner" of this slave was proverbially kind to her negroes; so much so, that the planters in the neighborhood said she spoiled them, and set a bad example, which might produce discontent among the surrounding slaves; yet I have seen this woman tremble with rage, when her slaves displeased her, and heard her use language to them which could only be expected from an inmate of Bridewell; and have known her in a gust of passion send a favorite slave to the workhouse to be severely whipped.

Another fact occurs to me. A young woman about eighteen, stated some circumstances relative to her young master, which were thought derogatory to his character; whether true or false, I am unable to say; she was threatened with punishment, but persisted in affirming that she had only spoken the truth. Finding her incorrigible, it was concluded to send her to the Charleston workhouse and have her whipt; she pleaded in vain for a commutation of her sentence, not so much because she dreaded the actual suffering, as because her delicate mind shrunk from the shocking exposure of her person to the eyes of brutal and licentious men; she declared to me that death would be preferable; but her entreaties were vain, and as there was no means of escaping but by running away, she resorted to it as a desperate remedy, for her timid nature never could have braved the perils necessarily encountered by fugitive slaves, had not her mind been thrown into a state of despair.——She was apprehended after a few weeks, by two slave-catchers, in a deserted house, and as it was late in the evening they concluded to spend the night there. What inhuman treatment she received from them has never been revealed. They tied her with cords to their bodies, and supposing they had secured their victim, soon fell into a deep sleep, probably rendered more profound by intoxication and fatigue; but the miserable captive slumbered not; by some means she disengaged herself from her bonds, and again fled through the lone wilderness. After a few days she was discovered in a wretched hut, which seemed to have been long uninhabited; she was speechless; a raging fever consumed her vitals, and when a physician saw her, he said she was dying of a disease brought on by over fatigue; her mother was permitted to visit her, but ere she reached her, the damps of death stood upon her brow, and she had only the sad consolation of looking on the death-struck form and convulsive agonies of her child.

A beloved friend in South Carolina, the wife of a slaveholder, with whom I often mingled my tears, when helpless and hopeless we deplored together the horrors of slavery, related to me some years since the following circumstance.

On the plantation adjoining her husband's, there was a slave of pre-eminent piety. His master was not a professor of religion, but the superior excellence of this disciple of Christ was not unmarked by him, and I believe he was so sensible of the good influence of his piety that he did not deprive him of the few religious privileges within his reach. A planter was one day dining with the owner of this slave, and in the course of conversation observed, that all profession of religion among slaves was mere hypocrisy. The other asserted a contrary opinion, adding, "I have a slave who I believe would rather die than deny his Saviour." This was ridiculed, and the master urged to prove the assertion. He accordingly sent for this man of God, and peremptorily ordered him to deny his belief in the Lord Jesus Christ. The slave pleaded to be excused, constantly affirming that he would rather die than deny the Redeemer, whose blood was shed for him. His master, after vainly trying to induce obedience by threats, had him terribly whipped. The fortitude of the sufferer was not to be shaken; he nobly rejected the offer of exemption from further chastisement at the expense of destroying his soul, and this blessed martyr *died in consequence of this severe infliction*. Oh, how bright a gem will this victim of irresponsible power be, in that crown which sparkles on the Redeemer's brow; and that many such will cluster there, I have not the shadow of a doubt.

Sarah M. Grimké.

Fort Lee, Bergen County,
　New Jersey, 3rd Month, 26th, 1830.

TESTIMONY OF THE LATE REV. JOHN GRAHAM

Mr. Graham of Townsend, Mass., resided in S. Carolina from 1831 to the latter part of 1833. Mr. Graham graduated at Amherst College in 1829, spent some time at the Theological Seminary, in New Haven, Ct., and went to South Carolina, for his health in 1830. He resided principally on the island of St. Helena, S. C., and most of the time in the family of James Tripp, Esq., a wealthy slave holding planter. During his residence at St. Helena, he was engaged as an instructer, and was most of the time the stated preacher on the island. Mr. G. was extensively known in Massachusetts; and his fellow students and instructors, at Amherst College, and at Yale Theological Seminary, can bear testimony to his integrity and moral worth. The following are extracts of letters, which he wrote while in South Carolina, to an intimate friend in Concord, Massachusetts, who has kindly furnished them for publication.

EXTRACTS

Springfield, St. Helena Isl., S. C., Oct. 22, 1832.

"Last night, about one o'clock, I was awakened by the report of a musket. I was out of bed almost instantly. On opening my window, I found the report proceeded from my host's chamber. He had let off his pistol, which he usually keeps by him night and day, at a slave, who had come into the yard, and as it appears, had been with one of his house servants. He did not hit him. The ball, taken from a pine tree the next morning, I will show you, should I be spared by Providence ever to return to you. The house servant was called to the master's chamber, where he received 75 lashes, very severe too; and I could not only hear every lash, but each groan which succeeded very distinctly as I lay in my bed. What was then done with the servant I know not. Nothing was said of this to me in the morning and I presume it will ever be kept from me with care, if I may judge of kindred acts. I shall make no comment."

In the same letter, Mr. Graham says:—

"You ask me of my hostess"—then after giving an idea of her character says: "To-day, she has I verily believe laid, in a very severe manner too, more than 300 *stripes,* upon the house servants," (17 in number).

Darlington, Court House, S. C., March, 28th, 1838.

"I walked up to the Court House to-day, where I heard one of the most interesting cases I ever heard. I say interesting, on account of its novelty to me, though it had no novelty for the people, as such cases are of frequent occurrence. The case was this: To know whether two ladies, present in court, were *white* or *black.* The ladies were dressed well, seemed modest, and were retiring and neat in their look, having blue eyes, black hair, and appeared to understand much of the etiquette of southern behaviour.

"A man, more avaricious than humane, as is the case with most of the rich planters, laid a remote claim to those two modest, unassuming, innocent and free young ladies as his property, with the design of putting them into the field, and thus increasing his STOCK! As well as the people of Concord are known to be of a peaceful disposition, and for their love of good order, I verily believe if a similar trial should be brought forward there and conducted as this was, the good people would drive the lawyers out of the house.

Such would be their indignation at their language, and at the mean under-handed manner of trying to ruin those young ladies, as to their standing in society in this district, if they could not succeed in dooming them for life to the degraded condition of slavery, and all its intolerable cruelties. Oh slavery! if statues of marble could curse you, they would speak. If bricks could speak, they would all surely thunder out their anathemas against you, accursed thing! How many white sons and daughters, have bled and groaned under the lash in this sultry climate," &c.

Under date of March, 1832, Mr. G. writes, "I have been doing what I hope never to be called to do again, and what I fear I have badly done, though performed to the best of my ability, namely, sewing up a very bad wound made by a wild hog. The slave was hunting wild hogs, when one, being closely pursued, turned upon his pursuer, who turning to run, was caught by the animal, thrown down, and badly wounded in the thigh. The wound is about five inches long and very deep. It was made by the tusk of the animal. The slaves brought him to one of the huts on Mr. Tripp's plantation and made every exertion to stop the blood by filling the wound with ashes, (their remedy for stopping blood) but finding this to fail they came to me (there being no other white person on the plantation, as it is now holidays) to know if I could stop the blood. I went and found that the poor creature must bleed to death unless it could be stopped soon. I called for a needle and succeeded in sewing it up as well as I could, and in stopping the blood. In a short time his master, who had been sent for came; and oh, you would have shuddered if you had heard the awful oaths that fell from his lips, threatening in the same breath "*to pay him for that!*" I left him as soon as decency would permit, with his hearty thanks that I had saved him $500! Oh, may heaven protect the poor, suffering, fainting slave, and show his master his wanton cruelty—oh slavery! slavery!"

Under date of July, 1832, Mr. G. writes, "I wish you could have been at the breakfast table with me this morning to have seen and heard what I saw and heard, not that I wish your ear and heart and soul pained as mine is, 'with every day's observation of wrong and outrage' with which this place is filled, but that you might have auricular and ocular evidence of the cruelty of slavery, of cruelties that mortal language can never describe—that you might see the tender mercies of a hardened slaveholder, one who bears the name of being *one of the mildest and most merciful masters of which this island can boast.* Oh, my friend, another is screaming under the lash, in the shed-room, but for what I know not. The scene this morning was truly distressing to me. It was this:—*After the blessing was asked* at the breakfast table, one of the servants, a woman grown, in giving one of the children some molasses, happened to pour out a little more than usual, though not more than the child usually eats. Her master was angry at the petty and indifferent mistake, or slip of the hand. He rose from the table, took both of her hands in one of his, and with the other began to beat her, first on one side of her head and then on the other, and repeating this, till, as he said on sitting down at table, it hurt his hand too much to continue it longer. He then took off his *shoe,* and with the heel began in the same manner as with his hand, till the poor creature could no longer endure it without screeches and raising her elbow as it is natural to ward off the blows. He then called a great overgrown negro *to hold her hands behind her* while he should wreak his vengeance upon the poor servant. In this position he began again to beat the poor suffering wretch. It now became intolerable to bear; she *fell, screaming to me for help.* After she fell, he beat her until I thought she would have died in his hands. She got up, however, went out and washed off the blood and came in before we rose from table, one of the most pitiable objects I ever saw till I came to the South. Her ears were almost as thick as my hand, her eyes awfully blood-shotten, her lips, nose, cheeks, chin, and whole head swollen so that no one would have known it was Etta—and for all this, she had to turn round as she was going out and *thank her master!* Now, all this was done while I was sitting at breakfast with the rest of the family. Think you not I wished myself sitting with the peaceful and happy circle around your table? Think of my feelings, but pity the poor negro slave, who not only fans his cruel master when he eats and sleeps, but bears the stripes his caprice may inflict. Think of this, and let heaven hear your prayers."

In a letter dated St. Helena Island, S. C., Dec. 3, 1832, Mr. G. writes, "If a slave here complains to his master, that his task is too great, his master at once calls him a scoundrel and tells him it is only because he has not enough to do, and orders the driver to increase his task, however unable he may be for the performance of it. I saw TWENTY-SEVEN *whipped at one time* just because they did not do more, when the poor creatures were so tired that they could scarcely drag one foot after the other."

TESTIMONY OF MR. WILLIAM POE

Mr. Poe is a native of Richmond, Virginia, and was formerly a slaveholder. He was for several years a merchant in Richmond, and subsequently in Lynchburg, Virginia. A few years since, he emancipated his slaves, and removed to Hamilton County, Ohio, near Cincinnati; where he is a highly respected ruling elder in the Presbyterian church. He says,—

I am pained exceedingly, and nothing but my duty to God, to the oppressors, and to the poor down-trodden slaves, who go mourning all their days, could move me to say a word. I will state to you a *few* cases of the abuse of the slaves, but time would fail, if I had language to tell how many and great are the inflictions of slavery, even in its mildest form.

Benjamin James Harris, a wealthy tobacconist of Richmond, Virginia, whipped a slave girl fifteen years old to death. While he was whipping her, his wife heated a smoothing iron, put it on her body in various places, and burned her severely. The verdict of the coroner's inquest was, "Died of excessive whipping." He was tried in Richmond, and acquitted. I attended the trial. Some years after, this same Harris whipped another slave to death. The man had not done so much work as was required of him. After a number of protracted and violent scourgings, with short intervals between, the slave died under the lash. Harris was tried, and again acquitted, because none but blacks saw it done. The same man afterwards whipped another slave severely, for not doing work to please him. After repeated and severe floggings in quick succession, for the same cause, the slave, in despair of pleasing him, cut off his own hand. Harris soon after became a bankrupt, went to New Orleans to recruit his finances, failed, removed to Kentucky, became a maniac, and died.

A captain in the United States' Navy, who married a daughter of the collector of the port of Richmond, and resided there, became offended with his negro boy, took him into the meat house, put him upon a stool, crossed his hands before him, tied a rope to them, threw it over a joist in the building, drew the boy up so that he could just stand on the stool with his toes, and kept him in that position, flogging him severely at intervals, until the boy became so exhausted that he reeled off the stool, and swung by his hands until he died. The master was tried and acquitted.

In Goochland County, Virginia, an overseer tied a slave to a tree, flogged him again and again with great severity, then piled brush around him, set it on fire, and burned him to death. The overseer was tried and imprisoned. The whole transaction may be found on the records of the court.

In traveling, one day, from Petersburg to Richmond, Virginia, I heard cries of distress at a distance, on the road. I rode up, and found two white men, beating a slave. One of them had hold of a rope, which was passed under the bottom of a fence; the other end was fastened around the neck of the slave, who was thrown flat on the ground, on his face, with his back bared. The other was beating him furiously with a large hickory.

A slaveholder in Henrico County, Virginia, had a slave who used frequently to work for my father. One morning he came into the field with his back completely *cut up*, and mangled from his head to his heels. The man was so stiff and sore he could scarcely walk. This same person got offended with another of his slaves, knocked him down, and struck out one of his eyes with a maul. The eyes of several of his slaves were injured by similar violence.

In Richmond, Virginia, a company occupied as a dwelling a large warehouse. They got angry with a negro lad, one of their slaves, took him into the cellar, tied his hands with a rope, bored a hole through the floor, and passed the rope up through it. Some of the family drew up the boy, while others whipped. This they continued until the boy died. The warehouse was owned by a Mr. Whitlock, on the scite of one formerly owned by a Mr. Philpot.

Joseph Chilton, a resident of Campbell County, Virginia, purchased a quart of tanners' oil, for the purpose, as he said, of putting it on one of his negro's heads, that he had sometime previous pitched or tarred over, for running away.

In the town of Lynchburg, Virginia, there was a negro man put in prison, charged with having pillaged some packages of goods, which he, as head man of a boat, received at Richmond, to be delivered at Lynchburg. The goods belonged to A. B. Nichols, of Liberty, Bedford County, Virginia. He came to Lynchburg, and desired the jailor to permit him to whip the negro, to make him confess, as there was *no proof against him*. Mr. Williams, (I think that is his name), a pious Methodist man, a great stickler for law and good order, professedly a great friend to the black man, delivered the negro into the hands of Nichols. Nichols told me that he took the slave,

tied his wrists together, then drew his arms down so far below his
knees as to permit a staff to pass above the arms under the knees,
thereby placing the slave in a situation that he could not move hand
or foot. He then commenced his bloody work, and continued, at
intervals, until 500 blows were inflicted. I received this statement
from Nichols himself, who was, by the way, a *son of the land of "steady
habits,"* where there are many like him, if we may judge from their
writings, sayings, and doings.

PRIVATIONS OF THE SLAVES

I. FOOD

We begin with the *food* of the slaves, because if they are ill treated
in this respect we may be sure that they will be ill treated in other
respects, and generally in a greater degree. For a man habitually to
stint his dependents in their food, is the extreme of meanness and
cruelty, and the greatest evidence he can give of utter indifference
to their comfort. The father who stints his children or domestics, or
the master his apprentices, or the employer his laborers, or the officer his soldiers, or the captain his crew, when able to furnish them
with sufficient food, is every where looked upon as unfeeling and
cruel. All mankind agree to call such a character inhuman. If any
thing can move a hard heart, it is the appeal of hunger. The Arab
robber whose whole life is a prowl for plunder, will freely divide his
camel's milk with the hungry stranger who halts at his tent door,
though he may have just waylaid him and stripped him of his money.
Even savages take pity on hunger. Who ever went famishing from
an Indian's wigwam. As much as hunger craves, is the Indian's free
gift even to an enemy. The necessity for food is such a universal
want, so constant, manifest and imperative, that the heart is more
touched with pity by the plea of hunger, and more ready to supply
that want than any other. He who can habitually inflict on others
the pain of hunger by giving them insufficient food, can habitually
inflict on them any other pain. He can kick and cuff and flog and
brand them, put them in irons or the stocks, can overwork them,

deprive them of sleep, lacerate their backs, make them work without clothing, and sleep without covering.

Other cruelties may be perpetrated in hot blood and the act regretted as soon as done—the feeling that prompts them is not a permanent state of mind, but a violent impulse stung up by sudden provocation. But he who habitually withholds from his dependents sufficient sustenance, can plead no such palliation. The fact itself shows, that his permanent state of mind toward them is a brutal indifference to their wants and sufferings—A state of mind which will naturally, necessarily, show itself in innumerable privations and inflictions upon them, when it can be done with impunity.

If, therefore, we find upon examination, that the slaveholders do not furnish their slaves with sufficient food, and do thus habitually inflict upon them the pain of hunger, we have a clue furnished to their treatment in other respects, and may fairly infer habitual and severe privations and inflictions; not merely from the fact that men are quick to feel for those who suffer from hunger, and perhaps more ready to relieve that want than any other; but also, because it is more for the interest of the slaveholder to supply that want than any other; consequently, if the slave suffer in this respect, he must as the general rule, suffer *more* in other respects.

We now proceed to show that the slaves have insufficient food. This will be shown first from the express declarations of slaveholders, and other competent witnesses who are, or have been residents of slave states, that the slaves generally are *under-fed*. And then, by the laws of slave states, and by the testimony of slaveholders and others, the *kind*, *quantity*, and *quality*, of their allowance will be given, and the reader left to judge for himself whether the slave *must* not be a sufferer.

THE SLAVES SUFFER FROM HUNGER—DECLARATIONS OF SLAVEHOLDERS AND OTHERS

WITNESSES	TESTIMONY
Hon. Alexander Smyth, a slaveholder, and for ten years, Member of Congress from Virginia, in his speech on the Missouri question, Jan 28th, 1820.	"By confining the slaves to the Southern states, where crops are raised for exportation, and bread and meat are purchased, you *doom them to scarcity and hunger.* It is proposed to hem in the blacks where they are ILL FED."

WITNESSES	TESTIMONY
Rev. George Whitefield, in his letter, to the slaveholders of Md., Va., N. C., S. C. and Ga. published in Georgia, just one hundred years ago, 1739.	"My blood has frequently run cold within me, to think how many of your slaves *have not sufficient food to eat;* they are scarcely permitted to *pick up the crumbs,* that fall from their master's table."
Rev. John Rankin, of Ripley, Ohio, a native of Tennessee, and for some year's a preacher in slave states.	"Thousands of the slaves are pressed with the gnawings of cruel hunger during their whole lives."
Report of the Gradual Emancipation Society, of North Carolina, 1826. Signed Moses Swain, President, and William Swain, Secretary.	Speaking of the condition of slaves, in the eastern part of that state, the report says,— "The master puts the unfortunate wretches upon short allowances, scarcely sufficient for their sustenance, so that a *great part* of them go *half starved* much of the time."
Mr. Asa A. Stone, a Theological Student, who resided near Natchez, Miss., in 1834–5.	"On almost every plantation, the hands suffer more or less from hunger at some seasons of almost every year. There is always a *good deal of suffering* from hunger. On many plantations, and particularly in Louisiana, the slaves are in a condition of *almost utter famishment,* during a great portion of the year."
Thomas Clay, Esq., of Georgia, a Slaveholder.	"From various causes this [the slave's allowance of food] is *often* not adequate to the support of a laboring man."
Mr. Tobias Boudinot, St. Albans, Ohio, a member of the Methodist Church. Mr. B. for some years navigated the Mississippi.	"The slaves down the Mississippi, are *half-starved,* the boats, when they stop at night, are constantly boarded by slaves, begging for something to eat."
President Edwards, the younger, in a sermon before the Conn. Abolition Society, 1791.	"The slaves are supplied with barely enough to keep them from *starving.*"

WITNESSES	TESTIMONY
Rev. Horace Moulton, a Methodist Clergyman of Marlborough, Mass., who lived five years in Georgia.	"As a general thing on the plantations, the slaves suffer extremely for the want of food."
Rev. George Bourne, late editor of the Protestant Vindicator, N. Y., who was seven years pastor of a church in Virginia.	"The slaves are deprived of *needful* sustenance."

1. KINDS OF FOOD

Hon. Robert Turnbull, a slaveholder of Charleston, South Carolina.	"The subsistence of the slaves consists, from March until August, of corn ground into grits, or meal, made into what is called *hommony,* or baked into corn bread. The other six months, they are fed upon the sweet potatoes. Meat, when given, is only by way of *indulgence or favor.*"
Mr. Eleazar Powell, Chippewa, Beaver Co., Penn., who resided in Mississippi, in 1836–7.	"The food of the slaves was generally corn bread, and *sometimes* meat or molasses."
Reuben G. Macy, a member of the Society of Friends, Hudson, N. Y., who resided in South Carolina.	"The slaves had no food allowed them besides *corn,* excepting at Christmas, when they had beef."
Mr. William Leftwich, a native of Virginia, and recently of Madison Co., Alabama, now member of the Presbyterian Church, Delhi, Ohio.	"On my uncle's plantation, the food of the slaves, was corn pone and a small allowance of meat."

WILLIAM LADD, Esq., of Minot, Me., president of the American Peace Society, and formerly a slaveholder of Florida, gives the following testimony as to the allowance of food to slaves.

"The usual food of the slaves was *corn*, with a modicum of salt. In some cases the master allowed no salt, but the slaves boiled the sea water for salt in their little pots. For about eight days near Christmas, i. e., from the Saturday evening before, to the Monday evening after Christmas day, they were allowed some *meat*. They always with one single exception ground their corn in a hand-mill, and cooked their food themselves.

Extract of a letter from Rev. D. C. EASTMAN, a preacher of the Methodist Episcopal church, in Fayette county, Ohio.

"In March, 1838, Mr. Thomas Larrimer, a deacon of the Presbyterian church in Bloomingbury, Fayette county, Ohio, Mr. G. S. Fullerton, merchant, and member of the same church, and Mr. William A. Ustick, an elder of the same church, spent a night with a Mr. Shepherd, about 30 miles North of Charleston, S. C., on the Monk's corner road. He owned five families of negroes, who, he said, were fed from the same meal and meat tubs as himself, but that 99 out of a 100 of all the slaves in that county *saw meat but once a year,* which was on Christmas holidays."

As an illustration of the inhuman experiments sometimes tried upon slaves, in respect to the *kind* as well as the quality and quantity of their food, we solicit the attention of the reader to the testimony of the late General Wade Hampton, of South Carolina. General Hampton was for some time commander in chief of the army on the Canada frontier during the last war, and at the time of his death, about three years since, was the largest slaveholder in the United States. The General's testimony is contained in the following extract of a letter, just received from a distinguished clergyman in the west, extensively known both as a preacher and a writer. His name is with the executive committee of the American Anti-Slavery Society.

"You refer in your letter to a statement made to you while in this place, respecting the late General Wade Hampton, of South Carolina, and task me to write out for you the circumstances of the case—considering them well calculated to illustrate two points in the history of slavery: 1st, That the habit of slaveholding dreadfully blunts the feelings toward the slave, producing such insensibility that his sufferings and death are regarded with indifference. 2d, That the slave often has insufficient food, both in quantity and quality.

"I received my information from a lady in the west of high respectability and great moral worth,—but think it best to withhold her name, although the statement was not made in confidence.

"My informant stated that she sat at dinner once in company with General Wade Hampton, and several others; that the conversation turned upon the treatment of their servants, &c.; when the General undertook to entertain the company with the relation of an experiment he had made in the feeding of his slaves on cotton seed. He said that he first mingled one-fourth cotton seed with three-fourths corn, on which they seemed to thrive tolerably well; that he then had measured out to them equal quantities of each, which did not seem to produce any important change; afterwards he increased the quantity of cotton seed to three-fourths, mingled with one-fourth corn, and then he declared, with an oath, that 'they died like rotten sheep!!' It is but justice to the lady to state that she spoke of his conduct with the utmost indignation; and she mentioned also that he received no countenance from the company present, but that all seemed to look at each other with astonishment. I give it to you just as I received it from one who was present, and whose character for veracity is unquestionable.

"It is proper to add that I had previously formed an acquaintance with Dr. Witherspoon, now of Alabama, if alive; whose former residence was in South Carolina; from whom I received a particular account of the manner of feeding and treating slaves on the plantations of General Wade Hampton, and others in the same part of the State; and certainly no one could listen to the recital without concluding that such masters and overseers as he described must have hearts like the nether millstone. The cotton seed experiment I had heard of before also, as having been made in other parts of the south; consequently, I was prepared to receive as true the above statement, even if I had not been so well acquainted with the high character of my informant."

2. QUANTITY OF FOOD

The legal allowance of food for slaves in North Carolina, is in the words of the law, "a quart of corn per day." See Haywood's Manual, 525. The legal allowance in Louisiana is more, a barrel [flour barrel] of corn, (in the ear), or its equivalent in other grain, and a pint of salt a month. In the other slave states the amount of food for the slaves is left to the option of the master.

WITNESSES	TESTIMONY
Thos. Clay, Esq., of Georgia, a slaveholder, in his address before the Georgia Presbytery, 1833.	"The quantity allowed by custom is *a peck of corn a week!*"
The Maryland Journal, and Baltimore Advertiser, May 30, 1788.	"*A single peck of corn a week, or the like measure of rice,* is the *ordinary* quantity of provision for a *hard-working* slave; to which a small quantity of meat is occasionally, though *rarely,* added."
W. C. Gildersleeve, Esq., a native of Georgia, and Elder in the Presbyterian Church, Wilksbarre, Penn.	"The weekly allowance to grown slaves on this plantation, where I was best acquainted, was *one peck of corn.*"
Wm. Ladd, of Minot, Maine, formerly a slaveholder in Florida.	"The usual allowance of food was *one quart of corn a day,* to a full task hand, with a modicum of salt; kind masters allowed *a peck of corn a week*; some masters allowed no salt."
Mr. Jarvis Brewster, in his "Exposition of the treatment of slaves in the Southern States," published in N. Jersey, 1815.	"The allowance of provisions for the slaves, is *one peck of corn, in the grain, per week.*"
Rev. Horace Moulton, a Methodist Clergyman of Marlborough, Mass., who lived five years in Georgia.	"In Georgia the planters give each slave only *one peck of their gourd seed corn per week,* with a small quantity of salt."
Mr. F. C. Macy, Nantucket, Mass., who resided in Georgia in 1820.	"The food of the slaves was three pecks of potatoes a week during the potato season, and *one peck of corn,* during the remainder of the year."
Mr. Nehemiah Caulkins, a member of the Baptist Church in Waterford, Conn., who resided in North Carolina, eleven winters.	"The subsistence of the slaves, consists of *seven quarts of meal* or *eight quarts of small rice for one week!*"

WITNESSES	TESTIMONY
William Savery, late of Philadelphia, an eminent Minister of the Society of Friends, who travelled extensively in the slave states, on a Religious Visitation, speaking of the subsistence of the slaves, says, in his published Journal,	"*A peck of corn* is their (the slaves), miserable subsistence *for a week*."
The late John Parrish, of Philadelphia, another highly respected Minister of the Society of Friends, who traversed the South, on a similar mission, in 1804 and 5, says in his "Remarks on the slavery of Blacks,"	"They allow them but *one peck of meal,* for a whole week, in some of the Southern states."
Richard Macy, Hudson, N. Y., a Member of the Society of Friends, who has resided in Georgia.	"Their usual allowance of food was one peck of corn per week, which was dealt out to them every first day of the week. They had nothing allowed them besides the corn, except one quarter of beef at Christmas."
Rev. C. S. Renshaw, of Quincy, Ill., (the testimony of a Virginian.)	"The slaves are generally allowanced: a pint of corn meal and a salt herring, or in lieu of the herring a "dab" of fat meat of about the same value. I have known the sour milk, and clauber to be served out to the hands, when there was an abundance of milk on the plantation. This is a luxury not often afforded."

Testimony of Mr. George W. Westgate, member of the Congregational Church, of Quincy, Illinois. Mr. W. has been engaged in the low country trade for twelve years, more than half of each year, principally on the Mississippi, and its tributary streams in the southwestern slave states.

"*Feeding is not sufficient,*—let facts speak. On the coast, i. e. Natchez and the Gulf of Mexico, the allowance was one barrel of ears of corn, and a pint of salt per month. They may cook this in what manner they please, but it must be done after dark; they have no day light to prepare it by. Some few planters, but only a few, let them prepare their corn on Saturday afternoon. Planters, overseers, and negroes, have told me, that in *pinching times,* i. e. when corn is high, they did not get near that quantity. In Miss., I know some planters who allowed their hands three and a half pounds of meat per week, when it was cheap. Many prepare their corn on the Sabbath, when they are not worked on that day, which however is frequently the case on sugar plantations. There are very many masters on "the coast" who will not suffer their slaves to come to the boats, because they steal molasses to barter for meat; indeed they generally trade more or less with stolen property. But it is impossible to find out what and when, as their articles of barter are of such trifling importance. They would often come on board our boats to beg a bone, and would tell how badly they were fed, that they were almost starved; many a time I have set up all night, to prevent them from stealing something to eat."

3. QUALITY OF FOOD

Having ascertained the kind and quantity of food allowed to the slaves, it is important to know something of its *quality*, that we may judge of the amount of sustenance which it contains. For, if their provisions are of an inferior quality, or in a damaged state, then, power to sustain labor must be greatly diminished.

WITNESSES	TESTIMONY
Thomas Clay, Esq., of Georgia, in an address to the Georgia Presbytery, 1834, speaking of the quality of the corn given to the slaves, says,	"There is *often a defect here.*"
Rev. Horace Moulton, a Methodist clergyman at Marlborough, Mass. and five years a resident of Georgia.	"The food, or 'feed' of slaves is generally of the *poorest* kind."

WITNESSES	TESTIMONY
The "Western Medical Reformer," in an article on the diseases peculiar to negroes, by a Kentucky physician, says of the diet of the slaves,	"They live on a coarse, *crude, unwholesome diet.*"
Professor A. G. Smith, of the New York Medical College; formerly a physician in Louisville, Kentucky.	"I have myself known numerous instances of large families of *badly fed* negroes swept off by a prevailing epidemic; and it is well known to many intelligent planters in the south, that the best method of preventing that horrible malady, *Chachexia Africana,* is to feed the negroes with *nutritious* food."

4. NUMBER AND TIME OF MEALS EACH DAY

In determining whether or not the slaves suffer for want of food, the number of hours intervening, and the labor performed between their meals, and the number of meals each day, should be taken into consideration.

WITNESSES	TESTIMONY
Philemon Bliss, Esq., a lawyer in Elyria, Ohio, and member of the Presbyterian church, who lived in Florida, in 1834, and 1835.	"The slaves go to the field in the morning; they carry with them corn meal wet with water, and at *noon* build a fire on the ground and bake it in the ashes. After the labors of the day are over, they take their *second* meal of ash-cake."
President Edwards, the younger.	"The slaves eat *twice* during the day."
Mr. Eleazar Powell, Chippewa, Beaver county, Penn., who resided in Mississippi in 1836 and 1837.	"The slaves received *two* meals during the day. Those who have their food cooked for them get their breakfast about eleven o'clock, and their other meal *after night.*"

WITNESSES	TESTIMONY
Mr. Nehemiah Caulkins, Waterford, Conn., who spent eleven winters in North Carolina.	"The *breakfast* of the slaves was generally about *ten or eleven* o'clock."
Rev. Phineas Smith, Centreville, N. Y., who has lived at the south some years.	"The slaves have usually *two* meals a day, viz: at eleven o'clock and at night."
Rev. C. S. Renshaw, Quincy, Illinois,—the testimony of a Virginian.	"The slaves have *two* meals a day. They breakfast at from ten to eleven, A. M., and eat their supper at from six to nine or ten at night, as the season and crops may be."

The preceding testimony establishes the following points.

1st. That the slaves are allowed, in general, *no meat*. This appears from the fact, that in the *only* slave states which regulate the slaves' rations *by law,* (North Carolina and Louisiana), the *legal ration* contains *no meat*. Besides, the late Hon. R. J. Turnbull, one of the largest planters in South Carolina, says expressly, "meat, when given, is only by the way of indulgence or favor." It is shown also by the direct testimony recorded above, of slaveholders and others, in all parts of the slaveholding south and west, that the *general* allowance on plantations is corn or meal and salt merely. To this there are doubtless many exceptions, but they are *only* exceptions; the number of slaveholders who furnish meat for their *field-hands*, is small, in comparison with the number of those who do not. The house slaves, that is, the cooks, chambermaids, waiters, &c., generally get some meat every day; the remainder bits and bones of their masters' tables. But that the great body of the slaves, those that compose the field gangs, whose labor and exposure, and consequent exhaustion, are vastly greater than those of house slaves, toiling as they do from day light till dark, in the fogs of the early morning, under the scorchings of mid-day, and amid the damps of evening, are *in general* provided with *no meat*, is abundantly established by the preceding testimony.

Now we do not say that meat *is necessary* to sustain men under hard and long continued labor, nor that it is *not*. This is not a treatise on dietetics; but it is a notorious fact, that the medical faculty in this country, with very few exceptions, do most strenuously insist that it is necessary; and that working men in all parts of the country do *believe* that meat is indispensable to sustain them, even those who work within doors, and only ten hours a day, every one knows. Further, it is notorious, that the slaveholders themselves *believe* the daily use of meat to be absolutely necessary to the comfort, not merely of those who labor, but of those who are idle, is proved by the fact of meat being a part of the daily ration of food provided for convicts in the prisons, in every one of the slave states, except in those rare cases where meat is expressly prohibited, and the convict is, by *way of extra punishment* confined to bread and water; he is occasionally, and for a little time only, confined to bread and water; that is, to the *ordinary diet* of slaves, with this difference in favor of the convict: his bread is made for him, whereas the slave is forced to pound or grind his own corn and make his own bread, when exhausted with toil.

The preceding testimony shows also, that *vegetables* form generally no part of the slaves' allowance. The *sole* food of the majority is *corn*: at every meal—from day to day—from week to week—from month to month, *corn*. In South Carolina, Georgia, and Florida, the sweet potato is, to a considerable extent, substituted for corn during a part of the year.

2d. The preceding testimony proves conclusively, that the *quantity of food* generally allowed to a full-grown field-hand, is a peck of corn a week, or a fraction over a quart and a gill of corn a day. The legal ration of North Carolina is *less*—in Louisiana it is *more*. Of the slaveholders and other witnesses, who give the foregoing testimony, the reader will perceive that no one testifies to a larger allowance of corn than a peck for a week; though a number testify, that within the circle of their knowledge, *seven* quarts was the usual allowance. Frequently a small quantity of meat is added; but this, as has already been shown, is not the general rule for *field-hands*. We may add, also, that in the season of "pumpkins," "cimblins," "cabbages," "greens," &c., the slaves on small plantations are, to some extent, furnished with those articles.

Now, without entering upon the vexed question of how much food is necessary to sustain the human system, under severe toil and exposure, and without giving the opinions of physiologists as to the insufficiency or sufficiency of the slaves' allowance, we affirm that all civilized nations have, in all ages, and in the most emphatic manner, declared, that *eight quarts of corn a week,* (the usual allowance of our slaves), is utterly insufficient to sustain the human body, under such toil and exposure as that to which the slaves are subjected.

To show this fully, it will be necessary to make some estimates, and present some statistics. And first, the northern reader must bear in mind, that the corn furnished to the slaves at the south, is almost invariably the *white gourd seed* corn, and that a quart of this kind of corn weighs five or six ounces *less* than a quart of "flint corn," the kind generally raised in the northern and eastern states; consequently a peck of the corn generally given to the slaves, would be only equivalent to a fraction more than six quarts and a pint of the corn commonly raised in the New England States, New York, New Jersey, &c. Now, what would be said of the northern capitalist, who should allow his laborers but *six quart, and five gills of corn for a week's provisions*?

Further, it appears in evidence, that the corn given to the slaves is often *defective*. This, the reader will recollect, is the voluntary testimony of Thomas Clay, Esq., the Georgia planter, whose testimony is given above. When this is the case, the amount of actual nutriment contained in a peck of the "gourd seed," may not be more than in five, or four, or even three quarts of "flint corn."

As a quart of southern corn weighs at least five ounces less than a quart of northern corn, it requires little arithmetic to perceive, that the daily allowance of the slave fed upon that kind of corn, would contain about one third of a pound less nutriment than, though his daily ration were the same quantity of, northern corn, which would amount, in a year, to more than a hundred and twenty pounds of human sustenance! which would furnish the slave with his full allowance of a peck of corn a week for two months! It is unnecessary to add, that this difference in the weight of the two kinds of corn, is an item too important to be overlooked. As one quart of the southern corn weighs one pound and eleven-sixteenths of a pound, it follows that it would be about one pound and six-eighths of a pound. We now solicit the attention of the reader to the following unanimous testimony, of the civilized world, to the utter insufficiency of this amount of food to sustain human beings under labor. This testimony is to be found in the laws of all civilized nations, which regulate the rations of soldiers and sailors, disbursements made by governments for the support of citizens in times of public calamity, the allowance to convicts in prisons. &c. We will begin with the United States.

The daily ration for each United States' soldier established by act of Congress, May 30, 1796 was the following: one pound of beef, one pound of bread, half a gill of spirits; and at the rate of one quart of salt, two quarts of vinegar, two pounds of soap, and one pound of candles to every hundred rations. To those soldiers "who were on the frontiers," (where the labor and exposure were greater), the ration was one pound two ounces of beef and one pound two ounces of bread. Laws U. S. vol. 3d, sec. 10, p. 431.

After an experiment of two years, the preceding ration being found *insufficient,* it was increased, by act of Congress, July 16, 1798, and was as follows: beef one pound and a quarter, bread one pound two ounces; salt two quarts, vinegar four quarts, soap four pounds, and candles one and a half pounds to the hundred rations. The preceding allowance was afterwards still further increased.

The *present daily ration* for the United States' soldiers, is, as we learn from an advertisement of Captain Fulton, of the United States' army, in a late number of the Richmond (Va.) Enquirer, as follows: one and a quarter pounds of beef, one and three-sixteenths pounds of bread; and at the rate of *eight quarts of beans, eight pounds of sugar,* four pounds of coffee, two quarts of salt, four pounds of candles, and four pounds of soap, to every hundred rations.

We have before us the daily rations provided for the emigrating Ottawa Indians, two years since, and for the emigrating Cherokees last fall. They were the same—one pound of fresh beef, one pound of flour, &c.

The daily ration for the United States' navy, is fourteen ounces of bread, half a pound of beef, six ounces of pork, three ounces of rice, three ounces of peas, one ounce of cheese, one ounce of sugar, half an ounce of tea, one-third of a gill molasses.

The daily ration in the British army is one and a quarter pounds of beef, one pound of bread, &c.

The daily ration in the French army is one pound of beef, one and a half pounds of bread, one pint of wine, &c.

The common daily ration for foot soldiers on the continent, is one pound of meat, and one and a half pounds of bread.

The *sea ration* among the Portuguese, has become the usual ration in the navies of European powers generally. It is as follows: "one and a half pounds of biscuit, one pound of salt meat, one pint of wine, with some dried fish and onions."

PRISON RATIONS.—Before giving the usual daily rations of food allowed to convicts, in the principal prisons in the United States, we will quote the testimony of the "American Prison Discipline Society," which is as follows:

"The common allowance of food in the penitentiaries, is equivalent to ONE POUND OF MEAT, ONE POUND OF BREAD, AND ONE POUND OF

VEGETABLES PER DAY. It varies a little from this in some of them, but it is generally equivalent to it." First Report of American Prison Discipline Society, page 13.

The daily ration of food to each convict, in the principal prisons in this country, is as follows:

In the New Hampshire State Prison, one and a quarter pounds of meal, and fourteen ounces of beef, for *breakfast and dinner*; and for supper, a soup or porridge of potatoes and beans, or peas, the *quantity not limited*.

In the Vermont prison, the convicts are allowed to eat *as much as they wish*.

In the Massachusetts penitentiary, one and a half pounds of bread, fourteen ounces of meat, half a pint of potatoes, and one gill of molasses, or one pint of milk.

In the Connecticut State Prison, one pound of beef, one pound of bread, two and a half pounds of potatoes, half a gill of molasses, with salt, pepper, and vinegar.

In the New York State Prison, at Auburn, one pound of beef, twenty-two ounces of flour and meal, half a gill of molasses; with two quarts of rye, four quarts of salt, two quarts of vinegar, one and a half ounces of pepper, and two and a half bushels of potatoes to every hundred rations.

In the New York State Prison at Sing Sing, one pound of beef, eighteen ounces of flour and meal, besides potatoes, rye coffee, and molasses.

In the New York City Prison, one pound of beef, one pound of flour; and three pecks of potatoes to every hundred rations, with other small articles.

In the New Jersey State Prison, one pound of bread, half a pound of beef, with potatoes and cabbage, (quantity not specified), one gill of molasses, and a bowl of mush for supper.

In the late Walnut Street Prison, Philadelphia, one and a half pounds of bread and meal, half a pound of beef, one pint of potatoes, one gill of molasses, and half a gill of rye, for coffee.

In the Baltimore prison, we believe the ration is the same with the preceding.

In the Pennsylvania Eastern Penitentiary, one pound of bread and one pint of coffee for breakfast, one pint of meat soup, with potatoes without limit, for dinner, and mush and molasses for supper.

In the Penitentiary for the District of Columbia, Washington city, one pound of beef, twelve ounces of Indian meal, ten ounces of wheat flour, half a gill of molasses; with two quarts of rye, four quarts of salt, four quarts of vinegar, and two and a half bushels of potatoes to every hundred rations.

RATIONS IN ENGLISH PRISONS.—The daily ration of food in the Bedfordshire Penitentiary, is *two pounds of bread*; and if at hard labor, *a quart of soup for dinner.*

In the Cambridge County House of Correction, three pounds of bread, and one pint of beer.

In the Millbank General Penitentiary, one and a half pounds of bread, one pound of potatoes, six ounces of beef, with half a pint of broth therefrom.

In the Gloucestershire Penitentiary, one and a half pounds of bread, three-fourths of a pint of peas, made into soup, with beef, quantity not stated. Also gruel, made of vegetables, quantity not stated, and one and a half ounces of oatmeal mixed with it.

In the Leicestershire House of Correction, two pounds of bread, and three pints of gruel; and when at hard labor, one pint of milk in addition, and twice a week a pint of meat soup at dinner, instead of gruel.

In the Buxton House of Correction, one and a half pounds of bread, one and a half pints of gruel, one and a half pints of soup, four-fifths of a pound of potatoes, and two-sevenths of an ounce of beef.

Notwithstanding the preceding daily ration in the Buxton Prison is about double the usual daily allowance of our slaves, yet the visiting physicians decided, that for those prisoners who were required to work the tread-mill, it was *entirely insufficient.* This question was considered at length, and publicly discussed at the sessions of the Surry magistrates, with the benefit of medical advice; which resulted in "large additions" to the rations of those who worked on the tread-mill. See London Morning Chronicle, Jan. 13, 1830.

To the preceding we add the *ration of the Roman slaves.* The monthly allowance of food to slaves in Rome was called "Dimensum." The "Dimensum" was an allowance of wheat or of other grain, which consisted of five *modii* a month to each slave. Ainsworth, in his Latin Dictionary estimates the *modius,* when used for the measurement of grain, at *a peck and a half* our measure, which would make the Roman slave's allowance *two quarts of grain a day*, just double the allowance provided for the slave by *law* in North Carolina, and *six* quarts more per week than the ordinary allowance of slaves in the slave states generally, as already established by the testimony of slaveholders themselves. But it must by no means be overlooked that this "dimensum," or *monthly* allowance, was far from being the sole allowance of food to Roman slaves. In *addition* to this, they had a stated *daily* allowance (*diarium*) besides a monthly allowance of *money,* amounting to about a cent a day.

Now without further trenching on the reader's time, we add, compare the preceding daily allowances of food to soldiers and sailors in this and other countries; to convicts in this and other countries; to bodies of emigrants rationed at public expense; and finally, with the fixed allowance given to Roman slaves, and we find the states of this Union, the *slave* states as well as the free, the United States' government, the different European governments, the old Roman empire, in fine, we may add, the *world,* ancient and modern, uniting in the testimony that to furnish men at hard labor from daylight till dark with but 1⅞ lbs. of *corn* per day, their sole sustenance, is to MURDER THEM BY PIECE-MEAL. The reader will perceive by examining the preceding statistics that the *average daily ration* throughout this country and Europe exceeds the usual slave's allowance *at least a pound a day*; also that one-third of this ration for soldiers and convicts in the United States, and for soldiers and sailors in Europe, is *meat,* generally beef; whereas the allowance of the mass of our slaves is corn, only. Further, the convicts in our prisons are sheltered from the heat of the sun, and from the damps of the early morning and evening, from cold, rain, &c.; whereas, the great body of the slaves are exposed to all of these, in their season, from daylight till dark; besides this, they labor more hours in the day than convicts, as will be shown under another head, and are obliged to prepare and cook their own food after they have finished the labor of the day, while the convicts have theirs prepared for them. These, with other circumstances, necessarily make larger and longer draughts upon the strength of the slave, produce consequently greater exhaustion, and demand a larger amount of food to restore and sustain the laborer than is required by the convict in his briefer, less exposed, and less exhausting toils.

That the slaveholders themselves regard the usual allowance of food to slaves as insufficient, both in kind and quantity, for hard-working men, is shown by the fact, that in all the slave states, we believe without exception, *white* convicts at hard labor, have a much *larger* allowance of food than the usual one of slaves; and generally more than *one third* of this daily allowance is meat. This conviction of slaveholders shows itself in various forms. When persons wish to hire slaves to labor on public works, in addition to the inducement of high wages held out to masters to hire out their slaves, the contractors pledge themselves that a certain amount of food shall be given the slaves, taking care to specify a *larger* amount than the usual allowance, and a part of it *meat*.

The following advertisement is an illustration. We copy it from the "Daily Georgian," Savannah, Dec. 14, 1838.

NEGROES WANTED

The Contractors upon the Brunswick and Altamaha Canal are desirous to hire a number of prime Negro Men, from the 1st October next, for fifteen months, until the 1st January, 1840. They will pay at the rate of eighteen dollars per month for each prime hand.

These negroes will be employed in the excavation of the Canal. They will be provided with *three and a half pounds of pork or bacon, and ten quarts of gourd seed corn per week,* lodged in comfortable shantees, and attended constantly by a skilful physician.

J. H. COUPER,
P. M. NIGHTINGALE.

But we have direct testimony to this point. The late Hon. John Taylor, of Caroline Co. Virginia, for many years Senator in Congress, and for many years president of the Agricultural Society of the State, says in his "Agricultural Essays," No. 30, page 97, "BREAD ALONE OUGHT NEVER TO BE CONSIDERED A SUFFICIENT DIET FOR SLAVES EXCEPT AS A PUNISHMENT." He urges upon the planters of Virginia to give their slaves, in addition to bread, "salt meat and vegetables," and adds, "we shall be ASTONISHED *to discover upon trial,* that this great comfort to them is a profit to the master."

The Managers of the American Prison Discipline Society, in their third Report, page 58, say, "In the Penitentiaries *generally*, in the United States, the *animal* food is equal to *one pound of meat per day* for each convict."

Most of the actual suffering from hunger on the part of the slaves, is in the sugar and cotton-growing region, where the crops are exported and the corn generally purchased from the upper country. Where this is the case *there cannot but be suffering*. The contingencies of bad crops, difficult transportation, high prices, &c. &c., naturally occasion short and often precarious allowances. The following extract from a New

Orleans paper of April 26, 1837, affords an illustration. The writer in describing the effects of the *money pressure* in Mississippi, says:

"They, (the planters), are now left without provisions and the means of living and using their industry, for the present year. In this dilemma, planters whose crops have been from 100 to 700 bales, find themselves forced to *sacrifice many of their slaves* in order to get the *common necessaries of life* for the support of themselves and the rest of their negroes. *In many places, heavy planters compel their slaves to fish for the means of subsistence, rather than sell them at such ruinous rates. There are at this moment* THOUSANDS OF SLAVES *in Mississippi, that* KNOW NOT WHERE THE NEXT MORSEL IS TO COME FROM. *The master must be ruined to save the wretches from being* STARVED."

II. LABOR

THE SLAVES ARE OVERWORKED

This is abundantly proved by the number of hours that the slaves are obliged to be in the field. But before furnishing testimony as to their hours of labor and rest, we will present the express declarations of slaveholders and others, that the slaves are severely driven in the field.

WITNESSES	TESTIMONY
The Senate and House of Representatives of the State of South Carolina.	"MANY OWNERS of slaves, and others who have the management of slaves, *do confine them so closely at hard labor that they have not sufficient time for natural rest.*—See 2 Brevard's Digest of the Laws of South Carolina, 243."
History of Carolina.— Vol. i, page 120.	"So *laborious* is the task of raising, beating, and cleaning rice, that had it been possible to obtain European servants in sufficient numbers, *thousands and tens of thousands* MUST HAVE PERISHED."

WITNESSES	TESTIMONY
Hon. Alexander Smyth, a slaveholder, and member of Congress from Virginia, in his speech on the "Missouri question," Jan. 28, 1820.	"Is it not obvious that the way to render their situation *more comfortable,* is to allow them to be taken where there is not the same motive to force the slave to INCESSANT TOIL that there is in the country where cotton, sugar, and tobacco are raised for exportation. It is proposed to hem in the blacks *where they are* HARD WORKED, that they may be rendered unproductive and the race be prevented from increasing. ★ ★ ★ The proposed measure would be EXTREME CRUELTY to the blacks. ★ ★ ★ You would ★ ★ ★ doom them to HARD LABOR."
"Travels in Louisiana," translated from the French by John Davies, Esq.— Page 81.	"At the rolling of sugars, an interval of from two to three months, they *work both night and day*. Abridged of their sleep, they *scarce retire to rest during the whole period.*"
The Western Review, No. 2,—article "Agriculture of Louisiana."	"The work is admitted to be severe for the hands, (slaves), requiring when the process is commenced to be *pushed night and day.*"
W. C. Gildersleeve, Esq., a native of Georgia, elder of the Presbyterian church, Wilkesbarre, Penn.	"*Overworked* I know they (the slaves) are."
Mr. Asa A. Stone, a theological student, near Natchez, Miss., in 1834 and 1835.	"Every body here knows *overdriving* to be one of the most common occurrences, the planters do not deny it, except, perhaps, to northerners."
Philemon Bliss, Esq., a lawyer of Elyria, Ohio, who lived in Florida in 1834 and 1835.	"During the cotton-picking season they usually labor in the field during the whole of the daylight, and then spend a good part of the night in ginning and baling. The labor required is very frequently *excessive,* and speedily impairs the constitution."

WITNESSES	TESTIMONY
Hon. R. J. Turnbull of South Carolina, a slave-holder, speaking of the harvesting of cotton, says:	*"All the pregnant women* even, on the plantation, and weak and *sickly* negroes incapable of other labor, are then *in requisition."*

HOURS OF LABOR AND REST

WITNESSES	TESTIMONY
Asa A. Stone, theological student, a classical teacher near Natchez, Miss., 1835.	"It is a general rule on all regular plantations, that the slaves be in the field as *soon as it is light enough for them to see to work,* and remain there until it is *so dark that they cannot see."*
Mr. Cornelius Johnson, of Farmington, Ohio, who lived in Mississippi a part of 1837 and 1838.	"It is the common rule for the slaves to be kept at work *fifteen hours in the day,* and in the time of picking cotton a certain number of pounds is required of each. If this amount is not brought in at night, the slave is whipped, and the number of pounds lacking is added to the next day's job; this course is often repeated from day to day."
W. C. Gildersleeve, Esq., Wilkesbarre, Penn., a native of Georgia.	"It was customary for the overseers to call out the gangs *long before day,* say three o'clock, in the winter, while dressing out the crops; such work as could be done by fire light (pitch pine was abundant), was provided."
Mr. William Leftwich, a native of Virginia and son of a slaveholder—he has recently removed to Delhi, Hamilton county Ohio.	*"From dawn till dark,* the slaves are required to bend to their work."
Mr. Nehemiah Caulkins, Waterford, Conn., a resident in North Carolina eleven winters.	"The slaves are obliged to work *from daylight till dark,* as long as they can see."
Mr. Eleazar Powell, Chippewa, Beaver county, Penn., who lived in Mississippi in 1836 and 1837.	"The slaves had to cook and eat their breakfast and be in the field by *daylight, and continue there till dark."*

WITNESSES	TESTIMONY
Philemon Bliss, Esq., a lawyer in Elyria, Ohio, who resided in Florida in 1834 and 1835.	"The slaves commence labor *by daylight* in the morning, and do not leave the field *till dark* in the evening."
"Travels in Louisiana," page 87.	"Both in summer and winter the slave must *be in the field by the first dawning of day*."
Mr. Henry E. Knapp, member of a Christian church in Farmington, Ohio, who lived in Mississippi in 1837 and 1838.	"The slaves were made to work, from *as soon as they could see* in the morning, till as late as they could see at night. Sometimes they were made to work till nine o'clock at night, in such work as they could do, as burning cotton stalks, &c."

A New Orleans paper, dated March 23, 1826, says: "To judge from the activity reigning in the cotton presses of the suburbs of St. Mary, and the *late hours* during which their slaves work, the cotton trade was never more brisk."

Mr. GEORGE W. WESTGATE, a member of the Congregational Church at Quincy, Illinois, who lived in the south western slave states a number of years, says, "The slaves are driven to the field in the morning *about four o'clock,* the general calculation is to get them at work by daylight; the time for breakfast is between nine and ten o'clock, this meal is sometimes eaten '*bite* and *work,*' others allow fifteen minutes, and this is the only rest the slave has while in the field. I have never known a case of stopping an hour, in Louisiana; in Mississippi the rule is milder, though entirely subject to the will of the master. On cotton plantations, in cotton picking time, that is from October to Christmas, each hand has a certain quantity to pick, and is flogged if his task is not accomplished; their tasks are such as to keep them all the while busy."

The preceding testimony under this head has sole reference to the actual labor of the slaves *in the field*. In order to determine how many hours are left for sleep, we must take into the account, the time spent in going to and from the field, which is often at a distance of one, two and sometimes three miles; also the time necessary for pounding, or grinding their corn, and preparing, over night, their food for the next day; also the preparation of tools, getting fuel and preparing it, making fires and cooking their suppers, if they have any, the occasional mending and washing of their clothes, &c. Besides this, as every one knows who has lived on a southern plantation, many little errands and *chores* are to be done for their masters and mistresses, old and young, which have accumulated during the day and been kept in reserve till the slaves return from the field at night. To this we may add that the slaves are *social* beings, and that during the day, silence is generally enforced by the whip of the overseer or driver.* When they return at night, their pent up social feelings will seek vent, it is a law of nature, and though the body may be greatly worn with toil, this law cannot be wholly stifled. Sharers of the same woes, they are drawn together by strong affinities, and seek the society and sympathy of their fellows; even *"tired* nature" will joyfully forego for a time needful rest, to minister to a want of its being equally permanent and imperative as the want of sleep, and as much more profound, as the yearnings of the higher nature surpass the instincts of its animal appendage.

All these things make drafts upon *time.* To show how much of the slave's time, which is absolutely indispensable for rest and sleep, is necessarily spent in various labors after his return from the field at night, we subjoin a few testimonies.

Mr. CORNELIUS JOHNSON, Farmington, Ohio, who lived in Mississippi in the years 1837 and 38, says:

"On all the plantations where I was acquainted, the slaves were kept in the field till dark; after which, those who had to grind their own corn, had that to attend to, get their supper, attend to other family affairs of their own and of their master, such as bringing water, washing clothes, &c. &c., and be in the field as soon as it was sufficiently light to commence work in the morning."

Mr. GEORGE W. WESTGATE, of Quincy, Illinois, who has spent several years in the south western slave states, says:

"Their time, after full dark until four o'clock in the morning is their own; this fact alone would seem to say they have sufficient rest, but there are other things to be considered; much of their making, mending and washing of clothes, preparing and cooking food, hauling

---

* We do not mean that they are not suffered to *speak,* but, that, as conversation would be a hindrance to labor, they are generally permitted to indulge in it but little.

and chopping wood, fixing and preparing tools, and a variety of little nameless jobs must be done between those hours."

PHILEMON BLISS, Esq., of Elyria, Ohio, who resided in Florida in 1834 and 5, gives the following testimony:

"After having finished their field labors, they are occupied till nine or ten o'clock in doing *chores,* such as grinding corn, (as all the corn in the vicinity is ground by hand), chopping wood, taking care of horses, mules, &c., and a thousand things necessary to be done on a large plantation. If any extra job is to be done, it must not hinder the 'niggers' from their work, but must be done in the night."

W. C. GILDERSLEEVE, Esq., a native of Georgia, an elder of the Presbyterian Church at Wilkesbarre, says:

"The corn is ground in a handmill by the slave *after his task is done*—generally there is but one mill on a plantation, and as but one can grind at a time, the mill is going sometimes *very late at night.*"

We now present another class of facts and testimony, showing that the slaves engaged in raising the large staples, are *overworked.*

In September, 1834, the writer of this had an interview with JAMES G. BIRNEY, Esq., who then resided in Kentucky, having removed with his family from Alabama the year before. A few hours before that interview, and on the morning of the same day, Mr. B. had spent a couple of hours with Hon. Henry Clay, at his residence, near Lexington. Mr. Birney remarked, that Mr. Clay had just told him, he had lately been led to mistrust certain estimates as to the increase of the slave population in the far south west—estimates which he had presented, I think, in a speech before the Colonization Society. He now believed, that the births among the slaves in that quarter were *not equal to the deaths*—and that, of course, the slave population, independent of immigration from the slave-selling states, was *not sustaining itself.*

Among other facts stated by Mr. Clay, was the following, which we copy *verbatim* from the original memorandum, made at the time by Mr. Birney, with which he has kindly furnished us.

"Sept. 16, 1834.—Hon. H. Clay, in a conversation at his own house, on the subject of slavery, informed me, that Hon. Outerbridge Horsey, formerly a senator in Congress from the state of Delaware, and the owner of a sugar plantation in Louisiana, declared to him, that his overseer worked his hands so closely, that one of the women brought forth a child whilst engaged in the labors of the field.

"Also, that a few years since, he was at a brick yard in the environs of New Orleans, in which one hundred hands were employed; among them were from *twenty to thirty young women,* in the prime of life. He was told by the proprietor, that there had *not been a child born among them for the last two or three years, although they all had husbands*."

The preceding testimony of Mr. Clay, is strongly corroborated by advertisements of slaves, by Courts of Probate, and by executors administering upon the estates of deceased persons. Some of those advertisements for the sale of slaves, contain the names, ages, accustomed employment, &c., of all the slaves upon the plantation of the deceased. These catalogues show large numbers of young men and women, almost all of them between twenty and thirty-eight years old; and yet the number of young children is *astonishingly small.* We have laid aside many lists of this kind, in looking over the newspapers of the slaveholding states; but the two following are all we can lay our hands on at present. One is in the "Planter's Intelligencer," Alexandria, La., March 22, 1837, containing one hundred and thirty slaves; and the other in the New Orleans Bee, a few days later, April 8, 1837, containing fifty-one slaves. The former is a "Probate sale" of the slaves belonging to the estate of Mr. Charles S. Lee, deceased, and is advertised by G. W. Keeton, Judge of the Parish of Concordia, La. The sex, name, and age of each slave are contained in the advertisement, which fills two columns. The following are some of the particulars.

The whole number of slaves is *one hundred and thirty.* Of these, *only three are over forty years old.* There are *thirty-five females* between the ages of *sixteen and thirty-three,* and yet there are only THIRTEEN children under the age of *thirteen years!*

It is impossible satisfactorily to account for such a fact, on any other supposition, than that these thirty-five females were so overworked, or underfed, or both, as to prevent child-bearing.

The other advertisement is that of a "Probate sale," ordered by the Court of the Parish of Jefferson—including the slaves of Mr. William Gormley. The whole number of slaves is fifty-one; the sex, age, and accustomed labors of each are given. The oldest of these slaves is but *thirty-nine years old*: of the females, *thirteen* are between the ages of sixteen and thirty-two, and the oldest female is but *thirty-eight*—and yet there are but *two children under eight years old!*

Another proof that the slaves in the southwestern states are overworked, is the fact, that so few of them live to old age. A large majority of them are *old* at middle age, and few live beyond fifty-five. In one of the preceding advertisements, out of one hundred and thirty slaves, only *three* are over forty years old! In the other, out of fifty-one slaves, only *two* are over *thirty-five*; the oldest is but thirty-nine, and the way in which he is designated in the advertisement, is an additional proof, that what to others is "middle age," is to the slaves in the south-west "old age": he is advertised as "*old* Jeffrey."

But the proof that the slave population of the south-west is so over-worked that it cannot *supply its own waste,* does not rest upon mere inferential evidence. The Agricultural Society of Baton Rouge, La., in its report, published in 1829, furnishes a labored estimate of the amount of expenditure necessarily incurred in conducting "a well-regulated sugar estate." In this estimate, the annual net loss of slaves, over and above the supply by propagation, is set down at TWO AND A HALF PER CENT! The late Hon. Josiah S. Johnson, a member of Congress from Louisiana, addressed a letter to the Secretary of the United States' Treasury, in 1830, containing a similar estimate, apparently made with great care, and going into minute details. Many items in this estimate differ from the preceding; but the estimate of the annual *decrease* of the slaves on a plantation was the same—TWO AND A HALF PER CENT!

The following testimony of Rev. Dr. CHANNING, of Boston, who resided some time in Virginia, shows that the over-working of slaves, to such an extent as to abridge life, and cause a decrease of population, is not confined to the far south and south-west.

"I heard of an estate managed by an individual who was considered as singularly successful, and who was able to govern the slaves without the use of the whip. I was anxious to see him, and trusted that some discovery had been made favorable to humanity. I asked him how he was able to dispense with corporal punishment. He replied to me, with a very determined look, 'The slaves know that the work *must* be done, and that it is better to do it without punishment than with it.' In other words, the certainty and dread of chastisement were so impressed on them, that they never incurred it.

"I then found that the slaves on this well-managed estate, *decreased* in number. I asked the cause. He replied, with perfect frankness and ease, 'The gang is not large enough for the estate.' In other words, they were not equal to the work of the plantation, and yet were *made to do it,* though with the certainty of abridging life.

"On this plantation the huts were uncommonly convenient. There was an unusual air of neatness. A superficial observer would have called the slaves happy. Yet they were living under a severe, subduing discipline, and were *over-worked* to a degree that *shortened life.*"— *Channing on Slavery,* page 162, first edition.

PHILEMON BLISS, Esq., a lawyer of Elyria, Ohio, who spent some time in Florida, gives the following testimony to the over-working of the slaves:

"It is not uncommon for hands, in hurrying times, beside working all day, to labor half the night. This is usually the case on sugar plantations, during the sugar-boiling season; and on cotton, during its gathering. Beside the regular task of picking cotton, averaging of the short staple, when the crop is good, 100 pounds a day to the hand, the ginning (extracting the seed), and baling was done in the night. Said Mr. ——— to me, while conversing upon the customary labor of slaves, 'I work my niggers in a hurrying time till 11 or 12 o'clock at night, and have them up by four in the morning.'

"Beside the common inducement, the desire of gain, to make a large crop, the desire is increased by that spirit of gambling, so common at the south. It is very common to *bet* on the issue of a crop. A. lays a wager that, from a given number of hands, he will make more cotton than B. The wager is accepted, and then begins the contest; and who bears the burden of it? How many tears, yea, how many broken constitutions, and premature deaths, have been the effect of this spirit? From the desperate energy of purpose with which the gambler pursues his object, from the passions which the practice calls into exercise, we might conjecture many. Such is the fact. In Middle Florida, a *broken-winded* negro is more common than a *broken-winded* horse; though usually, when they are declared unsound, or when their constitution is so broken that their recovery is despaired of, they are exported to New Orleans, to drag out the remainder of their days in the cane-field and sugar house. I would not insinuate that all planters gamble upon their crops; but I mention the practice as one of the common inducements to 'push niggers.' Neither would I assert that all planters drive the hands to the injury of their health. I give it as a *general rule* in the district of Middle Florida, and I have no reason to think that negroes are driven worse there than in other fertile sections. People there told me that the situation of the slaves was far better than in Mississippi and Louisiana. And from comparing the crops with those made in the latter states, and for other reasons, I am convinced of the truth of their statements."

Dr. DEMMING, a gentleman of high respectability, residing in Ashland, Richland county, Ohio, stated to Professor Wright, of New York city,

"That during a recent tour at the south, while ascending the Ohio river, on the steamboat Fame, he had an opportunity of conversing with a Mr. Dickinson, a resident of Pittsburg, in company with a number of cotton-planters and slave-dealers, from Louisiana, Alabama, and Mississippi. Mr. Dickinson stated as a fact, that the sugar planters upon the sugar coast in Louisiana had ascertained, that, as it was usually necessary to employ about *twice* the amount of labor during the boiling season, that was required during the season of raising, they could, by excessive driving, day and night, during the boiling season, accomplish the whole labor *with one set of hands*. By pursuing this plan, they could afford *to sacrifice a set of hands once in seven years*! He further stated that this horrible system was now practised to a considerable extent! The correctness of this statement was substantially admitted by the slaveholders then on board."

The late Mr. SAMUEL BLACKWELL, a highly respected citizen of Jersey city, opposite the city of New York, and a member of the Presbyterian church, visited many of the sugar plantations in Louisiana a few years since; and having for many years been the owner of an extensive sugar refinery in England, and subsequently in this country, he had not only every facility afforded him by the planters, for personal inspection of all parts of the process of sugar-making, but received from them the most unreserved communications, as to their management of their slaves. Mr. B., after his return, frequently made the following statement to gentlemen of his acquaintance,—"That the planters generally declared to him, that they were *obliged* so to over-work their slaves during the sugar-making season, (from eight to ten weeks), as to *use them up* in seven or eight years. For, said they, after the process is commenced, it must be pushed without cessation, night and day; and we cannot afford to keep a sufficient number of slaves to do the *extra* work at the time of sugar-making, as we could not profitably employ them the rest of the year."

It is not only true of the sugar planters, but of the slaveholders generally throughout the far south and south west, that they believe it for their interest to wear out the slaves by excessive toil in eight or ten years after they put them into the field.[*]

---

[*] Alexander Jones, Esq., a large planter in West Feliciana, Louisiana, published a communication in the "North Carolina True American," Nov. 25, 1838, in which, speaking of the horses employed in the mills on the plantations for

Rev. DOCTOR REED, of London, who went through Kentucky, Virginia and Maryland in the summer of 1834, gives the following testimony:

"I was told confidently and from *excellent authority,* that recently at a meeting of planters in South Carolina, the question was seriously discussed whether the slave is more profitable to the owner, if well fed, well clothed, and worked lightly, or if made the most of *at once,* and exhausted in some eight years. The decision was in favor of the last alternative. That decision will perhaps make many shudder. But to my mind this is not the chief evil. The greater and original evil is considering the *slave as property.* If he is only property and my property, then I have some right to ask how I may make that property *most available.*"

"Visit to the American Churches," by Rev. Drs. Reed and Matthe-son. Vol. 2. p. 173.

Rev. JOHN O. CHOULES, recently pastor of the Baptist Church at New Bedford, Massachusetts, now of Buffalo, New York, made substantially the following statement in a speech in Boston.

"While attending the Baptist Triennial Convention at Richmond, Virginia, in the spring of 1835, as a delegate from Massachusetts, I had a conversation on slavery, with an officer of the Baptist Church in that city, at whose house I was a guest. I asked my host if he did not apprehend that the slaves would eventually rise and exterminate their masters.

"'Why,' said the gentleman, 'I used to apprehend such a catastrophe, but God has made a providential opening, *a merciful safety valve,* and now I do not feel alarmed in the *prospect* of what is coming.' 'What do you mean,' said Mr. Choules, 'by providence opening a merciful safety valve?' 'Why,' said the gentleman, 'I will tell you; the slave traders come from the cotton and sugar plantations of the South and are willing to buy up more slaves than we can part with. We must keep a stock for the purpose of *rearing* slaves, but we part with the most valuable, and at the same time, the most *dangerous,* and the

---

ginning cotton, he says, they "are much whipped and jaded"; and adds, "In fact, this service is so severe on horses, as to shorten their lives in many instances, if not actually kill them in gear."

Those who work *one* kind of their "live stock" so as to "shorten their lives," or "kill them in gear," would not stick at doing the same thing to another kind.

demand is very constant and likely to be so, for when they go to these southern states, the average existence is ONLY FIVE YEARS!'"

Monsieur C. C. ROBIN, a highly intelligent French gentleman, who resided in Louisiana from 1802 to 1806, and published a volume of travels, gives the following testimony to the overworking of the slaves there:

"I have been a witness, that after the fatigue of the day, their labors have been prolonged several hours by the light of the moon; and then, before they could think of rest, they must pound and cook their corn; and yet, long before day, an implacable scold, whip in hand, would arouse them from their slumbers. Thus, of more than twenty negroes, who in twenty years should have doubled, the number *was reduced to four or five.*"

In conclusion we add, that slaveholders have in the most public and emphatic manner declared themselves guilty of barbarous inhumanity toward their slaves in exacting from them such *long continued daily labor.* The Legislatures of Maryland, Virginia and Georgia, have passed laws providing that convicts in their state prisons and penitentiaries, "shall be employed in work each day in the year except Sundays, not exceeding *eight* hours, in the months of November, December, and January; *nine* hours, in the months of February and October, and *ten* hours in the rest of the year." Now contrast this *legal* exaction of labor from CONVICTS with the exaction from slaves as established by the preceding testimony. The reader perceives that the amount of time, in which by the preceding laws of Maryland, Virginia, and Georgia, the *convicts* in their prisons are required to labor, is on an average during the year but little more than NINE HOURS daily. Whereas, the laws of South Carolina permit the master to *compel* his slaves to work FIFTEEN HOURS in the twenty-four, in summer, and FOURTEEN in the winter—which would be in winter, from daybreak in the morning until *four hours* after sunset!— See 2 Brevard's Digest, 243.

The other slave states, except Louisiana, have *no laws* respecting the labor of slaves, consequently if the master should work his slaves day and night without sleep till they drop dead, *he violates no law!*

The law of Louisiana provides for the slaves but TWO AND A HALF HOURS in the twenty-four for "rest!" See law of Louisiana, act of July 7. 1806, Martin's Digest 6. 10–12.

III. CLOTHING

We propose to show under this head, that the clothing of the slaves by day, and their covering by night, are inadequate, either for comfort or decency.

WITNESSES	TESTIMONY
Hon. T. T. Bouldin, a slaveholder, and member of Congress from Virginia, in a speech in Congress, Feb. 16, 1835.	Mr. Bouldin said *"he knew* that many negroes had *died* from exposure to weather," and added, "they are clad in a *flimsy fabric, that will turn neither wind nor water."*
George Buchanan, M. D., of Baltimore, member of the American Philosophical Society, in an oration at Baltimore, July 4, 1791.	"The slaves, *naked* and starved, *often* fall victims to the inclemencies of the weather."
Wm. Savery, of Philadelphia, an eminent Minister of the Society of Friends, who went through the Southern states in 1791, on a religious visit; after leaving Savannah, Ga., we find the following entry in his journal, 6th, month, 28, 1791.	"We rode through many rice swamps, where the blacks were very numerous, great droves of these poor slaves, working up to the middle in water, men and women nearly *naked."*
Rev. John Rankin, of Ripley, Ohio, a native of Tennessee.	"In every slave-holding state, *many slaves suffer extremely,* both while they labor and while they sleep, *for want of clothing* to keep them warm."
John Parrish, late of Philadelphia, a highly esteemed minister in the Society of Friends, who travelled through the South in 1804.	"It is shocking to the feelings of humanity, in travelling through some of those states, to see those poor objects, [slaves], especially in the inclement season, in *rags,* and *trembling with the cold."* "They suffer them, both male and female, *to go without clothing* at the age of ten and twelve years."

WITNESSES	TESTIMONY
Rev. Phineas Smith, Centreville, Allegany Co., N. Y. Mr. S. has just returned from a residence of several years at the south, chiefly in Virginia, Louisiana, and among the American settlers in Texas.	"The apparel of the slaves, is of the coarsest sort and *exceedingly deficient* in quantity. I have been on many plantations, where children of eight and ten years old, were in a state of *perfect nudity.* Slaves are *in general wretchedly clad.*"
Wm. Ladd, Esq., of Minot, Maine, recently a slaveholder in Florida.	"They were allowed two suits of clothes a year, viz. one pair of trowsers with a shirt or frock of osnaburg for summer; and for winter, one pair of trowsers, and a jacket of negro cloth, with a baize shirt and a pair of shoes. Some allowed hats, and some did not; and they were generally, I believe, allowed one blanket in two years. Garments of similar materials were allowed the women."
A Kentucky physician, writing in the Western Medical Reformer, in 1836, on the diseases peculiar to slaves, says.	"They are *imperfectly clothed* both summer and winter."
Mr. Stephen E. Maltby, Inspector of provisions, Skeneateles, N. Y., who resided sometime in Alabama.	"I was at Huntsville, Alabama, in 1818–19, I frequently saw slaves on and around the public square, *with hardly a rag of clothing on them,* and in a *great many* instances with but a single garment both in summer and in winter; generally the only bedding of the slaves was a *blanket.*"
Reuben G. Macy, Hudson, N. Y., member of the Society of Friends, who resided in South Carolina, in 1818 and 19.	"Their clothing consisted of a pair of trowsers and jacket, made of 'negro cloth.' The women a petticoat, a very short 'short-gown,' and *nothing else,* the same kind of cloth; some of the women had an old pair of shoes, but they *generally went barefoot.*"

WITNESSES	TESTIMONY
Mr. Lemuel Sapington, of Lancaster, Pa., a native of Maryland, and formerly a slaveholder.	"Their clothing is often made by themselves after night, though sometimes assisted by the old women, who are no longer able to do out-door work; consequently it is harsh and uncomfortable. And I have very frequently seen those who had not attained the age of twelve years *go naked.*"
Philemon Bliss, Esq., a lawyer in Elyria, Ohio, who lived in Florida in 1834 and 35.	"It is very common to see the younger class of slaves up to eight or ten *without any clothing,* and most generally the laboring men wear *no shirts* in the warm season. The perfect nudity of the younger slaves is so familiar to the whites of both sexes, that they seem to witness it with perfect indifference. I may add that the aged and feeble often *suffer from cold.*"
Richard Macy, a member of the Society of Friends, Hudson, N. Y., who has lived in Georgia.	"For *bedding* each slave was allowed *one blanket,* in which they rolled themselves up. I examined their houses, but could not find any thing like *a bed.*"
W. C. Gildersleeve, Esq., Wilkesbarre, Pa., a native of Georgia.	"It is an every day sight to see women as well as men, with no other covering than a *few filthy rags fastened above the hips,* reaching midway to the ankles. *I never knew any kind of covering for the head* given. Children of both sexes, from infancy to ten years are seen in companies on the plantations, *in a state of perfect nudity.* This was so common that the most refined and delicate beheld them unmoved."
Mr. William Leftwich, a native of Virginia, now a member of the Presbyterian Church, in Delhi, Ohio.	"The only bedding of the slaves generally consists of *two old blankets.*"

Advertisements like the following from the "New Orleans Bee," May 31, 1837, are common in the southern papers.

"10 DOLLARS REWARD.—Ranaway, the slave SOLOMON, about 28 years of age; BADLY CLOTHED. The above reward will be paid on application to FERNANDEZ & WHITING, No. 20, St. Louis St."

"RANAWAY from the subscriber the negress FANNY, always badly dressed, she is about 25 or 26 years old. JOHN MACOIN, 117 S. Ann st."

The Darien (Ga.), Telegraph, of Jan. 24, 1837, in an editorial article, hitting off the aristocracy of the planters, incidentally lets out some secrets, about the usual *clothing* of the slaves. The editor says,— "The planter looks down, with the most sovereign contempt, on the merchant and the storekeeper. He deems himself a lord, because he gets his two or three RAGGED servants, to row him to his plantation every day, that he may inspect the labor of his hands."

The following is an extract from a letter lately received from REV. C. S. RENSHAW, of Quincy, Illinois.

"I am sorry to be obliged to give more testimony without the *name*. An individual in whom I have great confidence, gave me the following facts. That I am not alone in placing confidence in him, I subjoin a testimonial from Dr. Richard Eells, Deacon of the Congregational Church, of Quincy, and Rev. Mr. Fisher, Baptist Minister of Quincy.

"We have been acquainted with the brother who has communicated to you some facts that fell under his observation, whilst in his native state; he is a professed follower of our Lord, and we have great confidence in him as a man of integrity, discretion, and strict Christian principle.

RICHARD EELLS.
EZRA FISHER.

Quincy, Jan. 9th, 1839.

TESTIMONY.—"I lived for thirty years in Virginia, and have travelled extensively through Fauquier, Culpepper, Jefferson, Stafford, Albemarle and Charlotte Counties; my remarks apply to these Counties.

"The negro houses are miserably poor, generally they are a shelter from neither the wind, the rain, nor the snow, and the earth is the floor. There are exceptions to this rule, but they are only exceptions; you may sometimes see puncheon floor, but never, or almost never a plank floor. The slaves are generally without *beds or bedsteads*; some few have cribs that they fasten up for themselves in the corner of the hut. Their bed-clothes are a nest of rags thrown upon a crib, or in the corner; sometimes there are three or four families in one small cabin. Where the slaveholders have more than one family, they put them in the same quarter till it is filled, then build another. I have seen exceptions to this, when only one family would occupy a hut, and where were tolerably comfortable bed-clothes.

"Most of the slaves in these counties are *miserably clad*, I have known slaves who went without shoes all winter, perfectly barefoot. The feet of many of them are frozen. As a general fact the planters do not serve out to their slaves, drawers, or any under clothing, or vests, or overcoats. Slaves sometimes, by working at night and on Sundays, get better things than their masters serve to them.

"Whilst these things are true of *field-hands,* it is also true that many slaveholders clothe their *waiters* and coachmen like gentlemen. I do not think there is any difference between the slaves of professing Christians and others; at all events, it is so small as to be scarcely noticeable.

"I have seen men and women at work in the field more than half naked: and more than once in passing, when the overseer was not near, they would stop and draw round them a tattered coat or some ribbons of a skirt to hide their nakedness and shame from the stranger's eye."

Mr. George W. Westgate, a member of the Congregational Church in Quincy, Illinois, who has spent the larger part of twelve years navigating the rivers of the south-western slave states with keel boats, as a trader, gives the following testimony as to the clothing and lodging of the slaves.

"In Lower Tennessee, Mississippi and Louisiana, the clothing of the slaves is wretchedly poor; and grows worse as you go south, in the order of the states I have named. The only material is cotton bagging, i. e. bagging in which cotton is *baled,* not bagging made of cotton. In Louisiana, especially in the lower country, I have frequently seen them with nothing but a tattered coat, not sufficient to hide their nakedness. In winter their clothing seldom serves the purpose of comfort, and frequently not even of decent covering. In Louisiana *the planters never think of serving out shoes to slaves*. In Mississippi they give one pair a year generally. I never saw or heard of an instance of masters allowing them *stockings*. A *small poor blanket is generally the only bed-clothing,* and this they frequently wear in the field when they have not sufficient clothing to hide their nakedness or to keep them warm. Their manner of sleeping varies with the season. In hot weather they stretch themselves anywhere and sleep. As it becomes cool they roll themselves in their blankets, and lay scattered about the cabin. In cold weather they nestle together with their feet towards the fire, promiscuously. As a general fact the earth is their only floor and bed—not one in ten have anything like a bedstead, and then it is a mere bunk put up by themselves."

Mr. GEORGE A. AVERY, an elder in the fourth Congregational Church, Rochester, N. Y., who spent four years in Virginia, says, "The slave children, very commonly of both sexes, up to the ages of eight and ten years, and I think in some instances beyond this age, go in a state of *disgusting* nudity. I have often seen them with their tow shirt (their only article of summer clothing) which, to all human appearance, had not been taken off from the time it was first put on, worn off from the bottom upwards, shred by shred, until nothing remained but the straps which passed over their shoulders, and the less exposed portions extending a very little way below the arms, leaving the principal part of the chest, as well as the limbs, entirely uncovered."

SAMUEL ELLISON, a member of the Society of Friends, formerly of Southampton Co., Virginia, now of Marlborough, Stark Co., Ohio, says, "I knew a Methodist who was the owner of a number of slaves. The children of both sexes, belonging to him, under twelve years of age, were *entirely* destitute of clothing. I have seen an old man compelled to labor in the fields, not having rags enough to cover his nakedness."

REV. H. LYMAN, late pastor of the Free Presbyterian Church, in Buffalo, N. Y., in describing a tour down and up the Mississippi river in the winter of 1832-3, says, "At the wood yards where the boats stop, it is not uncommon to see female slaves employed in carrying wood. Their dress which was quite uniform was provided without any reference to comfort. They had no covering for their heads; the stuff which constituted the outer garment was sackcloth, similar to that in which brown domestic goods are done up. It was then December, and I thought that in such a dress, and being as they were, without *stockings,* they must suffer from the cold."

Mr. Benjamin Anderson, Colerain, Lancaster Co., Pa., a member of the Society of Friends, in a recent letter describing a short tour through the northern part of Maryland in the winter of 1836, thus speaks of a place a few miles from Chestertown. "About this place there were a number of slaves; very few, if any, had *either stockings or shoes*; the weather was intensely cold, and the ground covered with snow."

The late Major Stoddard of the United States' artillery, who took possession of Louisiana for the U. S. government, under the cession of 1804, published a book entitled "Sketches of Louisiana," in which, speaking of the planters of Lower Louisiana, he says, "*Few of them allow any clothing to their slaves.*"

The following is an extract from the Will of the late celebrated John Randolph of Virginia.

"To my old and faithful servants, Essex and his wife Hetty, I give and bequeath a pair of strong shoes, a suit of clothes and a blanket each, to be paid them annually; also an annual hat to Essex."

No Virginia slaveholder has ever had a better name as a "kind master," and "good provider" for his slaves, than John Randolph. Essex and Hetty were *favorite* servants, and the memory of the long uncompensated services of those "old and faithful servants," seems to have touched their master's heart. Now as this master was *John Randolph,* and as those servants were "faithful," and favorite servants, advanced in years, and worn out in his service, and as their allowance was, in their master's eyes, of sufficient moment to constitute a paragraph in his last *will and testament*, it is fair to infer that it would be *very liberal,* far better than the ordinary allowance for slaves.

Now we leave the reader to judge what must be the *usual* allowance of clothing to common field slaves in the hands of common masters, when Essex and Hetty, the "old" and "faithful" slaves of John Randolph, were provided, in his last will and testament, with but *one* suit of clothes annually, with but *one blanket* each for bedding, with no *stockings,* nor *socks,* nor *cloaks*, nor overcoats, nor *handkerchiefs,* nor *towels,* and with no *change* either of under or outside garments!

IV. DWELLINGS

THE SLAVES ARE WRETCHEDLY SHELTERED AND LODGED

WITNESSES	TESTIMONY
Mr. Stephen E. Maltby, Inspector of provisions, Skaneateles, N. Y., who has lived in Alabama.	"The huts where the slaves slept, generally contained but *one* apartment, and that *without floor.*"

WITNESSES	TESTIMONY
Mr. George A. Avery, elder of the 4th Presbyterian Church, Rochester, N. Y., who lived four years in Virginia.	"Amongst all the negro cabins which I saw in Va., *I cannot call to mind one* in which there was any other floor than the *earth;* any thing that a northern laborer, or mechanic, white or colored, would call a *bed,* nor a solitary *partition,* to separate the sexes."
William Ladd, Esq., Minot, Maine. President of the American Peace Society, formerly a slave-holder in Florida.	"The dwellings of the slaves were palmetto huts, built by themselves of stakes and poles, thatched with the palmetto leaf. The door, when they had any, was generally of the same materials, sometimes boards found on the beach. They had *no floors,* no separate apartments, except the guinea negroes had sometimes a small inclosure for their 'god house.' These huts the slaves built themselves after task and on Sundays."
Rev. Joseph M. Sadd, Pastor Pres. Church, Castile, Greene Co., N. Y., who lived in Missouri five years previous to 1837.	"The slaves live *generally* in *miserable huts,* which are *without floors,* and have a single apartment only, where both sexes are herded promiscuously together."
Mr. George W. Westgate, member of the Congregational Church in Quincy, Illinois, who has spent a number of years in slave states.	"On old plantations, the negro quarters are of frame and clapboards, seldom affording a comfortable shelter from wind or rain; their size varies from 8 by 10, to 10 by 12, feet, and six or eight feet high; sometimes there is a hole cut for a window, but I never saw a sash, or glass in any. In the new country, and in the woods, the quarters are generally built of logs, of similar dimensions."
Mr. Cornelius Johnson, a member of a Christian Church in Farmington, Ohio. Mr. J. lived in Mississippi in 1837-8.	"Their houses were commonly built of logs, sometimes they were framed, often they had no floor, some of them have two apartments, commonly but one; each of those apartments contained a family. Sometimes these families consisted of a man and his wife and children, while in other instances persons of both sexes, were thrown together without any regard to family relationship."

WITNESSES	TESTIMONY
The Western Medical Reformer, in an article on the Cachexia Africana by a Kentucky physician, thus speaks of the huts of the slaves.	"They are *crowded* together in a *small hut,* and sometimes having an imperfect, and sometimes no floor, and seldom raised from the ground, ill ventilated, and surrounded with filth."
Mr. William Leftwich, a native of Virginia, but has resided most of his life in Madison Co., Alabama.	"The dwellings of the slaves are log huts, from 10 to 12 feet square, often without windows, doors, or floors, they have neither chairs, table, or bedstead."
Reuben L. Macy of Hudson, N. Y., a member of the Religious Society of Friends. He lived in South Carolina in 1818-19.	"The houses for the field slaves were about 14 feet square, built in the coarsest manner, with one room, *without any chimney or flooring, with a hole in the roof to let the smoke out.*"
Mr. Lemuel Sapington of Lancaster, Pa., a native of Maryland, formerly a slaveholder.	"The descriptions generally given of negro quarters, are correct; the quarters are *without floors, and not sufficient to keep off the inclemency of the weather;* they are uncomfortable both in summer and winter."
Rev. John Rankin, a native of Tennessee.	"When they return to their miserable huts at night, they find not there the means of comfortable rest; but *on the cold ground they must lie without covering, and shiver while they slumber.*"
Philemon Bliss, Esq. Elyria, Ohio., who lived in Forida, in 1835.	"The dwellings of the slaves are usually small *open* log huts, with but one apartment, and very generally *without floors.*"
Mr. W. C. Gildersleeve, Wilkesbarre, Pa., a native of Georgia.	"Their huts were generally put up without a nail, frequently without floors, and with a single apartment."
Hon. R. J. Turnbull, of South Carolina, a slaveholder.	"The slaves live in *clay cabins.*"

V. TREATMENT OF THE SICK

THE SLAVES SUFFER FROM INHUMAN NEGLECT WHEN SICK

In proof of this we subjoin the following testimony:

Rev. Dr. CHANNING of Boston, who once resided in Virginia, relates the following fact in his work on slavery, page 163, 1st edition.

"I cannot forget my feelings on visiting a hospital belonging to the plantation of a gentleman *highly esteemed for his virtues,* and whose manners and conversation expressed much *benevolence and conscientiousness.* When I entered with him the hospital, the first object on which my eye fell was a young woman, very ill, probably approaching death. She was stretched on the floor. Her head rested on something like a pillow; but *her body and limbs were extended on the hard boards.* The owner, I doubt not, had at least as much kindness as myself; but he was so used to see the slaves living without common comforts, that the idea of unkindness in the present instance did not enter his mind."

This *dying* young woman "was *stretched on the floor*"—"her body and limbs extended upon the hard boards,"—and yet her master "was highly esteemed for his virtues," and his general demeanor produced upon Dr. Channing the impression of "benevolence and conscientiousness." If the *sick and dying female* slaves of *such* a master, suffer such barbarous neglect, whose heart does not fail him, at the thought of that inhumanity, exercised by the *majority* of slaveholders, towards their aged, sick, and dying victims.

The following testimony is furnished by SARAH M. GRIMKÉ, a sister of the late Hon. Thomas S. Grimké, of Charleston, South Carolina.

"When the Ladies' Benevolent Society in Charleston, S. C., of which I was a visiting commissioner, first went into operation, we were applied to for the relief of several sick and aged colored persons; one case I particularly remember, of an aged woman who was dreadfully burnt from having fallen into the fire; she was living with some free blacks who had taken her in out of compassion. On inquiry, we found that *nearly all* the colored persons who had solicited aid, were *slaves,* who being no longer able to work for their "owners," were thus inhumanly cast out in their sickness and old age, and must have perished, but for the kindness of their friends.

"I was once visiting a sick slave in whose spiritual welfare peculiar circumstances had led me to be deeply interested. I knew that she had been early seduced from the path of virtue, as nearly all the female slaves are. I knew also that her mistress, though a professor of religion, had never taught her a single precept of Christianity, yet that she had had her severely punished for this departure from them, and that the poor girl was then ill of an incurable disease, occasioned partly by her own misconduct, and partly by the cruel treatment she had received, in a situation that called for tenderness and care. Her heart seemed truly touched with repentance for her sins, and she was inquiring, 'What shall I do to be saved?' I was sitting by her as she lay on the floor upon a blanket, and was trying to establish her trembling spirit in the fulness of Jesus, when I heard the voice of her mistress in loud and angry tones, as she approached the door. I read in the countenance of the prostrate sufferer, the terror which she felt at the prospect of seeing her mistress. I knew my presence would be very unwelcome, but staid, hoping that it might restrain, in some measure, the passions of the mistress. In this, however, I was mistaken; she passed me without apparently observing that I was there, and seated herself on the other side of the sick slave. She made no inquiry how she was, but in a tone of anger commenced a tirade of abuse, violently reproaching her with her past misconduct, and telling her in the most unfeeling manner, that eternal destruction awaited her. No word of kindness escaped her. What had then roused her temper I do not know. She continued in this strain several minutes, when I attempted to soften her by remarking, that ———— was very ill, and she ought not thus to torment her, and that I believed Jesus had granted her forgiveness. But I might as well have tried to stop the tempest in its career, as to calm the infuriated passions nurtured by the exercise of arbitrary power. She looked at me with ineffable scorn, and continued to pour forth a torrent of abuse and reproach. Her helpless victim listened in terrified silence, until nature could endure no more, when she uttered a wild shriek, and casting on her tormentor a look of unutterable agony, exclaimed, 'Oh, mistress, I am dying!' This appeal arrested her attention, and she soon left the room, but in the same spirit with which she entered it. The girl survived but a few days, and, I believe, saw her mistress *no more*.''

Mr. GEORGE A. AVERY, an elder of a Presbyterian church in Rochester, N. Y., who lived some years in Virginia, gives the following:

''The manner of treating the sick slaves, and especially in *chronic* cases, was to my mind peculiarly revolting. My opportunities for observation in this department were better than in, perhaps, any other, as the friend under whose direction I commenced my medical studies, enjoyed a high reputation as a *surgeon*. I rode considerably with him in his practice, and assisted in the surgical operations and dressings from time to time. In confirmed cases of disease, it was common for the master to place the subject under the care of a physician or surgeon, at whose expense the patient should be kept, and if death ensued to the patient, or the disease was not cured, no compensation was to be made, but if cured a bonus of one, two, or three hundred dollars was to be given. No provision was made against the *barbarity* or *neglect* of the physician, &c. I have seen *fifteen or twenty of these helpless sufferers* crowded together in the true spirit of slaveholding inhumanity, like the "brutes that perish," and driven from time to time *like* brutes into a common yard, where they had to suffer any and every operation and experiment, which interest, caprice, or professional curiosity might prompt,—unrestrained by law, public sentiment, or the claims of common humanity."

Rev. WILLIAM T. ALLAN, son of Rev. Dr. Allan, a slaveholder, of Huntsville, Alabama, says in a letter now before us:

"Colonel Robert H. Watkins, of Laurence county, Alabama, who owned about three hundred slaves, after employing a physician among them for some time, ceased to do so, alleging as the reason, that it was cheaper to lose a few negroes every year than to pay a physician. This Colonel Watkins was a Presidential elector in 1836."

A. A. GUTHRIE, Esq., elder in the Presbyterian church at Putnam, Muskingum county, Ohio, furnishes the testimony which follows.

"A near female friend of mine in company with another young lady, in attempting to visit a sick woman on Washington's Bottom, Wood county, Virginia, missed the way, and stopping to ask directions of a group of colored children on the outskirts of the plantation of Francis Keen, Sen., they were told to ask 'aunty, in the house.' On entering the hut, says my informant, I beheld such a sight as I hope never to see again; its sole occupant was a female slave of the said Keen—her whole wearing apparel consisted of a frock, made of the coarsest tow cloth, and so scanty, that it could not have been made more tight around her person. In the hut there was neither table, chair, nor chest—a stool and a rude fixture in one corner, were all its furniture. On this last were a little straw and a *few* old remnants of what had been bedding—all exceedingly filthy.

"The woman thus situated *had been for more than a day in travail, without any assistance, any nurse, or any kind of proper provision*—during the night she said some fellow slave woman would stay with her, and the aforesaid children through the day. From a woman, who

was a slave of Keen's at the same time, my informant learned, that
this poor woman suffered for three days, and then died—when too
late to save her life her master sent assistance. It was understood to
be a rule of his, to neglect his women entirely in such times of trial,
unless they previously came and informed him, and asked for aid."

Rev. PHINEAS SMITH, of Centreville, N. Y., who has resided four
years at the south, says: "Often when the slaves are sick, their
accustomed toil is exacted from them. Physicians are rarely called for
their benefit."

Rev. HORACE MOULTON, a minister of the Methodist Episcopal
church in Marlborough, Mass., who resided a number of years in
Georgia, says:

"Another dark side of slavery is the neglect of the *aged* and *sick*.
Many when sick, are suspected by their masters of *feigning* sickness,
and are therefore whipped out to work after disease has got fast hold
of them; when the masters learn, that they are really sick, they are
in many instances left alone in their cabins during work hours; not
a few of the slaves are left to die without having one friend to wipe
off the sweat of death. When the slaves are sick, the masters do not,
as a general thing, employ physicians, but "doctor" them themselves,
and their mode of practice in almost all cases is to bleed and give
salts. When women are confined they have no physician, but are
committed to the care of slave midwives. Slaves complain very little
when sick, when they die they are frequently buried at night without
much ceremony, and in many instances without any; their coffins
are made by nailing together rough boards, frequently with their feet
sticking out at the end, and sometimes they are put into the ground
without a coffin or box of any kind."

PERSONAL NARRATIVES

TESTIMONY OF THE REV. WILLIAM T. ALLAN, LATE OF ALABAMA

Mr. ALLAN is a son of the Rev. Dr. Allan, a slaveholder and pastor of the Presbyterian Church at Huntsville, Alabama. He has recently become the pastor of the Presbyterian Church in Chatham, Illinois.

"I was born and have lived most of my life in the slave states, mainly in the village of Huntsville, Alabama, where my parents still reside. I seldom went to a *plantation,* and as my visits were confined almost exclusively to the families of professing Christians, my *personal* knowledge of slavery, was consequently a knowledge of its *fairest* side, (if fairest may be predicated of foul.)

"There was one plantation just opposite my father's house in the suburbs of Huntsville, belonging to Judge Smith, formerly a Senator in Congress from South Carolina, now of Huntsville. The name of his overseer was Tune. I have often seen him flogging the slaves in the field, and have often heard their cries. Sometimes, too, I have met them with the tears streaming down their faces, and the marks of the whip, ('whelks,') on their bare necks and shoulders. Tune was so severe in his treatment, that his employer dismissed him after two or three years, lest, it was said, he should kill off all the slaves. But he was immediately employed by another planter in the neighborhood. The following fact was stated to me by my brother, James M. Allan, now residing at Richmond, Henry county, Illinois, and clerk of the circuit and county courts. Tune became displeased with one of the women who was pregnant, he made her lay down over a log, with her face towards the ground, and beat her so unmercifully, that she was soon after delivered of a *dead child*.

"My brother also stated to me the following, which occurred near my father's house, and within sight and hearing of the academy and public garden. Charles, a fine active negro, who belonged to a bricklayer in Huntsville, exchanged the burning sun of the brickyard to enjoy for a season the pleasant shade of an adjacent mountain. When his master got him back, he tied him by his hands so that his feet could just touch the ground—stripped off his clothes, took a paddle, bored full of holes, and paddled him leisurely all day long. It was two weeks before they could tell whether he would live or die. Neither of these cases attracted any particular notice in Huntsville.

"While I lived in Huntsville a slave was killed in the mountain near by. The circumstances were these. A white man (James Helton) hunting in the woods, suddenly came upon a black man, and commanded him to stop, the slave kept on running, Helton fired his rifle and the negro was killed.*

"Mrs. BARR, wife of Rev. H. Barr of Carrollton, Illinois, formerly from Courtland, Alabama, told me last spring, that she has very often stopped her ears that she might not hear the screams of slaves who were under the lash, and that sometimes she has left her house, and retired to a place more distant, in order to get away from their agonizing cries.

"I have often seen groups of slaves on the public squares in Huntsville, who were to be sold at auction, and I have often seen their tears gush forth and their countenances distorted with anguish. A considerable number were generally sold publicly every month.

"The following facts I have just taken down from the lips of Mr. L. Turner, a regular and respectable member of the Second Presbyterian Church in Springfield, our county town. He was born and brought up in Caroline county, Virginia. He says that the slaves are neither considered nor treated as human beings. One of his neighbors whose name was Barr, he says, on one occasion stripped a slave and lacerated his back with a handcard (for cotton or wool) and then washed it with salt and water, with pepper in it. Mr. Turner *saw* this. He further remarked that he believed there were *many* slaves there in advanced life whose backs had *never* been well since they began to work.

"He stated that one of his uncles had killed a woman—broke her skull with an ax helve: she had insulted her mistress! No notice was taken of the affair. Mr. T. said, further, that slaves were *frequently murdered.*

"He mentioned the case of one slaveholder, whom he had seen lay his slaves on a large log, which he kept for the purpose, strip

---

* This murder was committed about twelve years since. At that time, James G. Birney, Esq., now Corresponding Secretary of the American Anti-Slavery Society was the Solicitor (prosecuting attorney) for that judicial district. His views and feelings upon the subject of slavery were, even at that period, in advance of the mass of slaveholders, and he determined if possible to bring the murderer to justice. He accordingly drew up an indictment and procured the finding of a true bill against Helton. Helton, meanwhile, moved over the line into the state of Tennessee, and such was the apathy of the community, individual effort proved unavailing; and though the murderer had gone no further than to an adjoining county (where perhaps he still resides) he was never brought to trial.—ED.

them, tie them with the face downward, then have a kettle of hot water brought—take the paddle, made of hard wood, and perforated with holes, dip it into the hot water and strike—before every blow dipping it into the water—every hole at every blow would raise a 'whelk.' This was the usual punishment for *running away*.

"Another slaveholder had a slave who had often run away, and often been severely whipped. After one of his floggings he burnt his master's barn: this so enraged the man, that when he caught him he took a pair of pincers and pulled his toe nails out. The negro then murdered two of his master's children. He was taken after a desperate pursuit, (having been shot through the shoulder) and hung.

"One of Mr. Turner's cousins, was employed as overseer on a large plantation in Mississippi. On a certain morning he called the slaves together, to give some orders. While doing it, a slave came running out of his cabin, having a knife in his hand and eating his breakfast. The overseer seeing him coming with the knife, was somewhat alarmed, and instantly raised his gun and shot him dead. He said afterwards, that he believed the slave was perfectly innocent of any evil intentions, he came out hastily to hear the orders whilst eating. *No* notice was taken of the killing.

"Mr. T. related the whipping habits of one of his uncles in Virginia. He was a wealthy man, had a splendid house and grounds. A tree in his *front yard*, was used as a *whipping post*. When a slave was to be punished, he would frequently invite some of his friends, have a table, cards and wine set out under the shade; he would then flog his slave a little while, and then play cards and drink with his friends, occasionally taunting the slave, giving him the privilege of confessing such and such things, at his leisure, after a while flog him again, thus keeping it up for hours or half the day, and sometimes all day. This was his *habit*.

"*February 4th.*—Since writing the preceding, I have been to Carrollton, on a visit to my uncle, Rev. Hugh Barr, who was originally from Tennessee, lived 12 or 14 years in Courtland, Lawrence county, Alabama, and moved to Illinois in 1835. In conversation with the family, around the fireside, they stated a multitude of horrid facts, that were perfectly notorious in the neighborhood of Courtland.

"William P. Barr, an intelligent young man, and member of his father's church in Carrollton, stated the following. Visiting at a Mr. Mosely's, near Courtland, William Mosely came in with a bloody knife in his hand, having just stabbed a negro man. The negro was sitting quietly in a house in the village, keeping a woman company who had been left in charge of the house,—when Mosely, passing along, went in and demanded his business there. Probably his answer was not as civil as slaveholding requires, and Mosely rushed upon him and stabbed him. The wound laid him up for a season. Mosely was called to no account for it. When he came in with the bloody knife, he said he wished he had killed him.

"John Brown, a slaveholder, and a member of the Presbyterian church in Courtland, Alabama, stated the following a few weeks since, in Carrollton. A man near Courtland, of the name of Thompson, recently shot a negro *woman* through the head; and put the pistol so close that her hair was singed. He did it in consequence of some difficulty in his dealings with her as a concubine. He buried her in a log heap; she was discovered by the buzzards gathering around it.

"William P. Barr stated the following, as facts well known in the neighborhood of Courtland, but not witnessed by himself. Two men, by the name of Wilson, found a fine looking negro man at 'Dandridge's Quarter,' without a pass; and flogged him so that he died in a short time. They were not punished.

"Col. Blocker's overseer attempted to flog a negro—he refused to be flogged; whereupon the overseer seized an axe, and cleft his skull. The Colonel justified it.

"One Jones whipped a woman to death for 'grabbling' a potato hill. He owned 80 or 100 negroes. His own children could not live with him.

"A man in the neighborhood of Courtland, Alabama, by the name of Puryear, was so proverbially cruel that among the negroes he was usually called 'the Devil.' Mrs. Barr, wife of Rev. H. Barr, was at Puryear's house, and saw a negro girl about 13 years old, waiting around the table, with a single garment—and that in cold weather; arms and feet bare—feet wretchedly swollen—arms burnt, and full of sores from exposure. All the negroes under his care made a wretched appearance.

"Col. Robert H. Watkins had a runaway slave, who was called Jim Dragon. Before he was caught the last time, he had been out a year, within a few miles of his master's plantation. He never stole from any one but his master, except when necessity compelled him. He said he had a right to take from his master; and when taken, that he had, whilst out, seen his master a hundred times. Having been whipped, clogged with irons, and yoked, he was set at work in the field. Col. Watkins worked about 300 hands—generally had one negro out hunting runaways. After employing a physician for some time among his negroes, he ceased to do so, alleging as the reason, that it was cheaper to lose a few negroes every year than to pay a physician. He was a Presidential elector in 1836.

"Col. Ben Sherrod, another large planter in that neighborhood, is remarkable for his kindness to his slaves. He said to Rev. Mr. Barr, that he had no doubt he should be rewarded in heaven for his kindness to his slaves; and yet his overseer, Walker, had to sleep with loaded pistols, for fear of assassination. Three of the slaves attempted to kill him once, because of his *treatment of their wives*.

"Old Major Billy Watkins was noted for his severity. I well remember, when he lived in Madison county, to have often heard him yell at his negroes with the most savage fury. He would stand at his house, and watch the slaves picking cotton; and if any of them straitened their backs for a moment, his savage yell would ring, 'bend your backs.'

"Mrs. Barr stated, that Mrs. H——, of Courtland, a member of the Presbyterian church, sent a little negro girl to jail, suspecting that she had attempted to put poison into the water pail. The fact was, that the child had found a vial, and was playing in the water. This same woman (in high standing too), told the Rev. Mr. McMillan, that she could 'cut Arthur Tappan's throat from ear to ear.'

"The clothing of slaves is in many cases comfortable, and in many it is far from being so. I have very often seen slaves, whose tattered rags were neither comfortable nor decent.

"Their *huts* are sometimes comfortable, but generally they are miserable *hovels,* where male and female are herded promiscuously together.

"As to the *usual* allowance of food on the plantations in North Alabama, I cannot speak confidently, from *personal* knowledge. There was a slave named Hadley, who was in the habit of visiting my father's slaves occasionally. He had run away several times. His reason was, as he stated, that they would not give him any meat—said he could not work without meat. The last time I saw him, he had quite a heavy iron yoke on his neck, the two prongs twelve or fifteen inches long, extending out over his shoulders and bending upwards.

"*Legal* marriage is unknown among the slaves, they sometimes have a marriage form—generally, however, *none at all*. The pastor of the Presbyterian church in Huntsville had two families of slaves when I left there. One couple were married by a negro preacher—the man was robbed of his wife a number of months afterwards, by her '*owner*.' The other couple just 'took up together,' without any

form of marriage. They are both members of churches—the man a
Baptist deacon, sober and correct in his deportment. They have a
large family of children—all children of concubinage—living in a
minister's family.

"If these statements are deemed of any value by you, in forwarding
your glorious enterprize, you are at liberty to use them as you please.
The great wrong is *enslaving a man*; all other wrongs are pigmies,
compared with that. Facts might be gathered abundantly, to show
that it is *slavery itself,* and not cruelties merely, that make slaves
unhappy. Even those that are most kindly treated, are generally far
from being happy. The slaves in my father's family are almost as
kindly treated as *slaves* can be, yet they pant for liberty.

"May the Lord guide you in this great movement.

In behalf of the perishing,
Your friend and brother,
WILLIAM T. ALLAN."

NARRATIVE OF MR. WILLIAM LEFTWICH, A NATIVE OF VIRGINIA

Mr. Leftwich is a grandson of Gen. Jabez Leftwich, who was for
some years a member of Congress from Virginia. Though born in
Virginia, he has resided most of his life in Alabama. He now lives in
Delhi, Hamilton county, Ohio, near Cincinnati.

As an introduction to his letter, the reader is furnished with the
following testimonial to his character, from the Rev. Horace Bushnell,
pastor of the Presbyterian church in Delhi. Mr. B. says:

"Mr. Leftwich is a worthy member of this church, and is a young
man of sterling integrity and veracity.   H. BUSHNELL."

The following is the letter of Mr. Leftwich, dated Dec. 26, 1838.

"DEAR BROTHER—Though I am not ranked among the abolitionists,
yet I cannot, as a friend of humanity, withhold from the public such
facts in relation to the condition of the slaves, as have fallen under
my own observation. That I am somewhat acquainted with slavery
will be seen, as I narrate some incidents of my own life. My parents
were slaveholders, and moved from Virginia to Madison county,
Alabama, during my infancy. My mother soon fell a victim to the
climate. Being the youngest of the children, I was left in the care of

my aged grandfather, who never held a slave, though his sons owned from 90 to 100 during the time I resided with him. As soon as I could carry a hoe, my uncle, by the name of Neely, persuaded my grandfather that I should be placed in his hands, and brought up in habits of industry. I was accordingly placed under his tuition. I left the domestic circle, little dreaming of the horrors that awaited me. My mother's own brother took me to the cotton field, there to learn habits of industry, and to be benefited by his counsels. But the sequel proved, that I was there to feel in my own person, and witness by experience many of the horrors of slavery. Instead of kind admonition, I was to endure the frowns of one, whose sympathies could neither be reached by the prayers and cries of his slaves, nor by the entreaties and sufferings of a sister's son. Let those who call slaveholders kind, hospitable and humane, mark the course the slaveholder pursues with one born free, whose ancestors fought and bled for liberty; and then say, if they can without a blush of shame, that he who robs the helpless of every *right,* can be truly kind and hospitable.

"In a short time after I was put upon the plantation, there was but little difference between me and the slaves, except being *white,* I ate at the master's table. The slaves were my companions in misery, and I well learned their condition, both in the house and field. Their dwellings are log huts, from ten to twelve feet square; often without windows, doors or floors. They have neither chairs, tables or bedsteads. These huts are occupied by eight, ten or twelve persons each. Their bedding generally consists of two old blankets. Many of them sleep night after night sitting upon their blocks or stools; others sleep in the open air. Our task was appointed, and from dawn till dark all must bend to their work. Their meals were taken without knife or plate, dish or spoon. Their food was corn *pone,* prepared in the coarsest manner, with a small allowance of meat. Their meals in the field were taken from the hands of the carrier, wherever he found them, with no more ceremony than in the feeding of swine. My uncle was his own overseer. For punishing in the field, he preferred a large hickory stick; and wo to him whose work was not done to please him, for the hickory was used upon our heads as remorselessly as if we had been mad dogs. I was often the object of his fury, and shall bear the marks of it on my body till I die. Such was my suffering and degradation, that at the end of five years, I hardly dared to say I was *free.* When thinning cotton, we went mostly on our knees. One day, while thus engaged, my uncle found my row behind; and, by way of admonition, gave me a few blows with his hickory, the marks of which I carried for weeks. Often I followed the example of the fugitive slaves, and betook myself to the mountains; but hunger and fear drove me back, to share with the wretched slave his toil and stripes. But I have talked enough about my own bondage; I will now relate a few facts, showing the condition of the slaves *generally*.

"My uncle wishing to purchase what is called a good 'house wench,' a *trader* in human flesh soon produced a woman, recommending her as highly as ever a jockey did a horse. She was purchased, but on trial was found wanting in the requisite qualifications. She then fell a victim to the disappointed rage of my uncle; innocent or guilty, she suffered greatly from his fury. He used to tie her to a peach tree in the yard, and whip her till there was no sound place to lay another stroke, and repeat it so often that her back was kept continually sore. Whipping the females around the legs was a favorite mode of punishment with him. They must stand and hold up their clothes, while he plied his hickory. He did not, like some of his neighbors, keep a pack of hounds for hunting runaway negroes, but he kept one dog for that purpose, and when he came up with a runaway, it would have been death to attempt to fly, and it was nearly so to stand. Sometimes, when my uncle attempted to whip the slaves, the dog would rush upon them and relieve them of their rags, if not of their flesh. One object of my uncle's special hate was 'Jerry,' a slave of a proud spirit. He defied all the curses, rage and stripes of his tyrant. Though he was often overpowered—for my uncle would frequently wear out his stick upon his head—yet he would never submit. As he was not expert in picking cotton, he would sometimes run away in the fall, to escape abuse. At one time, after an absence of some months, he was arrested and brought back. As is customary, he was stripped, tied to a log, and the cow-skin applied to his naked body till his master was exhausted. Then a large log chain was fastened around one ankle, passed up his back, over his shoulders, then across his breast, and fastened under his arm. In this condition he was forced to perform his daily task. Add to this he was chained each night, and compelled to chop wood every Sabbath, to make up lost time. After being thus manacled for some months, he was released—but his spirit was unsubdued. Soon after, his master, in a paroxysm of rage, fell upon him, wore out his staff upon his head, loaded him again with chains, and after a month, sold him farther south. Another slave, by the name of Mince, who was a man of great strength, purloined some bacon on a Christmas eve. It was missed in the morning, and he being absent, was of course suspected. On returning home, my uncle commanded him to come to him, but he refused. The master strove in vain to lay hands on him; in vain he ordered his slaves to seize him—they dared not. At length the master hurled a stone at his head sufficient to have felled a bullock—but he did not heed it. At that instant my aunt sprang forward, and presenting the gun to my uncle, exclaimed, 'Shoot him! shoot him!' He made the attempt, but the gun missed fire, and Mince fled. He was taken eight or ten months after that, while crossing the Ohio. When brought back, the master, and an overseer on another plantation, took him to the mountain and punished him to their satisfaction in secret; after which he was loaded with chains and set to his task.

"I have spent nearly all my life in the midst of slavery. From being the son of a slaveholder, I descended to the condition of a slave, and from that condition I rose (if you please to call it so), to the station of a '*driver*.' I have lived in Alabama, Tennessee, and Kentucky; and I *know* the condition of the slaves to be that of unmixed wretchedness and degradation. And on the part of slaveholders, there is cruelty *untold*. The labor of the slave is constant toil, wrung out by fear. Their food is scanty, and taken without comfort. Their clothes answer the purposes neither of comfort nor decency. They are not allowed to read or write. Whether they may worship God or not, depends on the will of the master. The young children, until they can work, often go naked during the warm weather. I could spend months in detailing the sufferings, degradation and cruelty inflicted upon slaves. But my soul sickens at the remembrance of these things."

TESTIMONY OF MR. LEMUEL SAPINGTON, A NATIVE OF MARYLAND

Mr. Sapington is a repentant "soul driver" or slave trader, now a citizen of Lancaster, Pa. He gives the following testimony in a letter dated, Jan. 21, 1839.

"I was born in Maryland, afterwards moved to Virginia, where I commenced the business of farming and trafficking in slaves. In my neighborhood the slaves were 'quartered.' The description generally given of negro quarters is correct. The quarters are without floors, and not sufficient to keep off the inclemency of the weather, they are uncomfortable both in summer and winter. The food there consists of potatoes, pork, and corn, which were given to them daily, by weight and measure. The sexes were huddled together promiscuously. Their clothing is made by themselves after night, though sometimes assisted by the old women who are no longer able to do out door work, consequently it is harsh and uncomfortable. I have frequently seen those of both sexes who have not attained the age of twelve years go naked. Their punishments are invariably cruel. For the slightest offence, such as taking a hen's egg, I have seen them stripped and suspended by their hands, their feet tied together, a fence rail of ordinary size placed between their ankles, and then most cruelly whipped, until, from head to foot, they were completely lacerated, a pickle made for the purpose of salt and water, would then be applied by a fellow-slave, for the purpose of healing the wounds as well as giving pain. Then they were taken down and without the least respite sent to work with their hoe.

"Pursuing my assumed right of driving souls, I went to the Southern part of Virginia for the purpose of trafficking in slaves. In that part of the state, the cruelties practised upon the slaves are far greater than where I lived. The punishments there often resulted in death to the slave. There was no law for the negro, but that of the overseer's whip. In that part of the country, the slaves receive nothing for food, but an ear of corn, which has to be prepared for baking after working hours, by grinding it with a hand-mill. This they take to the fields with them, and prepare it for eating, by holding it on their hoes over a fire made by a stump. Among the gangs are often young women, who bring their children to the fields and lay them in a fence corner while they are at work, only being permitted to nurse them at the option of the overseer. When a child is three weeks old, a woman is considered in working order. I have seen a woman, with her young child strapped to her back, laboring the whole day, beside a man, perhaps the father of the child, and he not being permitted to give her any assistance, himself being under the whip. Only the uncommon humanity of the driver would allow her the comfort of doing so. I was then selling a drove of slaves, which I had brought by water from Baltimore, my conscience not allowing me to drive, as was generally the case uniting the slaves by collars and chains, and thus driving them under the whip. About that time an unaccountable something, which I now know was an interposition of Providence, prevented me from prosecuting any farther this unholy traffic; but though I had quitted it, I still continued to live in a slave state, witnessing every day its evil effects upon my fellow beings. Among which was a heart-rending scene that took place in my father's house, which led me to leave a slave state, as well as all the imaginary comforts arising from slavery. On preparing for my removal to the state of Pennsylvania, it became necessary for me to go to Louisville, in Kentucky, where, if possible, I became more horrified with the impositions practiced upon the negro than before. There a slave was sold to go farther south, and was handcuffed for the purpose of keeping him secure. But choosing death rather than slavery, he jumped overboard and was drowned. When I returned four weeks afterwards his body, that had floated three miles below, was yet unburied. One fact; it is impossible for a person to pass through a slave state, if he has eyes open, without beholding every day cruelties repugnant to humanity.

Respectfully Yours,

LEMUEL SAPINGTON."

TESTIMONY OF MRS. NANCY LOWRY, A NATIVE OF KENTUCKY

Mrs. Lowry, is a member of the non-conformist church in Osnaburg, Stark County, Ohio, she is a native of Kentucky. We have received from her the following testimony.

"I resided in the family of Reuben Long, the principal part of the time, from seven to twenty-two years of age. Mr. Long had 16 slaves, among whom were three who were treated with severity, although Mr. Long was thought to be a very humane master. These three, namely John, Ned, and James, had wives; John and Ned had theirs at some distance, but James had his with him. All three died a premature death, and it was generally believed by his neighbors, that extreme whipping was the cause. I believe so too. Ned died about the age of 25 and John 34 or 35. The cause of their flogging was commonly staying a little over the time, with their wives. Mr. Long would tie them up by the wrist, so high that their toes would just touch the ground, and then with a cow-hide lay the lash upon the naked back, until he was exhausted, when he would sit down and rest. As soon as he had rested sufficiently, he would ply the cowhide again, thus he would continue until the whole back of the poor victim was lacerated into one uniform coat of blood. Yet he was a strict professor of the Christian religion, in the southern church. I frequently washed the wounds of John, with salt water, to prevent putrefaction. This was the usual course pursued after a severe flogging; their backs would be full of gashes, so deep that I could almost lay my finger in them. They were generally laid up after the flogging for several days. The last flogging Ned got, he was confined to the bed, which he never left till he was carried to his grave. During John's confinement in his last sickness on one occasion while attending on him, he exclaimed, 'Oh, Nancy, Miss Nancy, I haven't much longer in this world, I feel as if my whole body inside and all my bones were beaten into a jelly.' Soon after he died. John and Ned were both professors of religion.

"John Ruffner, a slaveholder, had one slave named Piney, whom he as well as Mrs. Ruffner would often flog very severely. I frequently saw Mrs. Ruffner flog her with the broom, shovel, or any thing she could seize in her rage. She would knock her down and then kick and stamp her most unmercifully, until she would he apparently so lifeless, that I more than once thought she would never recover. Often Piney would try to shelter herself from the blows of her mistress, by creeping under the bed, from which Mrs. Ruffner would draw her by the feet, and then stamp and leap on her body, till her breath would be gone. Often Piney, would cry, 'Oh Missee, don't kill me!' 'Oh Lord, don't kill me!' 'For God's sake don't kill me!' But Mrs. Ruffner would beat and stamp away, with all the venom of a demon. The cause of Piney's flogging was, not working enough, or making some mistake in baking, &c. &c. Many a night Piney had to lie on the bare floor, by the side of the cradle, rocking the baby of her mistress, and if she would fall asleep, and suffer the child to cry, so as to waken Mrs. Ruffner, she would be sure to receive a flogging."

TESTIMONY OF MR. WM. C. GILDERSLEEVE, A NATIVE OF GEORGIA

Mr. W. C. GILDERSLEEVE, a native of Georgia, is an elder of the Presbyterian Church at Wilkesbarre, Pa.

"*Acts of cruelty, without number, fell under my observation* while I lived in Georgia. I will mention but one. A slave of a Mr. Pinkney, on his way with a wagon to Savannah, 'camped' for the night by the road side. That night, the nearest hen-roost was robbed. On his return, the hen-roost was again visited, and the fowl counted one less in the morning. The oldest son, with some attendants made search, and came upon the poor fellow, in the act of dressing his spoil. He was too nimble for them, and made his retreat good into a dense swamp. When much effort to start him from his hiding place had proved unsuccessful, it was resolved to lay an ambush for him, some distance ahead. The wagon, meantime, was in charge of a lad, who accompanied the teamster as an assistant. The little boy lay still till nearly night, (in the hope probably that the teamster would return), when he started with his wagon. After travelling some distance, the lost one made his appearance, when the ambush sprang upon him. The poor fellow was conducted back to the plantation. He expected little mercy. He begged for himself, in the most suplicating manner, 'pray massa give me 100 lashes and let me go.' He was then tied by the hands, to a limb of a large mulberry tree, which grew in the yard, so that his feet were raised a few inches from the ground, while a *sharpened stick* was driven underneath, that he might rest his weight on it, or swing by his hands. In this condition 100 lashes were laid on his bare body. I stood by and witnessed the whole, without as I recollect, feeling the least compassion. So hardening is the influence of slavery, that it very much destroys feeling for the slave."

TESTIMONY OF MR. HIRAM WHITE—
A NATIVE OF NORTH CAROLINA

Mr. WHITE resided thirty-two years in Chatham county, North Carolina, and is now a member of the Baptist Church, at Otter Creek Prairie, Illinois.

About the 20th December, 1830, a report was raised that the slaves in Chatham county, North Carolina, were going to rise on Christmas day, in consequence of which a considerable commotion ensued among the inhabitants; orders were given by the Governor to the militia captains, to appoint patrolling captains in each district, and orders were given for every man subject to military duty to patrol as their captains should direct. I went two nights in succession, and after that refused to patrol at all. The reason why I refused was this, orders were given to search every negro house for books or prints of any kind, and *Bibles* and *Hymn books* were particularly mentioned. And should we find any, our orders were to inflict punishment by whipping the slave until he *informed who* gave them to him, or how they came by them.

As regards the comforts of the slaves in the vicinity of my residence, I can say they had nothing that would bear that name. It is true, the slaves in general, of a good crop year, were tolerably well fed, but of a bad crop year, they were, as a general thing, cut short of their allowance. Their houses were pole cabins, without loft or floor. Their beds were made of what is there called "broom-straw." The men more commonly sleep on benches. Their clothing would compare well with their lodging. Whipping was common. It was hardly possible for a man with a common pair of ears, if he was out of his house but a short time on Monday mornings, to miss of hearing the sound of the lash, and the cries of the sufferers pleading with their masters to desist. These scenes were more common throughout the time of my residence there, from 1799 to 1831.

Mr. HEDDING of Chatham county, held a slave woman. I traveled past Hedding's as often as once in two weeks during the winter of 1828, and always saw her clad in a single cotton dress, sleeves came half way to the elbow, and in order to prevent her running away, a child, supposed to be about seven years of age, was connected with her by a long chain fastened round her neck, and in this situation she was compelled all the day to *grub* up the roots of shrubs and saplings to prepare ground for the plough. It is not uncommon for slaves to make up on Sundays what they are not able to perform through the week of their tasks.

At the time of the rumored insurrection above named, Chatham jail was filled with slaves who were said to have been concerned in the plot. Without the least evidence of it, they were punished in divers ways; some were whipped, some had their *thumbs screwed in a vice* to make them confess, but no proof satisfactory was ever obtained that the negroes had ever thought of an insurrection, nor did any so far as I could learn, acknowledge that an insurrection had ever been projected. From this time forth, the slaves were prohibited from assembling together for the worship of God, and many of those who had previously been authorized to preach the gospel were prohibited.

Amalgamation was common. There was scarce a family of slaves that had females of mature age where there were not some mulatto children.

HIRAM WHITE.

Otter Creek Prairie, Jan. 22, 1839.

TESTIMONY OF MR. JOHN M. NELSON—
A NATIVE OF VIRGINIA

Extract of a letter, dated January 3, 1839, from John M. Nelson, Esq., of Hillsborough. Mr. Nelson removed from Virginia to Highland county, Ohio, many years since, where he is extensively known and respected.

I was born and raised in Augusta county, Virginia; my father was an elder in the Presbyterian Church, and was "owner" of about twenty slaves; he was what was generally termed a "good master." His slaves were generally tolerably well fed and clothed, and not over worked, they were sometimes permitted to attend church, and called in to family worship; few of them, however, availed themselves of these privileges. On *some occasions* I have seen him whip them severely, particularly for the crime of trying to obtain their liberty, or for what was called, "running away." For *this* they were scourged more severely than for any thing else. After they have been retaken, I have seen them stripped naked and suspended by the hands, sometimes to a tree, sometimes to a post, until their toes barely touched the ground, and whipped with a cowhide until the blood dripped from their backs. A boy named Jack, particularly, I have seen served in this way more than once. When I was quite a child, I recollect it grieved me very much to see one *tied up* to be whipped, and I used to intercede with tears in their behalf, and mingle my cries with theirs, and feel almost willing to take part of the punishment; I have been severely rebuked by my father for this kind of sympathy. Yet, such is the hardening nature of such scenes, that from this kind of commisseration for the suffering slave, I became so blunted that I could not only witness their stripes with composure, but *myself* inflict them, and that without remorse. One case I have often looked back to with sorrow and contrition, particularly since I have been convinced that "negroes are men." When I was perhaps fourteen or fifteen years of age, I undertook to correct a young fellow named Ned, for some supposed offence; I think it was leaving a bridle out of its proper place; he being larger and stronger than myself took hold of my arms and held me, in order to prevent my striking him; this I considered the height of insolence, and cried for help, when my father and mother both came running to my rescue. My father stripped and tied him, and took him into the orchard, where switches were plenty, and directed me to whip him; when one switch wore out he supplied me with others. After I had whipped him a while, he fell on his knees to implore forgiveness, and I kicked him in the face; my father said, "don't kick him, but whip him"; this I did until his back was literally covered with *welts*. I know I have repented, and trust I have obtained pardon for these things.

My father owned a woman, (we used to call aunt Grace), she was purchased in Old Virginia. She has told me that her old master, in his *will,* gave her her freedom, but at his death, his sons had sold her to my father: when he bought her she manifested some unwillingness to go with him, when she was put in irons and taken by force. This was before I was born; but I remember to have seen the irons, and was told that was what they had been used for. Aunt Grace is still living, and must be between seventy and eighty years of age; she has, for the last forty years, been an exemplary Christian. When I was a youth I took some pains to learn her to read; this is now a great consolation to her. Since age and infirmity have rendered her of little value to her "owners," she is permitted to read as much as she pleases; this she can do, with the aid of glasses, in the old family Bible, which is almost the only book she has ever looked into. This with some little mending for the black children, is all she does; she is still held as a slave. I well remember what *a heart-rending scene* there was in the family when *my father sold her husband*; this was, I suppose, thirty-five years ago. And yet my father was considered one of the best of masters. I know of few who were better, but of *many* who were worse.

The last time I saw my father, which was in the fall of 1832, he promised me that he would free all his slaves at his death. He died however without doing it; and I have understood since, that he omitted it, through the influence of Rev. Dr. Speece, a Presbyterian minister, who lived in the family, and was *a warm friend of the Colonization Society*.

About the year 1809 or 10, I became a student of Rev. George Bourne; he was the first abolitionist I had ever seen, and the first I had ever heard pray or plead for the oppressed, which gave me the first misgivings about the *innocence* of slaveholding. I received impressions from Mr. Bourne which I could not get rid of,* and determined in my own mind that when I settled in life, it should be in a free state; this determination I carried into effect in 1813, when I removed to this place, which I supposed at that time, to be all the opposition to slavery that was necessary, but the moment I became convinced that all slaveholding was in itself *sinful,* I became an abolitionist, which was about four years ago.

TESTIMONY OF ANGELINA GRIMKÉ WELD

Mrs. Weld is the youngest daughter of the late Judge Grimké, of the Supreme Court of South Carolina, and a sister of the late Hon. Thomas S. Grimké, of Charleston.

FORT LEE, Bergen Co., New Jersey. }
Fourth month 6th, 1839. }

I sit down to comply with thy request, proffered in the name of the Executive Committee of the American Anti-Slavery Society. The responsibility laid upon me by such a request, leaves me no option. While I live, and slavery lives, I *must* testify against it. If I should hold my peace, "the stone would cry out of the wall, and the beam out of the timber would answer it." But though I feel a necessity upon me, and "a woe unto me," if I withhold my testimony, I give it with a heavy heart. My flesh crieth out, "if it be possible, let *this* cup pass from me"; but, "Father, *thy* will be done," is, I trust, the breathing of my spirit. Oh, the slain of the daughter of my people! they lie in all the ways; their tears fall as the rain, and are their meat day and night; their blood runneth down like water; their plundered hearths are desolate; they weep for their husbands and children, because they are not; and the proud waves do continually go over them, while no eye pitieth, and no man careth for their souls.

---

* Mr. Bourne resided seven years in Virginia, "in perils among false brethren," fiercely persecuted for his faithful testimony against slavery. More than twenty years since he published a work entitled "The Book and Slavery Irreconcileable."

But it is not alone for the sake of my poor brothers and sisters in bonds, or for the cause of truth, and righteousness, and humanity, that I testify; the deep yearnings of affection for the mother that bore me, who is still a slaveholder, both in fact and in heart; for my brothers and sisters, (a large family circle), and for my numerous other slave-holding kindred in South Carolina, constrain me to speak: for even were slavery no curse to its victims, the exercise of arbitrary power works such fearful ruin upon the hearts of *slaveholders,* that I should feel impelled to labor and pray for its overthrow with my last energies and latest breath.

I think it important to premise, that I have seen almost nothing of slavery on *plantations.* My testimony will have respect exclusively to the treatment of "*house-servants,*" and chiefly those belonging to the first families in the city of Charleston, both in the religious and in the fashionable world. And here let me say, that the treatment of *plantation* slaves cannot be fully known, except by the poor sufferers themselves, and their drivers and overseers. In a multitude of instances, even the master can know very little of the actual condition of his own field-slaves, and his wife and daughters far less. A few facts concerning my own family will show this. Our permanent residence was in Charleston; our country-seat (Bellemont), was 200 miles distant, in the north-western part of the state; where, for some years, our family spent a few months annually. Our *plantation* was three miles from this family mansion. There, all the field-slaves lived and worked. Occasionally, once a month, perhaps, some of the family would ride over to the plantation, but I never visited the *fields where the slaves were at work,* and knew almost nothing of their condition; but this I do know, that the overseers who had charge of them, were generally unprincipled and intemperate men. But I rejoice to know, that the general treatment of slaves in that region of country, was far milder than on the plantations in the lower country.

Throughout all the eastern and middle portions of the state, the planters very rarely reside permanently on their plantations. They have almost invariably *two* residences, and spend less than half the year on their estates. Even while spending a few months on them, politics, field-sports, races, speculations, journeys, visits, company, literary pursuits, &c., absorb so much of their time, that they must, to a considerable extent, take the condition of their slaves on *trust,* from the reports of their overseers. I make this statement, because these slaveholders (the wealthier class), are, I believe, almost the only ones who visit the north with their families;—and northern opinions of slavery are based chiefly on their testimony.

But not to dwell on preliminaries, I wish to record my testimony to the faithfulness and accuracy with which my beloved sister, Sarah M. Grimké, has, in her 'narrative and testimony,' on a preceding page, described the condition of the slaves, and the effect upon the hearts of slaveholders, (even the best), caused by the exercise of unlimited power over moral agents. Of the *particular acts* which she has stated, I have no personal knowledge, as they occurred before my remembrance; but of the spirit that prompted them, and that constantly displays itself in scenes of similar horror, the recollections of my childhood, and the effaceless imprint upon my riper years, with the breaking of my heart-strings, when, finding that I was powerless to shield the victims, I tore myself from my home and friends, and became an exile among strangers—all these throng around me as witnesses, and their testimony is graven on my memory with a pen of fire.

Why I did not become totally hardened, under the daily operation of this system, God only knows; in deep solemnity and gratitude, I say, it was the *Lord's* doing, and marvellous in mine eyes. Even before my heart was touched with the love of Christ, I used to say, "Oh that I had the wings of a dove, that I might flee away and be at rest"; for I felt that there could be no rest for me in the midst of such outrages and pollutions. And yet I saw *nothing* of slavery in its most vulgar and repulsive forms. I saw it in the *city,* among the fashionable and the honorable, where it was garnished by refinement, and decked out for show. A few *facts* will unfold the state of society in the circle with which I was familiar, far better than any general assertions I can make.

I will first introduce the reader to a woman of the highest respectability—one who was foremost in every benevolent enterprise, and stood for many years, I may say, at the *head* of the fashionable élite of the city of Charleston, and afterwards at the head of the moral and religious female society there. It was after she had made a profession of religion, and retired from the fashionable world, that I knew her; therefore I will present her in her religious character. This lady used to keep cowhides, or small paddles, (called 'pancake sticks,') in four different apartments in her house; so that when she wished to punish, or to have punished, any of her slaves, she might not have the trouble of sending for an instrument of torture. For many years,

one or other, and *often* more of her slaves, were flogged *every day*;
particularly the young slaves about the house, whose faces were slapped,
or their hands beat with the 'pancake stick,' for every trifling offence—
and often for no fault at all. But the floggings were not all; the scoldings
and abuse daily heaped upon them all, were worse: 'fools' and 'liars,'
'sluts' and 'husseys,' 'hypocrites' and 'good-for-nothing creatures,'
were the *common* epithets with which her mouth was filled, when
addressing her slaves, adults as well as children. Very often she would
take a position at her window, in an upper story, and scold at her
slaves while working in the garden, at some distance from the house,
(a large yard intervening), and occasionally order a flogging. I have
known her thus on the watch, scolding for more than an hour at a
time, in so loud a voice that the whole neighborhood could hear her;
and this without the least apparent feeling of shame. Indeed, it was
no disgrace among slaveholders, and did not in the least injure her standing,
either as a lady or a Christian, in the aristocratic circle in which she
moved. After the 'revival' in Charleston, in 1825, she opened her
house to social prayer-meetings. The room in which they were held
in the evening, and where the voice of prayer was heard around the
family altar, and where she herself retired for private devotion thrice
each day, was the very place in which, when her slaves were to be
whipped with the cowhide, they were taken to receive the infliction;
and the wail of the sufferer would be heard, where, perhaps only a
few hours previous, rose the voices of prayer and praise. This mistress
would occasionally send her slaves, male and female, to the Charleston
work-house to be punished. One poor girl, whom she sent there to
be flogged, and who was accordingly stripped *naked* and whipped,
showed me the deep gashes on her back—I might have laid my whole
finger in them—*large pieces of flesh had actually been cut out by the torturing
lash.* She sent another female slave there, to be imprisoned and worked
on the tread-mill. This girl was confined several days, and forced to
work the mill while in a state of suffering from another cause. For
ten days or two weeks after her return, she was lame, from the violent
exertion necessary to enable her to keep the step on the machine. She
spoke to me with intense feeling of this outrage upon her, as a *woman*.
Her men servants were sometimes flogged there; and so exceedingly
offensive has been the putrid flesh of their lacerated backs, for days
after the infliction, that they would be kept out of the house—the
smell arising from their wounds being too horrible to be endured.
They were always stiff and sore for some days, and not in a condition
to be seen by visitors.

This professedly Christian woman was a most awful illustration of the ruinous influence of arbitrary power upon the temper—her bursts of passion upon the heads of her victims were dreaded even by her own children, and very often, all the pleasure of social intercourse around the domestic board, was destroyed by her ordering the cook into her presence, and storming at him, when the dinner or breakfast was not prepared to her taste, and in the presence of all her children, commanding the waiter to slap his face. *Fault-finding,* was with her the constant accompaniment of every meal, and banished that peace which should hover around the social board, and smile on every face. It was common for her to order brothers to whip their own sisters, and sisters their own brothers, and yet no woman visited among the poor more than she did, or gave more liberally to relieve their wants. This may seem perfectly unaccountable to a northerner, but these seeming contradictions vanish when we consider that over *them* she possessed no arbitrary power, they were always presented to her mind as unfortunate sufferers, towards whom her sympathies most freely flowed; she was ever ready to wipe the tears from *their* eyes, and open wide her purse for *their* relief, but the others were her *vassals,* thrust down by public opinion beneath her feet, to be at her beck and call, ever ready to serve in all humility, her, whom God in his providence had set over them—it was their *duty* to abide in abject submission, and hers to *compel* them to do so—*it was thus that she reasoned.* Except at family prayers, none were permitted to *sit* in her presence, but the seamstresses and waiting maids, and they, however delicate might be their circumstances, were forced to sit upon low stools, without backs, that they might be constantly reminded of their inferiority. A slave who waited in the house, was guilty on a particular occasion of going to visit his wife, and kept dinner waiting a little, (his wife was the slave of a lady who lived at a little distance.) When the family sat down to the table, the mistress began to scold the waiter for the offence—he attempted to excuse himself—she ordered him to hold his tongue—he ventured another apology; her son then rose from the table in a rage, and beat the face and ears of the waiter so dreadfully that the blood gushed from his mouth, and nose, and ears. This mistress was *a professor of religion;* her daughter who related the circumstance, was a *fellow member* of the Presbyterian church *with the poor outraged slave*—instead of feeling indignation at this outrageous abuse of her brother in the church, she justified the deed, and said "he got just what he deserved." I solemnly believe this to be a true picture of *slaveholding religion.*

The following is another illustration of it:

A mistress in Charleston sent a grey headed female slave to the workhouse, and had her severely flogged. The poor old woman went to an acquaintance of mine and begged her to buy her, and told her how cruelly she had been whipped. My friend examined her *lacerated back,* and out of compassion did purchase her. The circumstance was mentioned to one of the former owner's relatives, who asked her if it were true. The mistress told her it was, and said that she had made the severe whipping of this aged woman a *subject of prayer,* and that she believed she had done right to have it inflicted upon her. The last 'owner' of the poor old slave, said she, had no fault to find with her as a servant.

I remember very well that when I was a child, our next door neighbor whipped a young woman so brutally, that in order to escape his blows she rushed through the drawing-room window in the second story, and fell upon the street pavement below and broke her hip. This circumstance produced no excitement or inquiry.

The following circumstance occurred in Charleston, in 1828:

A slaveholder, after flogging a little girl about thirteen years old, set her on a table with her feet fastened in a pair of stocks. He then locked the door and took out the key. When the door was opened she was found dead, having fallen from the table. When I asked a prominent lawyer, who belonged to one of the first families in the State, whether the murderer of this helpless child could not be indicted, he coolly replied, that the slave was Mr. ———'s property, and if he chose to suffer the *loss,* no one else had any thing to do with it. The loss of *human life,* the distress of the parents and other relatives of the little girl, seemed utterly out of his thoughts: it was the loss of *property* only that presented itself to his mind.

I knew a gentleman of great benevolence and generosity of character, so essentially to injure the eye of a little boy, about ten years old, as to destroy its sight, by the blow of a cowhide, inflicted whilst he was whipping him.* I have heard the same individual speak of "breaking down the spirit of a slave under the lash" as perfectly right.

---

* The Jewish law would have set this servant free, for his eye's sake, but he was held in slavery and sold from hand to hand, although, besides this title to his liberty according to Jewish law, he was a *mulatto,* and therefore free under the Constitution of the United States, in whose preamble our fathers declare that they established it expressly to "secure the blessings of *liberty* to themselves and *their posterity*."—ED.

I also know that an aged slave of his, (by marriage), was allowed to get a scanty and precarious subsistence, by begging in the streets of Charleston—he was too old to work, and therefore *his allowance was stopped,* and he was turned out to make his living by begging.

When I was about thirteen years old, I attended a seminary, in Charleston, which was superintended by a man and his wife of superior education. They had under their instruction the daughters of nearly all the aristocracy. Their cruelty to their slaves, both male and female, I can never forget. I remember one day there was called into the school room to open a window, a boy whose head had been shaved in order to disgrace him, and he had been so dreadfully whipped that he could hardly walk. So horrible was the impression produced upon my mind by his heart-broken countenance and crippled person that I fainted away. The sad and ghastly countenance of one of their female mulatto slaves who used to sit on a low stool at her sewing in the piazza, is now fresh before me. She often told me, secretly, how cruelly she was whipped when they sent her to the work-house. I had known so much of the terrible scourgings inflicted in that house of blood, that when I was once obliged to pass it, the very sight smote me with such horror that my limbs could hardly sustain me. I felt as if I was passing the precincts of hell. A friend of mine who lived in the neighborhood, told me she often heard the screams of the slaves under their torture.

I once heard a physician of a high family, and of great respectability in his profession, say, that when he sent his slaves to the work-house to be flogged, he always went to *see* it done, that he might be sure they were properly, i. e. *severely* whipped. He also related the following circumstance in my presence. He had sent a youth of about eighteen to this horrible place to be whipped and *afterwards* to be worked upon the treadmill. From not keeping the step, which probably he COULD NOT do, in consequence of the lacerated state of his body; his arm got terribly torn, from the shoulder to the wrist. This physcian said, he went every day to attend to it himself, in order that he might use those restoratives, which *would inflict the greatest possible pain*. This poor boy, after being imprisoned there for some weeks, was then brought home, and compelled to wear iron clogs on his ankles for one or two months. I saw him with those irons on one day when I was at the house. This man was, when young, remarkable in the fashionable world for his elegant and fascinating manners, but the exercise of the slaveholder's power has thrown the fierce air of tyranny even over these.

I heard another man of equally high standing say, that he believed he suffered far more than his waiter did, whenever he flogged him, for he felt the *exertion* for days afterward, but he could not let his servant go on in the neglect of his business, it was *his duty* to chastise him. "His duty" to flog this boy of seventeen so severely that he felt *the exertion* for days after! and yet he never felt it to be his duty to instruct him, or have him instructed, even in the common principles of morality. I heard the mother of this man say, it would be no surprise to her, if he killed a slave some day, for, that, when transported with passion he did not seem to care what he did. He once broke a *large* stick over the back of a slave, and at another time the ivory butt-end of a long coach whip over the *head* of another. This last was attacked with epileptic fits some months after, and has ever since been subject to them, and occasionally to violent fits of insanity.

Southern mistresses sometimes flog their slaves themselves, though generally one slave is compelled to flog another. Whilst staying at a friend's house some years ago, I one day saw the mistress with a cow-hide in her hand, and heard her scolding in an under tone, her waiting man, who was about twenty-five years old. Whether she actually inflicted the blows I do not know, for I hastened out of sight and hearing. It was not the first time I had seen a mistress thus engaged. I knew she was a cruel mistress, and had heard her daughters disputing, whether their mother did right or wrong, to send the slave *children,* (whom she sent out to sweep chimneys) to the work-house to be whipped if they did not bring in their wages regularly. This woman moved in the most fashionable circle in Charleston. The income of this family was derived mostly from the hire of their slaves, about one hundred in number. Their luxuries were blood-bought luxuries indeed. And yet what stranger would ever have inferred their cruelties from the courteous reception and bland manners of the parlor. Every thing cruel and revolting is carefully concealed from strangers, especially those from the north. Take an instance. I have known the master and mistress of a family to send to their friends to *borrow* servants to wait on company, because their own slaves had been so cruelly flogged in the work-house, that they could not walk without limping at every step, and their putrified flesh emitted such an intolerable smell that they were not fit to be in the presence of company. How can northerners know these things when they are hospitably received at southern tables and firesides? I repeat it, no one who has not been an *integral part* of a slaveholding community, can have any idea of its abominations. It is a whited sepulchre full of dead men's bones and all uncleanness. Blessed be God, the Angel of *Truth* has descended and rolled away the stone from the mouth of the sepulchre, and *sits* upon it. The abominations so long hidden are now brought forth before all Israel and the sun. Yes, the Angel of Truth *sits upon this stone,* and it can never be rolled back again.

The utter disregard of the comfort of the slaves, in *little* things, can scarcely be conceived by those who have not been a *component part* of slaveholding communities. Take a few particulars out of hundreds that might be named. In South Carolina musketoes swarm in myriads, more than half the year—they are so excessively annoying at night, that no family thinks of sleeping without nets or "musketoe-bars" hung over their bedsteads, yet slaves are never provided with them, unless it be the favorite old domestics who get the cast-off pavilions; and yet these very masters and mistresses will be so kind to their *horses* as to provide them with *fly nets.* Bedsteads and bedding too, are rarely provided for any of the slaves—if the waiters and coachmen, waiting maids, cooks, washers, &c., have beds at all, they must generally get them for themselves. Commonly they lie down at night on the bare floor, with a small blanket wrapped round them in winter, and in summer a coarse osnaburg sheet, or nothing. Old slaves generally have beds, but it is because when younger *they have provided them for themselves*.

Only two meals a day are allowed the house slaves—the *first at twelve* o'clock. If they eat before this time, it is by stealth, and I am sure there must be a good deal of suffering among them from *hunger,* and particularly by children. Besides this, they are often kept from their meals by way of punishment. No table is provided for them to eat from. They know nothing of the comfort and pleasure of gathering round the social board—each takes his plate or tin pan and iron spoon and holds it in the hand or on the lap. I *never* saw slaves seated round a *table* to partake of any meal.

As the general rule, no lights of any kind, no firewood—no towels, basins, or soap, no tables, chairs, or other furniture, are provided. Wood for cooking and washing *for the family* is found, but when the master's work is done, the slave must find wood for himself if he has a fire. I have repeatedly known slave children kept the whole winter's evening, sitting on the stair-case in a cold entry, just to be at hand to snuff candles or hand a tumbler of water from the side-board, or go on errands from one room to another. It may be asked why they were not permitted to stay in the parlor, when they would be still more at hand. I answer, because waiters are not allowed to *sit* in the presence of their owners, and as children who were kept running all day, would of course get very tired of standing for two or three hours, they were allowed to go into the entry and sit on the staircase until rung for. Another reason is, that even slaveholders at times find the presence of slaves very annoying; they cannot exercise entire freedom of speech before them on all subjects.

I have also known instances where seamstresses were kept in cold entries to work by the stair case lamps for one or two hours, every evening in winter—they could not see without standing up all the time, though the work was often too large and heavy for them to sew upon it in that position without great inconvenience, and yet they were expected to do their work as *well* with their cold fingers, and standing up, as if they had been sitting by a comfortable fire and provided with the necessary light. House slaves suffer a great deal also from not being allowed to leave the house without permission. If they wish to go even for a draught of water, they must *ask leave,* and if they stay longer than the mistress thinks necessary, they are liable to be punished, and often are scolded or slapped, or kept from going down to the next meal.

It frequently happens that relatives, among slaves, are separated for weeks or months, by the husband or brother being taken by the master on a journey, to attend on his horses and himself.—When they return, the white husband seeks the wife of his love; but the black husband must wait to see *his* wife, until mistress pleases to let her chambermaid leave her room. Yes, such is the despotism of slavery, that wives and sisters dare not run to meet their husbands and brothers after such separations, and hours sometimes elapse before they are allowed to meet; and, at times, a fiendish pleasure is taken in keeping them asunder—this furnishes an opportunity to vent feelings of spite for any little neglect of "duty."

The sufferings to which slaves are subjected by separations of various kinds, cannot be imagined by those unacquainted with the working out of the system behind the curtain. Take the following instances.

Chambermaids and seamstresses often sleep in their mistresses' apartments, but with no bedding at all. I know an instance of a woman who has been married eleven years, and yet has never been allowed to sleep out of her mistress's chamber.—This is a *great* hardship to slaves. When we consider that house slaves are rarely allowed social intercourse during *the day,* as their work generally *separates* them; the barbarity of such an arrangement is obvious. It is peculiarly a hardship in the above case, as the husband of the woman does not "belong" to her "owner"; and because he is subject to dreadful attacks of illness, and can have but little attention from his wife in the *day*. And yet her mistress, who is an old lady, gives her the highest character as a faithful servant, and told a friend of mine, that she was "entirely dependent upon her for *all* her comforts; she dressed and undressed her, gave her all her food, and was so *necessary* to her that she could not do without her." I may add, that this couple are tenderly attached to each other.

I also know an instance in which the husband was a slave and the wife was free: during the illness of the former, the latter was *allowed* to come and nurse him; she was obliged to leave the work by which she had made a living, and come to stay with her husband, and thus lost weeks of her time, or he would have suffered for want of proper attention; and yet his "owner" made her no compensation for her services. He had long been a faithful and a favorite slave, and his owner was a woman very benevolent to the poor whites.—She went a great deal among these, as a visiting commissioner of the Ladies' Benevolent Society, and was in the constant habit of *paying* the *relatives of the poor whites* for nursing *their* husbands, fathers, and other relations; because she thought it very hard, when their time was taken up, so that they could not earn their daily bread, that they should be left to suffer. Now, such is the stupifying influence of the "*chattel* principle" on the minds of slaveholders, that I do not suppose it ever occurred to her that this poor *colored* wife ought to be paid for her services, and particularly as she was spending her time and strength in taking care of *her "property."* She no doubt only thought how kind she was, to *allow* her to come and stay so long in her yard; for, let it be kept in mind, that slaveholders have unlimited power to separate husbands and wives, parents and children, however and whenever they please; and if this mistress had chosen to do it, she could have debarred this woman from all intercourse with her husband, by forbidding her to enter her premises.

Persons who own plantations and yet live in cities, often take children from their parents as soon as they are weaned, and send them into the country; because they do not want the time of the mother taken up by attendance upon her own children, it being too valuable to the mistress. As a *favor,* she is, in some cases, permitted to go to see them once a year. So, on the other hand, if field slaves happen to have children of an age suitable to the convenience of the master, they are taken from their parents and brought to the city.

Parents are almost never consulted as to the disposition to be made of their children; they have as little control over them, as have domestic animals over the disposal of their young. Every natural and social feeling and affection are violated with indifference; slaves are treated as though they did not possess them.

Another way in which the feelings of slaves are trifled with and often deeply wounded, is by changing their names; if, at the time they are brought into a family, there is another slave of the same name; or if the owner happens, for some other reason, not to like the name of the new comer. I have known slaves very much grieved at having the names of their children thus changed, when they had been called after a dear relation. Indeed it would be utterly impossible to recount the multitude of ways in which the *heart* of the slave is continually lacerated by the total disregard of his feelings as a social being and a human creature.

The slave suffers also greatly from being continually *watched*. The system of espionage which is constantly kept up over slaves is the most worrying and intolerable that can be imagined. Many mistresses are, in fact, during the absence of their husbands, really their drivers; and the pleasure of returning to their families often, on the part of the husband, is entirely destroyed by the complaints preferred against the slaves when he comes home to his meals.

A mistress of my acquaintance asked her servant boy, one day, what was the reason she could not get him to do his work whilst his master was away, and said to him, "Your master works a great deal harder than you do; he is at his office all day, and often has to study his law cases at night." "Master," said the boy, "is working for himself, and for you, ma'am, but I am working for *him*." The mistress turned and remarked to a friend, that she was so struck with the truth of the remark, that she could not say a word to him.

But I forbear—the sufferings of the slaves are not only innumerable, but they are *indescribable*. I may paint the agony of kindred torn from each other's arms, to meet no more in time; I may depict the inflictions of the blood-stained lash, but I *cannot describe* the daily, hourly, ceaseless torture, endured by the heart that is constantly trampled under the foot of despotic power. This is a part of the horrors of slavery which, I believe, no one has ever attempted to delineate; I wonder not at it, it mocks all power of language. Who can describe the anguish of that mind which feels itself impaled upon the iron of arbitrary power— its living, writhing, helpless victim! every human susceptibility tortured, its sympathies torn, and stung, and bleeding—always feeling the death-weapon in its heart, and yet not so deep as to *kill* that humanity which is made the curse of its existence.

In the course of my testimony I have entered somewhat into the *minutiæ* of slavery, because this is a part of the subject often overlooked, and cannot be appreciated by any but those who have been witnesses, and entered into sympathy with the slaves as human beings. Slaveholders think nothing of them, because they regard their slaves as *property,* the mere instruments of their convenience and pleasure. *One who is a slaveholder at heart never recognises a human being in a slave.*

As thou hast asked me to testify respecting the *physical condition* of the slaves merely, I say nothing of the awful neglect of their *minds* and *souls* and the systematic effort to imbrute them. A wrong and an impiety, in comparison with which all the other unutterable wrongs of slavery are but as the dust of the balance.

ANGELINA G. WELD.

GENERAL TESTIMONY

TO THE CRUELTIES INFLICTED UPON SLAVES

Before presenting to the reader particular details of the cruelties inflicted upon American slaves, we will present in brief the well-weighed declarations of slaveholders and other residents of slave states, testifying that the slaves are treated with barbarous inhumanity. All *details* and particulars will be drawn out under their appropriate heads. We propose in this place to present testimony of a *general character*— the solemn declarations of slaveholders and others, that the slaves are treated with great cruelty.

To discredit the testimony of witnesses who insist upon convicting themselves, would be an anomalous scepticism.

To show that American slavery has *always* had one uniform character of diabolical cruelty, we will go back one hundred years, and prove it by unimpeachable witnesses, who have given their deliberate testimony to its horrid barbarity, from 1739 to 1839.

TESTIMONY OF REV. GEORGE WHITEFIELD

In a letter written by him in Georgia, and addressed to the slaveholders of Maryland, Virginia, North and South Carolina and Georgia, in 1739.—See Benezet's "Caution to Great Britain and her Colonies."

"As I lately passed through your provinces on my way hither, I was sensibly touched with a fellow-feeling of the miseries of the poor negroes.

"Sure I am, it is sinful to use them as bad, nay worse than if they were brutes; and whatever particular *exceptions* there may be, (as I would charitably hope there are *some*), I fear the *generality* of you that own negroes, *are liable to such a charge.* Not to mention what numbers have been given up to the inhuman usage of cruel *taskmasters,* who by their unrelenting scourges, have ploughed their backs and made long furrows, and at length brought them to the grave! ★ ★ ★

"*The blood of them, spilt for these many years, in your respective provinces, will ascend up to heaven against you!*"

The following is the testimony of the celebrated JOHN WOOLMAN, an eminent minister of the Society of Friends, who traveled extensively in the slave states. We copy it from a "Memoir of JOHN WOOLMAN, chiefly extracted from a Journal of his Life and Travels." It was published in Philadelphia, by the "Society of Friends."

The following reflections, were written in 1757, while he was traveling on a religious account among slaveholders.

"Many of the white people in these provinces, take little or no care of negro marriages; and when negroes marry, after their own way, some make so little account of those marriages, that, with views of outward interest, they often part men from their wives, by selling them far asunder; which is common when estates are sold by executors at vendue.

"Many whose labor is heavy, being followed at their business in the field by a man with a whip, hired for that purpose,—have, in common, little else allowed them but *one peck* of Indian corn and some salt for one week, with a few potatoes. (The potatoes they commonly raise by their labor on the first day of the week.) The correction ensuing on their disobedience to overseers, or slothfulness in business, is often *very severe,* and sometimes *desperate.* Men and women have many times *scarce clothes enough to hide their nakedness*—and boys and girls, ten and twelve years old, are often *quite naked* among their masters' children. Some use endeavors to instruct those (negro children) they have in reading; but in common, this is not only neglected, but disapproved."

TESTIMONY OF THE 'MARYLAND JOURNAL AND BALTIMORE ADVERTISER,' OF MAY 30, 1788

"In the ordinary course of the business of the country, the punishment of relations frequently happens on the same farm, and in view of each other: the father often sees his beloved son—the son his venerable sire—the mother her much loved daughter—the daughter her affectionate parent—the husband sees the wife of his bosom, and she the husband of her affection, *cruelly bound up* without delicacy or mercy, and without daring to interpose in each other's behalf, and punished with all the *extremity of incensed rage, and all the rigor of unrelenting severity*. Let us reverse the case, and suppose it ours: ALL IS SILENT HORROR!"

TESTIMONY OF THE HON. WILLIAM PINCKNEY, OF MARYLAND

In a speech before the Maryland House of Delegates, in 1789, Mr. P. calls slavery in that state, "a speaking picture of *abominable oppression*"; and adds: "It will not do thus to . . . . . act like *unrelenting tyrants,* perpetually sermonizing it with liberty as our text, and actual *oppression* for our commentary. Is she [Maryland] not . . . . the foster mother of petty *despots,*—the patron of *wanton oppression*?"

Extract from a speech of Mr. RICE, in the Convention for form ing the Constitution of Kentucky, in 1790:

"The master may, and *often does, inflict upon him all the seve punishment the human body is capable of bearing.*"

President Edwards, the Younger, in a sermon before t necticut Abolition Society, 1791, says:

"From these drivers, for every imagined, as well as rea want of exertion, they receive the lash—the smack of day long in the ears of those who are on the plantati vicinity; and it is used with such dexterity and severity to lacerate the skin, but to tear out small portions of the f every stroke.

"This is the general treatment of the slaves. But many individuals suffer still more severely. *Many, many are knocked down; some have their eyes beaten out: some have an arm or a leg broken, or chopped off;* and many, for a very small, or for no crime at all, have been beaten to death, merely to gratify the fury of an enraged master or overseer."

Extract from an oration, delivered at Baltimore, July 4, 1791, by GEORGE BUCHANAN, M. D., member of the American Philosophical Society.

"Their situation (the slaves') is *insupportable*; misery inhabits their cabins, and pursues them in the field. Inhumanly beaten, they *often* fall sacrifices to the turbulent tempers of their masters! Who is there, unless inured to savage cruelties, that can hear of the inhuman punishments *daily inflicted* upon the unfortunate blacks, without feeling for them? Can a man who calls himself a Christian, coolly and deliberately tie up, *thumbscrew, torture with pincers,* and beat unmercifully a poor slave, for perhaps a trifling neglect of duty?"

TESTIMONY OF HON. JOHN RANDOLPH, OF ROANOKE—
A SLAVEHOLDER

In one of his Congressional speeches, Mr. R. says: "Avarice alone can drive, as it does drive, this *infernal* traffic, and the wretched victims of it, like so many post-horses *whipped to death* in a mail coach. Ambition has its cover-sluts in the pride, pomp, and circumstance of glorious war; but where are the trophies of avarice? *The handcuff, the manacle, the blood-stained cowhide!*"

MAJOR STODDARD, of the United States' army, who took possession of Louisiana in behalf of the United States, under the cession of 1804, in his *Sketches of Louisiana,* page 332, says:

"The feelings of humanity are outraged—the most odious tyranny exercised in a land of freedom, and hunger and nakedness prevail amidst plenty. ★ ★ ★ Cruel, and even unusual punishments are daily inflicted on these wretched creatures, enfeebled with hunger, labor and the lash. The scenes of misery and distress constantly witnessed along the coast of the Delta, [of the Mississippi], the wounds and ulcerations occasioned by demoralized masters and overseers, torture the feelings of the passing stranger, and wring blood from the heart."

Though only the third of the following series of resolutions is strictly relevant to the subject now under consideration, we insert the other resolutions, both because they are explanatory of the third, and also serve to reveal the public sentiment of Indiana, at the date of the resolutions. As a large majority of the citizens of Indiana at that time, were *natives of slave states,* they well knew the actual condition of the slaves.

1. "RESOLVED UNANIMOUSLY, by the Legislative Council and House of Representatives of Indiana Territory, that a suspension of the sixth article of compact between the United States and the territories and states north west of the river Ohio, passed the 13th day of January, 1783, for the term of ten years, would be highly advantageous to the territory, and meet the approbation of at least nine-tenths of the good citizens of the same.

2. "RESOLVED UNANIMOUSLY, that the abstract question of liberty and slavery, is not considered as involved in a suspension of the said article, inasmuch as the number of slaves in the United States would not be augmented by the measure.

3. "RESOLVED UNANIMOUSLY, that the suspension of the said article would be equally advantageous to the territory, to the states from whence the negroes would be brought, and *to the negroes themselves.* The states which are overburthened with negroes, would be benefited by disposing of the negroes which they cannot comfortably support; * * * and THE NEGRO HIMSELF WOULD EXCHANGE A SCANTY PITTANCE OF THE COARSEST FOOD, for a plentiful and nourishing diet; and a situation which admits not the most distant prospect of emancipation, for one which presents no considerable obstacle to his wishes.

4. "RESOLVED UNANIMOUSLY, that a copy of these resolutions be delivered to the delegate to Congress from this territory, and that he be, and he hereby is, instructed to use his best endeavors to obtain a suspension of the said article.

J. B. THOMAS,
Speaker of the House of Representatives.
PIERRE MINARD,
President pro tem. of the Legislative Council. Vincennes, Dec. 20, 1806.
"Forwarded to the Speaker of the United States' Senate, by WILLIAM HENRY HARRISON, Governor."—*American State Papers,* vol 1. p. 467.

MONSIEUR C. C. ROBIN, who resided in Louisiana from 1802 to 1806, and published a volume containing the results of his observations there, thus speaks of the condition of the slaves:

"While they are at labor, the manager, the master, or the driver has commonly the whip in hand to strike the idle. But those of the negroes who are judged guilty of serious faults, are punished twenty, twenty-five, forty, fifty, or one hundred lashes. The manner of this cruel execution is as follows: four stakes are driven down, making a long square; the culprit is extended naked between these stakes, face downwards; his hands and his feet are bound separately, with strong cords, to each of the stakes, so far apart that his arms and legs, stretched in the form of St. Andrew's cross, give the the poor wretch no chance of stirring. Then the executioner, who is ordinarily a negro, armed with the long whip of a coachman, strikes upon the reins and thighs. The crack of his whip resounds afar, like that of an angry cartman beating his horses. The blood flows, the long wounds cross each other, strips of skin are raised without softening either the hand of the executioner or the heart of the master, who cries 'sting him harder.'

"The reader is moved; so am I: my agitated hand refuses to trace the bloody picture, to recount how many times the piercing cry of pain has interrupted my silent occupations; how many times I have shuddered at the faces of those barbarous masters, where I saw inscribed the number of victims sacrificed to their ferocity.

"The women are subjected to these punishments as rigorously as the men—not even pregnancy exempts them; in that case, before binding them to the stakes, a hole is made in the ground to accommodate the enlarged form of the victim.

"It is remarkable that the white creole women are ordinarily more inexorable than the men. Their slow and languid gait, and the trifling services which they impose, betoken only apathetic indolence; but should the slave not promptly obey, should he even fail to divine the meaning of their gestures, or looks, in an instant they are armed with a formidable whip; it is no longer the arm which cannot sustain the weight of a shawl or a reticule—it is no longer the form which but feebly sustains itself. They themselves order the punishment of one of these poor creatures, and with a dry eye see their victim bound to four stakes; they count the blows, and raise a voice of menace, if the arm that strikes relaxes, or if the blood does not flow in sufficient abundance. Their sensibility changed to fury must needs feed itself for a while on the hideous spectacle; they must, as if to revive themselves, hear the piercing shrieks, and see the flow of fresh blood; there are some of them who, in their frantic rage, pinch and bite their victims.

"It is by no means wonderful that the laws designed to protect the slave, should be little respected by the generality of such masters. I have seen some masters pay those unfortunate people the miserable overcoat which is their due; but others give them nothing at all, and do not even leave them the hours and Sundays granted to them by law. I have seen some of those barbarous masters leave them, during the winter, in a state of revolting nudity, even contrary to their own true interests, for they thus weaken and shorten the lives upon which repose the whole of their own fortunes. I have seen some of those negroes obliged to conceal their nakedness with the long moss of the country. The sad melancholy of these wretches, depicted upon their countenances, the flight of some, and the death of others, do not reclaim their masters; they wreak upon those who remain, the vengeance which they can no longer exercise upon the others."

WHITMAN MEAD, Esq., of New York, in his journal, published nearly a quarter of a century ago, under date of
"SAVANNAH, January 28, 1817.
"To one not accustomed to such scenes as slavery presents, the condition of the slaves is *impressively shocking*. In the course of my walks, I was every where witness to their wretchedness. Like the brute creatures of the north, they are driven about at the pleasure of all who meet them: *half naked and half starved,* they drag out a pitiful existence, apparently almost unconscious of what they suffer. A threat accompanies every command, and a bastinado is the usual reward of disobedience."

TESTIMONY OF REV. JOHN RANKIN

A native of Tennessee, educated there, and for a number of years a preacher in slave states—now pastor of a church in Ripley, Ohio.
"Many poor slaves are stripped naked, stretched and tied across barrels, or large bags, *and tortured with the lash during hours, and even whole days, until their flesh is mangled to the very bones.* Others are stripped and hung up by the arms, their feet are tied together and the end of a heavy piece of timber is put between their legs in order to stretch their bodies, and so prepare them for the torturing lash—and in this situation they are often whipped until their bodies are covered *with blood and mangled flesh*—and in order to add the greatest keenness to their sufferings, their wounds are washed with *liquid salt*! And some of the miserable creatures are permitted to hang in that position until they actually *expire*; some die under the lash, others linger about for a time, and at length die of their wounds, and many survive, and endure again similar torture. These bloody scenes are *constantly exhibiting in every slaveholding country—thousands of whips are every day*

stained in African blood! Even the poor *females* are not permitted to escape these shocking cruelties."—*Rankin's Letters, pages* 57, 58.

These letters were published fifteen years ago.—They were addressed to a brother in Virginia, who was a slaveholder.

TESTIMONY OF THE AMERICAN COLONIZATION SOCIETY

"We have heard of slavery as it exists in Asia, and Africa, and Turkey—we have heard of the feudal slavery under which the peasantry of Europe have groaned from the days of Alaric until now, but excepting only the horrible system of the West India Islands, we have never heard of slavery in any country, ancient or modern, Pagan, Mohammedan, or *Christian! so terrible in its character*, as the slavery which exists in these United States."—*Seventh Report American Colonization Society*, 1824.

TESTIMONY OF THE GRADUAL EMANCIPATION SOCIETY OF NORTH CAROLINA

Signed by Moses Swain, President, and William Swain, Secretary

"In the eastern part of the state, the slaves considerably outnumber the free population. Their situation is there wretched beyond description. Impoverished by the mismanagement which we have already attempted to describe, the master, unable to support his own grandeur and maintain his slaves, puts the unfortunate wretches upon short allowances, scarcely sufficient for their sustenance, so that a great part of them go half naked and half starved much of the time. Generally, throughout the state, the African is an *abused, a monstrously outraged creature.*"—See Minutes of the American Convention, convened in Baltimore, Oct. 25, 1826.

FROM NILES' BALTIMORE REGISTER FOR 1829, VOL. 35, P. 4

"Dealing in slaves has become a *large business*. Establishments are made at several places in Maryland and Virginia, at which they are sold like cattle. These places of deposit are strongly built, and well supplied with *iron thumb-screws and gags,* and ornamented with *cowskins and other whips—often times bloody.*"

JUDGE RUFFIN, of the Supreme Court of North Carolina, in one of his judicial decisions, says—

"The slave, to remain a slave, must feel that there is NO APPEAL FROM HIS MASTER. No man can anticipate the provocations which the slave would give, nor the consequent wrath of the master, prompting him to BLOODY VENGEANCE on the turbulent traitor, a vengeance *generally* practiced with impunity, by reason of its PRIVACY."—See *Wheeler's Law of Slavery*, p. 247.

MR. MOORE, OF VIRGINIA, in his speech before the Legislature of that state, Jan. 15, 1832, says:

"It must be confessed, that although the treatment of our slaves is in the general, as mild and humane as it can be, that it must always happen, that there will be found hundreds of individuals, who, owing either to the natural ferocity of their dispositions, or to the effects of intemperance, will be guilty of cruelty and barbarity towards their slaves, which is *almost intolerable,* and at which humanity revolts."

TESTIMONY OF B. SWAIN, ESQ., OF NORTH CAROLINA

"Let any man of spirit and feeling, for a moment cast his thoughts over this land of slavery—think of the *nakedness* of some, the *hungry yearnings* of others, the *flowing tears and heaving sighs* of parting relations, the *wailings and wo, the bloody cut of the keen lash, and the frightful scream that rends the very skies*—and all this to gratify ambition, lust, pride, avarice, vanity, and other depraved feelings of the human heart. . . . *THE WORST IS NOT GENERALLY KNOWN*. Were all the miseries, the horrors of slavery, to burst at once into view, a peal of seven-fold thunder could scarce strike greater alarm."—See *"Swain's Address,"* 1830.

TESTIMONY OF DR. JAMES C. FINLEY

Son of Dr. Finley, one of the founders of the Colonization Society, and brother of R. S. Finley, agent of the American Colonization Society

Dr. J. C. Finley was formerly one of the editors of the Western Medical Journal, at Cincinnati, and is well known in the west as utterly hostile to immediate abolition.

"In almost the last conversation I had with you before I left Cincinnati, I promised to give you some account of some scenes of atrocious cruelty towards slaves, which I witnessed while I lived at the south. I almost regret having made the promise, for not only are they *so atrocious* that you will with difficulty believe them, but I also fear that they will have the effect of driving you into that *abolitionism*, upon the borders of which you have been so long hesitating. The people of the north *are ignorant of the horrors of slavery*—of the *atrocities* which it commits upon the unprotected slave. ★ ★ ★

"I do not know that any thing could be gained by particularizing the scenes of *horrible barbarity,* which fell under my observation during my *short* residence in one of the wealthiest, most intelligent, and most moral parts of Georgia. Their *number* and *atrocity* are such, that I am confident they would gain credit with none but *abolitionists*. Every thing will be conveyed in the remark, that in a state of society calculated to foster the worst passions of our nature, the slave derives *no protection* either from *law* or *public opinion,* and that ALL the cruelties which the Russians are reported to have acted towards the Poles, after their late subjugation, ARE SCENES OF EVERY-DAY OCCURRENCE in the southern states. This statement, incredible as it may seem, falls short, very far short of the truth."

The foregoing is extracted from a letter written by Dr. Finley to Rev. Asa Mahan, his former pastor, then of Cincinnati, now President of Oberlin Seminary.

TESTIMONY OF REV. WILLIAM T. ALLAN, OF ILLINOIS

Son of a Slaveholder, Rev. Dr. Allan of Huntsville, Ala.

"At our house it is so common to hear their (the slaves') screams, that we think nothing of it: and lest any one should think that in *general* the slaves are well treated, let me be distinctly understood:— *cruelty* is the *rule,* and *kindness* the *exception.*"

Extract of a letter dated July 2d, 1834, from Mr. NATHAN COLE, of St. Louis, Missouri, to Arthur Tappan, Esq., of this city:

"I am not an advocate of the immediate and unconditional emancipation of the slaves of our country, yet *no man has ever yet depicted the wretchedness of the situation of the slaves in colors too dark for the truth.* . . . I know that many good people *are not aware of the treatment to which slaves are usually subjected,* nor have they any just idea of the extent of the evil."

TESTIMONY OF REV. JAMES A. THOME

A native of Kentucky—Son of Arthur Thome, Esq., till recently a Slaveholder

"Slavery is the parent of more suffering than has flowed from any one source since the date of its existence. Such sufferings too! *Sufferings inconceivable and innumerable—unmingled wretchedness* from the ties of nature rudely broken and destroyed, the *acutest bodily tortures, groans, tears and blood*—lying for ever in weariness and painfulness, in watchings, in hunger and in thirst, in cold and nakedness.

"Brethren of the North, be not deceived. *These sufferings still exist,* and despite the efforts of their cruel authors to hush them down, and confine them within the precincts of their own plantations, they will ever and anon, struggle up and reach the ear of humanity."—*Mr. Thome's Speech at New York, May,* 1834.

TESTIMONY OF THE MARYVILLE (TENNESSEE) INTELLIGENCER, OF OCT. 4, 1835

The Editor, in speaking of the sufferings of the slaves which are taken by the internal trade to the South West, says:

"Place yourself in imagination, for a moment, in their condition. With *heavy galling chains,* riveted upon your person; *half-naked, half-starved;* your back *lacerated* with the 'knotted Whip;' traveling to a region where your *condition through time will be second only to the wretched creatures in Hell.*

"This depicting is not visionary. Would to God that it was."

TESTIMONY OF THE PRESBYTERIAN SYNOD OF KENTUCKY

A large majority of whom are slaveholders

"This system licenses and produces *great cruelty.*

"Mangling, imprisonment, starvation, every species of torture, may be inflicted upon him, (the slave), and he has no redress.

"There are now in our whole land two millions of human beings, exposed, defenceless, to every insult, and every injury short of maiming or death, which their fellow-men may choose to inflict. *They suffer all* that can be inflicted by wanton caprice, by grasping avarice, by brutal lust, by malignant spite, and by insane anger. Their happiness is the sport of every whim, and the prey of every passion that may, occasionally, or habitually, infest the master's bosom. If we could calculate the amount of woe endured by ill-treated slaves, it would overwhelm every compassionate heart—it would move even the obdurate to sympathy. There is also a vast sum of suffering inflicted upon the slave by humane masters, as a punishment for that idleness and misconduct which slavery naturally produces. ★ ★ ★

"*Brutal stripes* and all the varied kinds of personal indignities, are not the only species of cruelty which slavery licenses." ★ ★

TESTIMONY OF THE REV. N. H. HARDING, Pastor of the Presbyterian Church, in Oxford, North Carolina, a slaveholder.

"I am greatly surprised that you should in any form have been the apologist of a system so full of deadly poison to all holiness and benevolence as slavery, the concocted essence of fraud, selfishness, and cold hearted tyranny, and the fruitful parent of unnumbered evils, both to the oppressor and the oppressed, THE ONE THOUSANDTH PART OF WHICH HAS NEVER BEEN BROUGHT TO LIGHT."

MR. ASA A. STONE, a theological student, who lived near Natchez, (Mi.), in 1834 and 5, sent the following with other testimony, to be published under his own name, in the N. Y. Evangelist, while he was still residing there.

"Floggings for all offences, including deficiencies in work, are *frightfully common,* and *most terribly severe.*

"*Rubbing with salt and red pepper is very common after a severe whipping.*"

TESTIMONY OF REV. PHINEAS SMITH, Centreville, Allegany, Co., N. Y., who lived four years at the south.

"They are badly clothed, badly fed, wretchedly lodged, unmercifully whipped, from month to month, from year to year, from childhood to old age."

REV. JOSEPH M. SADD, Castile, Genessee Co., N. Y., who was till recently a preacher in Missouri, says,

"It is true that barbarous cruelties are inflicted upon them, such as terrible lacerations with the whip, and excruciating tortures are sometimes experienced from the thumb screw."

Extract of a letter from SARAH M. GRIMKÉ, dated 4th Month, 2nd, 1839.

"If the following extracts from letters which I have received from South Carolina, will be of any use thou art at liberty to publish them. I need not say, that the names of the writers are withheld of necessity, because such sentiments if uttered at the south would peril their lives.

EXTRACTS

————. South Carolina, 4th Month, 5th, 1835.

'With regard to slavery I must confess, though we had heard a great deal on the subject, we found on coming South the *half,* the *worst* half too, had not been told us; not that we have ourselves *seen* much oppression, though truly we have felt its deadening influence, but the accounts we have received from every tongue that nobly dares to speak upon the subject, are indeed *deplorable.* To quote the language of a lady, who with true Southern hospitality, received us at her mansion. "The *northern* people don't know anything of slavery at all, they think it is *perpetual bondage merely,* but of the *depth* of *degradation* that that word involves, they have no conception; if they had any just idea of it, they would I am sure use every effort until an end was put to such a shocking system.'

"Another friend writing from South Carolina, and who sustains herself the legal relation of slaveholder, in a letter dated April 4th, 1838, says—'I have some time since, given you my views on the subject of slavery, which so much engrosses your attention. I would most willingly forget what I have seen and heard in my own family, with regard to the slaves. *I shudder when I think of it,* and increasingly feel that slavery is a curse since it leads to such *cruelty.*'"

PUNISHMENTS

I. FLOGGINGS

The slaves are terribly lacerated with whips, paddles, &c.; red pepper and salt are rubbed into their mangled flesh; hot brine and turpentine are poured into their gashes; and innumerable other tortures inflicted upon them.

We will in the first place, prove by a cloud of witnesses, that the slaves are whipped with such inhuman severity, as to lacerate and mangle their flesh in the most shocking manner, leaving permanent scars and ridges; after establishing this, we will present a mass of testimony, concerning a great variety of other tortures. The testimony, for the most part, will be that of the slaveholders themselves, and in their own chosen words. A large portion of it will be taken from the advertisements, which they have published in their own newspapers, describing by the scars on their bodies made by the whip, their own runaway slaves. To copy these advertisements *entire* would require a great amount of space, and flood the reader with a vast mass of matter irrelevant to the *point* before us; we shall therefore insert only so much of each, as will intelligibly set forth the precise point under consideration. In the column under the word "witnesses," will be found the name of the individual, who signs the advertisement, or for whom it is signed, with his or her place of residence, and the name and date of the paper, in which it appeared, and generally the name of the place where it is published. Opposite the name of each witness, will be an extract, from the advertisement, containing his or her testimony.

WITNESSES	TESTIMONY
Mr. D. Judd, jailor, Davidson Co., Tennessee, in the "Nashville Banner," Dec. 10th, 1838.	"Committed to jail as a runaway, a negro woman named Martha, 17 or 18 years of age, has *numerous scars of the whip* on her back."
Mr. Robert Nicoll, Dauphin st. between Emmanuel and Conception st's, Mobile, Alabama, in the "Mobile Commercial Advertiser."	"Ten dollars reward for my woman Siby, *very much scarred about the neck and ears by whipping.*"
Mr. Bryant Johnson, Fort Valley, Houston Co., Georgia, in the "Standard of Union," Milledgeville Ga. Oct. 2, 1838.	"Ranaway, a negro woman, named Maria, *some soars on her back occasioned by the whip.*"
Mr. James T. De Jarnett, Vernon, Autauga Co., Alabama, in the "Pensacola Gazette," July 14, 1838.	"Stolen a negro woman, named Celia. On examining her back you will find *marks caused by the whip.*"

WITNESSES	TESTIMONY
Maurice Y. Garcia, Sheriff of the County of Jefferson, La., in the "New Orleans Bee," August 14, 1838.	"Lodged in jail, a mulatto boy, *having large marks of the whip, on* his shoulders and other parts of his body."
R. J. Bland, Sheriff of Claiborne Co, Miss., in the "Charleston (S.C.) Courier," August 28, 1838.	"Was committed a negro boy, named Tom, is *much marked with the whip.*"
Mr. James Noe, Red River Landing, La., in the "Sentinel," Vicksburg, Miss., August 22, 1837.	"Ranaway, a negro fellow named Dick—has *many scars* on his back from being *whipped.*"
William Craze, jailor, Alexandria, La. in the "Planter's Intelligencer," Sept. 26, 1838.	"Committed to jail, a negro slave—his back is *very badly scarred.*"
John A. Rowland, jailor, Lumberton, North Carolina, in the "Fayetteville (N. C.) Observer," June 20, 1838.	"Committed, a mulatto fellow—his back shows *lasting impressions of the whip*, and leaves no doubt of his being A SLAVE."
J. K. Roberts, sheriff, Blount county, Ala., in the "Huntsville Democrat," Dec. 9, 1838.	"Committed to jail, a negro man—his back *much marked* by the whip."
Mr. H. Varillat, No. 23 Girod street, New Orleans—in the "Commercial Bulletin," August 27, 1838.	"Ranaway, the negro slave named Jupiter—has a *fresh mark* of a cowskin on one of his cheeks."
Mr. Cornelius D. Tolin, Augusta, Ga., in the "Chronicle and Sentinel," Oct. 18, 1838.	"Ranaway, a negro man named Johnson—he has a *great many marks of the whip* on his back."
W. H. Brasseale, sheriff, Blount county, Ala., in the "Huntsville Democrat," June 9, 1838.	"Committed to jail, a negro slave named James—*much scarred* with a whip on his back."

WITNESSES	TESTIMONY
Mr. Robert Beasley, Macon, Ga., in the "Georgia Messenger," July 27, 1837.	"Ranaway, my man Fountain—he is marked *on the back with the whip.*"
Mr. John Wotton, Rockville, Montgomery county, Maryland, in the "Baltimore Republican," Jan. 13, 1838.	"Ranaway, Bill—has *several* LARGE SCARS on his back from a *severe* whipping in *early* life."
D. S. Bennett, sheriff, Natchitoches, La., in the "Herald," July 21, 1838.	"Committed to jail, a negro boy who calls himself Joe—said negro bears *marks of the whip.*"
Messrs. C. C. Whitehead, and R. A. Evans, Marion, Georgia, in the Milledgeville (Ga.) "Standard of Union," June 26, 1838.	"Ranaway, negro fellow John—from being whipped, has *scars on his back, arms, and thighs.*"
Mr. Samuel Stewart, Greensboro', Ala., in the "Southern Advocate," Huntsville, Jan. 6, 1838.	"Ranaway, a boy named Jim—with the marks of the *whip* on the small of the back, reaching round to the flank."
Mr. John Walker, No. 6, Banks' Arcade, New Orleans, in the "Bulletin," August 11, 1838.	"Ranaway, the mulatto boy Quash—*considerably marked* on the back and other places with the lash."
Mr. Jesse Beene, Cahawba, Ala., in the "State Intelligencer," Tuskaloosa, Dec. 25, 1837.	"Ranaway, my negro man Billy—he has the *marks of the* whip."
Mr. John Turner, Thomaston, Upson county, Georgia—in the "Standard of Union," Milledgeville, June 26, 1838.	"Left, my negro man named George—has *marks of the whip very plain* on his thighs."

WITNESSES	TESTIMONY
James Derrah, deputy sheriff, Claiborne county, Mi., in the "Port Gibson Correspondent," April 15, 1837.	"Committed to jail, negro man Toy—he has been *badly whipped*."
S. B. Murphy, sheriff, Wilkinson county, Georgia—in the Milledgeville "Journal," May 15, 1838.	"Brought to jail, a negro man named George—he has a *great many scars from the lash*."
Mr. L. E. Cooner, Branchville Orangeburgh District, South Carolina—in the Macon "Messenger," May 25, 1837.	"One hundred dollars reward, for my negro Glasgow, and Kate, his wife. Glasgow is 24 years old—has *marks of the whip* on his back. Kate is 26—has a *scar* on her cheek, *and several marks of a whip*."
John H. Hand, jailor, parish of West Feliciana, La., in the St. "Francisville Journal," July 6, 1837.	"Committed to jail, a negro boy named John, about 17 years old—his back *badly marked* with the *whip*, his upper lip and chin *severely bruised*."

The preceding are extracts from advertisements published in southern papers, mostly in the year 1838. They are the mere *samples* of hundreds of similar ones published during the same period, with which, as the preceding are quite sufficient to show the *commonness* of inhuman floggings in the slave states, we need not burden the reader.

The foregoing testimony is, as the reader perceives, that of the slaveholders themselves, voluntarily certifying to the outrages which their own hands have committed upon defenceless and innocent men and women, over whom they have assumed authority. We have given to *their* testimony precedence over that of all other witnesses, for the reason that when men testify against *themselves* they are under no temptation to exaggerate.

We will now present the testimony of a large number of individuals, with their names and residences, of persons who witnessed the inflictions to which they testify. Many of them have been slaveholders, and *all* residents for longer or shorter periods in slave states.

Rev. JOHN H. CURTISS, a native of Keep Creek, Norfolk county, Virginia, now a local preacher of the Methodist Episcopal Church in Portage co., Ohio, testifies as follows:—

"In 1829 or 30, one of my father's slaves was accused of taking the key to the office and stealing four or five dollars: he denied it. A constable by the name of Hull was called; he took the negro, very deliberately tied his hands, and whipped him till the blood ran freely down his legs. By this time Hull appeared tired, and stopped; he then took a rope, put a slip noose around his neck, and told the negro he was going to *kill* him, at the same time drew the rope and began whipping: the negro fell; his cheeks looked as though they would burst with strangulation. Hull whipped and kicked him, till I really thought he was going to kill him; when he ceased, the negro was in a complete gore of blood from head to foot."

Mr. DAVID HAWLEY, a class–leader in the Methodist Church, at St. Alban's, Licking county, Ohio, who moved from Kentucky to Ohio in 1831, testifies as follows:—

"In the year 1821 or 2, I saw a slave hung for killing his master. The master had whipped the slave's mother to DEATH, and, locking him in a room, threatened him with the same fate; and, cowhide in hand, had begun the work, when the slave joined battle and slew the master."

SAMUEL ELLISON, a member of the Society of Friends, formerly of Southampton county, Virginia, now of Marlborough, Stark county, Ohio, gives the following testimony:—

"While a resident of Southampton county, Virginia, I knew two men, after having been severely treated, endeavor to make their escape. In this they failed—were taken, tied to trees, and whipped to *death* by their overseer. I lived a mile from the negro quarters, and, at that distance, could frequently hear the screams of the poor creatures when beaten, and could also hear the blows given by the overseer with some heavy instrument."

Major HORACE NYE, of Putnam, Ohio, gives the following testimony of Mr. Wm. Armstrong, of that place, a captain and supercargo of boats descending the Mississippi river:—

"At Bayou Sarah, I saw a slave *staked out,* with his face to the ground, and whipped with a large whip, which laid open the flesh for about two and a half inches *every stroke*. I stayed about five minutes, but could stand it no longer, and left them whipping."

Mr. STEPHEN E. MALTBY, inspector of provisions, Skeneateles, New York, who has resided in Alabama, speaking of the condition of the slaves, says:—

"I have seen them cruelly whipped. I will relate one instance. One Sabbath morning, before I got out of my bed, I heard an outcry, and got up and went to the window, when I saw some six or eight boys, from eight to twelve years of age, near a rack (made for tying horses) on the public square. A man on horseback rode up, got off his horse, took a cord from his pocket, *tied one of the boys* by the *thumbs* to the rack, and with his horsewhip lashed him most severely. He then untied him and rode off without saying a word.

"It was a general practice, while I was at Huntsville, Alabama, to have a patrol every night; and, to my knowledge, this patrol was in the habit of traversing the streets with cow-skins, and, if they found any slaves out after eight o'clock without a pass, to whip them until they were out of reach, or to confine them until morning."

Mr. J. G. BALDWIN, of Middletown, Connecticut, a member of the Methodist Episcopal Church, gives the following testimony:—

"I traveled at the south in 1827: when near Charlotte, N. C. a free colored man fell into the road just ahead of me, and went on peaceably.—When passing a public-house, the landlord ran out with a large cudgel, and applied it to the head and shoulders of the man with such force as to shatter it in pieces. When the reason of his conduct was asked, he replied, that he owned slaves, and he would not permit free blacks to come into his neighborhood.

"Not long after, I stopped at a public-house near Halifax, N. C., between nine and ten o'clock P. M., to stay over night. A slave sat upon a bench in the bar-room asleep. The master came in, seized a large horsewhip, and, without any warning or apparent provocation, laid it over the face and eyes of the slave. The master cursed, swore, and swung his lash—the slave cowered and trembled, but said not a word. Upon inquiry the next morning, I ascertained that the only offence was falling asleep, and this too in consequence of having been up nearly all the previous night, in attendance upon company."

Rev. JOSEPH M. SADD, of Castile, N. Y., who has lately left Missouri, where he was pastor of a church for some years, says:—

"In one case, near where we lived, a runaway slave, when brought back, was most cruelly beaten—bathed in the *usual* liquid—laid in the sun, and a physician employed to heal his wounds:—then the same process of punishment and healing was *repeated,* and *repeated again,* and then the poor creature was sold for the New Orleans market. This account we had from the *physician himself.*"

Mr. ABRAHAM BELL, of Poughkeepsie, New York, a member of the Scotch Presbyterian Church, was employed, in 1837 and 38, in levelling and grading for a rail-road in the state of Georgia: he had under his direction, during the whole time, thirty slaves. Mr. B. gives the following testimony:—

"*All* the slaves had their backs scarred, from the oft-repeated whippings they had received."

Mr. ALONZO BARNARD, of Farmington, Ohio, who was in Mississippi in 1837 and 8, says:—

"The slaves were often severely whipped. I saw one *woman* very severely whipped for accidentally cutting up a stalk of cotton.* When they were whipped they were commonly *held down by four men:* if these could not confine them, they were fastened by stakes driven firmly into the ground, and then lashed often so as to draw blood at each blow. I saw one woman who had lately been delivered of a child in consequence of cruel treatment."

Rev. H. LYMAN, late pastor of the Free Presbyterian Church at Buffalo, N. Y. says:—

"There was a steam cotton press, in the vicinity of my boarding-house at New Orleans, which was driven night and day, without intermission. My curiosity led me to look at the interior of the establishment. There I saw several slaves engaged in rolling cotton bags, fastening ropes, lading carts, &c.

"The presiding genius of the place was a driver, who held a rope four feet long in his hand, which he wielded with cruel dexterity. He used it in single blows, just as the men were lifting to *tighten* the bale cords. It seemed to me that he was desirous to edify me with a specimen of his authority; at any rate the cruelty was horrible."

Mr. JOHN VANCE, a member of the Baptist Church, in St. Albans, Licking county, Ohio, who moved from Culpepper county, Va., his native state, in 1814, testifies as follows:—

---

* Mr. Cornelius Johnson, of Farmington, Ohio, was also a witness to this inhuman outrage upon an unprotected woman, for the unintentional destruction of a stalk of cotton! In his testimony he is more particular, and says, that the number of lashes inflicted upon her by the overseer was "ONE HUNDRED AND FIFTY."

"In 1826, I saw a woman by the name of Mallix, flog her female slave with a horse-whip so horribly that she was washed in salt and water several days, to keep her bruises from mortifying.

"In 1811, I was returning from mill, in Shenandoah county, when I heard the cry of murder, in the field of a man named Painter. I rode to the place to see what was going on. Two men, by the names of John Morgan and Michael Siglar, had heard the cry and came running to the place. I saw Painter beating a negro with a tremendous club, or small handspike, swearing he would kill him; but he was rescued by Morgan and Siglar. I learned that Painter had commenced flogging the slave for not getting to work soon enough. He had escaped, and taken refuge under a pile of rails that were on some timbers up a little from the ground. The master had put fire to one end, and stood at the other with his club, to kill him as he came out. The pile was still burning. Painter said he was a turbulent fellow and he *would* kill him. The apprehension of P. was TALKED ABOUT, but, as a compromise, the negro was sold to another man."

EXTRACT FROM THE PUBLISHED JOURNAL OF THE LATE WM. SAVERY, of Philadelphia, an eminent minister of the religious Society of Friends:—

"6th mo. 22d, 1791. We passed on to Augusta, Georgia. They can scarcely tolerate us, on account of our abhorrence of slavery. On the 28th we got to Savannah, and lodged at one Blount's, a hard-hearted slaveholder. One of his lads, aged about fourteen, was ordered to go and milk the cows: and falling asleep, through weariness, the master called out and ordered him a flogging. I asked him what he meant by a flogging. He replied, the way we serve them here is, we cut their backs until they are raw all over, and then salt them. Upon this my feelings were roused; I told him that was too bad, and queried if it were possible; he replied it was, with many curses upon the blacks. At supper this unfeeling wretch *craved a blessing*!

"Next morning I heard some one begging for mercy, and also the lash as of a whip. Not knowing whence the sound came, I rose, and presently found the poor boy tied up to a post, his toes scarcely touching the ground, and a negro whipper. He had already cut him in an unmerciful manner, and the blood ran to his heels. I stepped in between them, and ordered him untied immediately, which, with some reluctance and astonishment, was done. Returning to the house I saw the landlord, who then showed himself in his true colors, the most abominably wicked man I ever met with, full of horrid execrations and threatenings upon all northern people; but I did not spare him; which occasioned a bystander to say, with an oath, that I should be "popped over." We left them, and were in full expectation of their way-laying or coming after us, but the Lord restrained them. The next house we stopped at we found the same wicked spirit."

Col. ELIJAH ELLSWORTH, of Richfield, Ohio, gives the following testimony:—

"Eight or ten years ago I was in Putnam county, in the state of Georgia, at a Mr. Slaughter's, the father of my brother's wife. A negro, that belonged to Mr. Walker, (I believe), was accused of stealing a pedlar's trunk. The negro denied, but, without ceremony, was lashed to a tree—the whipping commenced—six or eight men took turns—the poor fellow begged for mercy, but without effect, until he was literally *cut to pieces, from his shoulders to his hips,* and covered with a gore of blood. When he said the trunk was in a stack of fodder, he was unlashed. They proceeded to the stack, but found no trunk. They asked the poor fellow, what he lied about it for; he said, "Lord, Massa, to keep from being whipped to death; I know nothing about the trunk." They commenced the whipping with redoubled vigor, until I really supposed he would be whipped to death on the spot: and such shrieks and crying for mercy!—Again he acknowledged, and again they were defeated in finding, and the same reason given as before. Some were for whipping again, others thought he would not survive another, and they ceased. About two months after, the trunk was found, and it was then ascertained who the thief was: and the poor fellow, after being nearly beat to death, and twice made to lie about it, was as innocent as I was."

The following statements are furnished by Major HORACE NYE, of Putnam, Muskingum county, Ohio.

"In the summer of 1837, Mr. JOHN H. MOOREHEAD, a partner of mine, descended the Mississippi with several boat loads of flour. He told me that floating in a place in the Mississippi, where he could see for miles a head, he perceived a concourse of people on the bank, that for at least a mile and a half above he saw them, and heard the screams of some person, and for a great distance, the crack of a whip, he ran near the shore, and saw them whipping a black man, who was on the ground, and at that time nearly unable to scream, but the whip continued to be plied without intermission, as long as he was in sight, say from one mile and a half, to two miles below—he probably saw and heard them for one hour in all. He expressed the opinion that the man could not survive.

"About four weeks since I had a conversation with Mr. Porter, a respectable citizen of Morgan county, of this state, of about fifty years of age. He told me that he formerly traveled about five years in the southern states, and that on one occasion he stopped at a private house, to stay all night; (I think it was in Virginia), while he was conversing with the man, his wife came in, and complained that the wench had broken some article in the kitchen, and that she must be whipped. He took the *woman* into the door yard, stripped her clothes down to her hips—tied her hands together, and drawing them up to a limb, so that she could just touch the ground, took a very large cowskin whip, and commenced flogging; he said that every stroke at first raised the skin, and immediately the blood came through; this he continued, until the blood stood in a puddle at her feet. He then turned to my informant and said, "Well, Yankee, what do you think of that?"

EXTRACT OF A LETTER FROM MR. W. DUSTIN, a member of the Methodist Episcopal Church, and, when the letter was written, 1835, a student of Marietta College, Ohio.

"I find by looking over my journal that the murdering, which I spoke of yesterday, took place about the first of June, 1834.

"Without commenting upon this act of cruelty, or giving vent to my own feelings, I will simply give you a statement of the fact, as known from *personal* observation.

"Dr. K. a man of wealth, and a practising physician in the county of Yazoo, state of Mississippi, personally known to me, having lived in the same neighborhood more than twelve months, after having scourged one of his negroes for running away, declared with an oath, that if he ran away again, he would kill him. The negro, so soon as an opportunity offered, ran away again. He was caught and brought back. Again he was scourged, until his flesh, mangled and torn, and thick mingled with the clotted blood, rolled from his back. He became apparently insensible, and beneath the heaviest stroke would scarcely utter a groan. The master got tired, laid down his whip and nailed the negro's ear to a tree; in this condition, nailed fast to the rugged wood, he remained all night!

"Suffice it to say, in the conclusion, that the next day he was found DEAD!

"Well, what did they do with the master? The sum total of it is this: He was taken before a magistrate and gave bonds, for his appearance at the next court. Well, to be sure he had plenty of cash, so he paid up his bonds and moved away, and there the matter ended.

"If the above fact will be of any service to you in exhibiting to the world the condition of the unfortunate negroes, you are at liberty to make use of it in any way you think best."

Mr. ALFRED WILKINSON, a member of the Baptist Church in Skeneateles, N. Y. and the assessor of that town, has furnished the following:

"I went down the Mississippi in December, 1808, and saw twelve or fourteen negroes punished, on one plantation, by stretching them on a ladder and tying them to it; then stripping off their clothes, and whipping them on the naked fresh with a heavy whip, the lash seven or eight feet long: most of the strokes cut the skin. I understood they were whipped for not doing the tasks allotted to them."

FROM THE PHILANTHROPIST, Cincinnati, Ohio, Feb. 26, 1839.

"A very intelligent lady, the widow of a highly respectable preacher of the gospel, of the Presbyterian Church, formerly a resident of a free state, and a colonizationist, and a strong anti-abolitionist, who, although an enemy to slavery, was opposed to abolition on the ground that it was for carrying things too rapidly, and without regard to circumstances, and especially who believed that abolitionists exaggerated with regard to the evils of slavery, and used to say that such men ought to go to slave states and see for themselves, to be convinced that they did the slaveholders injustice, has gone and seen for herself. Hear her testimony.

Kentucky, Dec. 25, 1835.

"Dear Mrs. W.—I am still in the land of oppression and cruelty, but hope soon to breathe the air of a free state. My soul is sick of slavery, and I rejoice that my time is nearly expired; but the scenes that I have witnessed have made an impression that never can be effaced, and have inspired me with the determination to unite my feeble efforts with those who are laboring to suppress this horrid system. I am *now* an *abolitionist*. You will cease to be surprised at this, when I inform you, that I have just seen a poor slave who was beaten by his inhuman master until he could neither walk nor stand. I saw him from my window carried from the barn where he had been whipped to the cabin, by two negro men; and he now lies there, and if he recovers, will be a sufferer for months, and probably for life. You will doubtless suppose that he committed some great crime; but it was not so. He was called upon by a young man (the son of his master), to do something, and not moving as quickly as his young master wished him to do, he drove him to the barn, knocked him down, and jumped upon him, stamped, and then cowhided him until he was almost dead. This is not the first act of cruelty that I have seen, though it is the *worst*; and I am convinced that those who have described the cruelties of slaveholders, have not exaggerated."

EXTRACT OF A LETTER FROM GERRIT SMITH, Esq., of Peterboro', N. Y.

PETERBORO', December 1, 1838.

To the Editor of the Union Herald:

"My dear Sir:—You will be happy to hear, that the two fugitive slaves, to whom in the brotherly love of your heart, you gave the use of your horse, are still making undisturbed progress towards the *monarchical* land whither *republican* slaves escape for the enjoyment of liberty. They had eaten their breakfast, and were seated in my wagon, before day-dawn, this morning.

"Fugitive slaves have before taken my house in their way, but never any, whose lips and persons made so forcible an appeal to my sensibilities, and kindled in me so much abhorrence of the hell-concocted system of American slavery.

"The fugitives exhibited their bare backs to myself and a number of my neighbors. Williams' back is comparatively scarred. But, I speak within bounds, when I say, that one-third to one-half of the whole surface of the back and shoulders of poor Scott, *consists of scars and wales resulting from innumerable gashes*. His natural complexion being yellow and the callous places being nearly black, his back and shoulders remind you of a spotted animal."

The LOUISVILLE REPORTER (Kentucky), Jan. 15, 1839, contains the report of a trial for inhuman treatment of a female slave. The following is some of the testimony given in court.

"Dr. CONSTANT testified that he saw Mrs. Maxwell at the kitchen door, whipping the negro severely, without being particular whether she struck her in the face or not. The negro was lacerated by the whip, and the blood flowing. Soon after, on going down the steps, he saw quantities of blood on them, and on returning, saw them again. She had been thinly clad—barefooted in very cold weather. Sometimes she had shoes—sometimes not. In the beginning of the winter she had linsey dresses, since then, calico ones. During the last four months, had noticed many scars on her person. At one time had one of her eyes tied up for a week. During the last three months seemed declining, and had become stupified. Mr. Winters was passing along the street, heard cries, looked up through the window that was hoisted, saw the boy whipping her, as much as forty or fifty licks, while he staid. The girl was stripped down to the hips. The whip seemed to be a cow-hide. Whenever she turned her face to him, he would hit her across the face either with the butt end or small end of the whip to make her turn her back round square to the lash, that he might get a fair blow at her.

"Mr. Say had noticed several wounds on her person, chiefly bruises.

"Captain Porter, keeper of the work-house, into which Milly had been received, thought the injuries on her person very bad— some of them appeared to be burns—some bruises or stripes, as of a cow-hide."

LETTER OF REV. JOHN RANKIN, of Ripley, Ohio, to the Editor of the Philanthropist.

RIPLEY, Feb. 20, 1839.
"Some time since, a member of the Presbyterian Church of Ebenezer, Brown county, Ohio, landed his boat at a point on the Mississippi. He saw some disturbance among the colored people on the bank. He stepped up, to see what was the matter. A black man was stretched naked on the ground; his hands were tied to a stake, and one held each foot. He was doomed to receive fifty lashes; but by the time the overseer had given him twenty-five with his great whip, the blood was standing round the wretched victim in little puddles. It appeared just as if it had rained blood.—Another observer stepped up, and advised to defer the other twenty-five to another time, lest the slave might die; and he was released, to receive the balance when he should have so recruited as to be able to bear it and live. The offence was, coming one hour too late to work."

Mr. RANKIN, who is a native of Tennessee, in his letters on slavery, published fifteen years since, says:

"A respectable gentleman, who is now a citizen of Flemingsburg, Fleming county, Kentucky, when in the state of South Carolina, was invited by a slaveholder, to walk with him and take a view of his farm. He complied with the invitation thus given, and in their walk they came to the place where the slaves were at work, and found the overseer whipping one of them very severely for not keeping pace with his fellows—in vain the poor fellow alleged that he was sick, and could not work. The master seemed to think all was well enough, hence he and the gentleman passed on. In the space of an hour they returned by the same way, and found that the poor slave, who had been whipped as they first passed by the field of labor, was actually dead! This I have from unquestionable authority."

Extract of a letter from a MEMBER OF CONGRESS, to the Editor of the New York American, dated Washington, Feb. 18, 1839. The name of the writer is with the Executive Committee of the American Anti-Slavery Society.

"Three days ago, the inhabitants in the vicinity of the new Patent Building were alarmed by an outcry in the street, which proved to be that of a slave who had just been knocked down with a brick-bat by his pursuing master. Prostrate on the ground, with a large gash in his head, the poor slave was receiving the blows of his master on one side, and the kicks of his master's son on the other. His cries brought a few individuals to the spot; but no one dared to interfere, save to exclaim—You will kill him—which was met by the response, "He is mine, and I have a right to do what I please with him." The heart-rending scene was closed from *public* view by dragging the poor bruised and wounded slave from the public street into his master's stable. What followed is not known. The outcries were heard by members of Congress and others at the distance of near a quarter of a mile from the scene.

"And now, perhaps, you will ask, is not the city aroused by this flagrant cruelty and breach of the peace? I answer—not at all. Every thing is quiet. If the occurrence is mentioned at all, it is spoken of in whispers."

From the Mobile Examiner, *August* 1, 1837.
"POLICE REPORT—MAYOR'S OFFICE.
Saturday morning, August 12, 1837.
"His Honor the Mayor presiding.

"Mr. MILLER, of the foundry, brought to the office this morning a small negro girl aged about eight or ten years, whom he had taken into his house some time during the previous night. She had crawled under the window of his bed room to screen herself from the night air, and to find a warmer shelter than the open canopy of heaven afforded. Of all objects of pity that have lately come to our view, this poor little girl most needs the protection of authority, and the sympathies of the charitable. From the cruelty of her master and mistress, she has been whipped, worked and starved, until she is now a breathing skeleton, hardly able to stand upon her feet.

"The back of the poor little sufferer, (which we ourselves saw), *was actually cut into strings, and so perfectly was the flesh worn from her limbs,* by the wretched treatment she had received, that *every joint showed distinctly* its crevices and protuberances through the skin. Her little lips clung closely over her teeth—her cheeks were sunken and her head narrowed, and when her eyes were closed, the lids resembled film more than flesh or skin.

"We would desire of our northern friends such as choose to publish to the world their own version of the case we have related, not to forget to add, in conclusion, that the owner of this little girl is a foreigner, speaks against slavery as an institution, and reads his Bible to his wife, with the view of finding proofs for his opinions."

Rev. WILLIAM SCALES, of Lyndon, Vermont, gives the following testimony in a recent letter:

"I had a class-mate at the Andover Theological Seminary, who spent a season at the south,—in Georgia, I think—who related the following fact in an address before the Seminary. It occasioned very deep sensation on the part of opponents. The gentleman was Mr. Julius C. Anthony, of Taunton, Mass. He graduated at the Seminary in 1835. I do not know where he is now settled. I have no doubt of the fact, as he was an *eye-witness* of it. The man with whom he resided had a very athletic slave—a valuable fellow—a blacksmith. On a certain day a small strap of leather was missing. The man's little son accused this slave of stealing it. He denied the charge, while the boy most confidently asserted it. The slave was brought out into the yard and bound—his hands below his knees, and a stick crossing his knees, so that he would lie upon either side in form of the letter S. One of the overseers laid on fifty lashes—he still denied the theft—was turned over and fifty more put on. Sometimes the master and sometimes the overseers whipping—as they relieved each other to take breath. Then he was for a time left to himself, and in the course of the day received FOUR HUNDRED LASHES—still denying the charge. Next morning Mr. Anthony walked out—the sun was just rising—he saw the man greatly enfeebled, leaning against a stump. It was time to go to work—he attempted to rise, but fell back—again attempted, and again fell back—still making the attempt, and still falling back, Mr. Anthony thought, nearly *twenty times* before he succeeded in standing—he then staggered off to his shop. In course of the morning Mr. A. went to the door and looked in. Two overseers were standing by. The slave was feverish and sick—his skin and mouth dry and parched. He was very thirsty. One of the overseers, while Mr. A. was looking at him, inquired of the other whether it were not best to give him a little water. 'No, damn him, he will do well enough,' was the reply from the other overseer. This was all the relief gained by the poor slave. A few days after, the slaveholder's *son confessed that he stole the strap himself.*"

Rev. D. C. EASTMAN, a minister of the Methodist Episcopal church at Bloomingburg, Fayette county, Ohio, has just forwarded a letter, from which the following is an extract:

"GEORGE ROEBUCK, an old and respectable farmer, near Bloomingburg, Fayette county, Ohio, a member of the Methodist Episcopal church, says, that almost forty-three years ago, he saw in Bath county, Virginia, a slave girl with a sore between the shoulders of the size and shape of a *smoothing iron*. The girl was 'owned' by one M'Neil. A slaveholder who boarded at M'Neil's stated that Mrs. M'Neil had placed the aforesaid iron when hot, between the girl's shoulders, and produced the sore.

"Roebuck was once at this M'Neil's father's, and whilst the old man was at morning prayer, he heard the son plying the whip upon a slave out of doors.

"ELI WEST, of Concord township, Fayette county, Ohio, formerly of North Carolina, a farmer and an exhorter in the Methodist Protestant church, says, that many years since he went to live with an uncle who owned about fifty negroes. Soon after his arrival, his uncle ordered his waiting boy, who was *naked,* to be tied—his hands to a horse rack, and his feet together, with a rail passed between his legs, and held down by a person at each end. In this position he was whipped, from neck to feet, till covered with blood; after which he was *salted.*

"His uncle's slaves received one quart of corn each day, and that only, and were allowed one hour each day to cook and eat it. They had no meat but once in the year. Such was the general usage in that country.

"West, after this, lived one year with Esquire Starky and mother. They had two hundred slaves, who received the usual treatment of starvation, nakedness, and the cowhide. They had one likely negro woman who bore no children. For this neglect, her mistress had her back made naked and a severe whipping inflicted. But as she continued barren, she was sold to the 'negro buyers.'

"THOMAS LARRIMER, a deacon in the Presbyterian church at Bloomingburg, Fayette county, Ohio, and a respectable farmer, says, that in April, 1837, as he was going down the Mississippi river, about fifty miles below Natchez, he saw ahead, on the left side of the river, a colored person tied to a post, and a man with a driver's whip, the lash about eight or ten feet long. With this the man commenced, with much deliberation, to whip, with much apparent force, and continued till he got out of sight.

"When coming up the river forty or fifty miles below Vicksburg, a Judge Owens came on board the steamboat. He was owner of a cotton plantation below there, and on being told of the above whipping, he said that slaves were often whipped to death for great offences, such as *stealing,* &c.—but that when death followed, the overseers were generally severely *reproved*!

"About the same time, he spent a night at Mr. Casey's, three miles from Columbia, South Carolina. Whilst there they heard him giving orders as to what was to be done, and amongst other things, 'That nigger must be buried.' On inquiry, he learnt that a gentleman traveling with a servant, had a short time previous called there, and said his servant had just been taken ill, and he should be under the necessity of leaving him. He did so. The slave became worse, and Casey called in a physician, who pronounced it an old case, and said that he must shortly die. The slave said, if that was the case he would now tell the truth. He had been attacked, a long time since, with a difficulty in the side—his master swore he would 'have his own out of him,' and started off to sell him, with a threat to kill him if he told he had been sick, more than a few days. They saw them making a rough plank box to bury him in.

"In March, 1833, twenty-five or thirty miles south of Columbia, on the great road through Sumpterville district, they saw a large company of female slaves carrying rails and building fence. Three of them were far advanced in pregnancy.

"In the month of January, 1838, he put up with a drove of mules and horses, at one Adams', on the Drovers' road, near the south border of Kentucky. His son-in-law, who had lived in the south, was there. In conversation about picking cotton, he said, 'some hands cannot get the sleight of it. I have a girl who to-day has done as good a day's work at grubbing as any *man,* but I could not make her a hand at cotton-picking. I whipped her, and if I did it once I did it five hundred times, but I found she *could* not; so I put her to carrying rails with the men. After a few days I found her shoulders were so *raw* that every rail was *bloody* as she laid it down. I asked her if she would not rather pick cotton than carry rails. 'No,' said she, 'I don't get whipped now.'"

WILLIAM A. USTICK, an elder of the Presbyterian church at Bloomingburg, and Mr. G. S. Fullerton, a merchant and member of the same church, were with Deacon Larrimer on this journey, and are witnesses to the preceding facts.

Mr. SAMUEL HALL, a teacher in Marietta College, Ohio, and formerly secretary of the Colonization society in that village, has recently communicated the facts which follow. We quote from his letter.

"The following horrid flagellation was witnessed in part, till his soul was sick, by MR. GLIDDEN, an inhabitant of Marietta, Ohio, who went down the Mississippi river, with a boat load of produce in the autumn of 1837; it took place at what is called 'Matthews' or 'Matheses Bend' in December, 1837. Mr. G. is worthy of credit.

"A negro was tied up, and flogged until the blood ran down and filled his shoes, so that when he raised either foot and set it down again, the blood would run over their tops. I could not look on any longer, but turned away in horror; the whipping was continued to the number of 500 lashes, as I understood; a quart of spirits of turpentine was then applied to his lacerated body. The same negro came down to my boat, to get some apples, and was so weak from his wounds and loss of blood, that he could not get up the bank, but fell to the ground. The crime for which the negro was whipped, was that of telling the other negroes, that *the overseer had lain with his wife.*"

Mr. Hall adds:—

"The following statement is made by a young man from Western Virginia. He is a member of the Presbyterian Church, and a student in Marietta College. All that prevents the introduction of his *name*, is the peril to his life, which would probably be the consequence, on his return to Virginia. His character for integrity and veracity is above suspicion.

'On the night of the great meteoric shower, in Nov. 1833, I was at Remley's tavern, 12 miles west of Lewisburg, Greenbrier Co., Virginia. A drove of 50 or 60 negroes stopped at the same place that night. They usually 'camp out,' but as it was excessively muddy, they were permitted to come into the house. So far as my knowledge extends, 'droves,' on their way to the south, eat but twice a day, early in the morning and at night. Their supper was a compound of 'potatoes and meal,' and was, without exception, *the dirtiest, blackest looking mess I ever saw*. I remarked at the time that the food was not as clean, in appearance, as that which was given to a *drove of hogs,* at the same place the night previous. Such as it was, however, a black woman brought it on her head, in a tray or trough two and a half feet long, where the men and women were promiscuously herded. The slaves rushed up and seized it from the trough in handfulls, before the woman could take it off her head. They jumped at it as if half-famished.

'They slept on the floor of the room which they were permitted to occupy, lying in every form imaginable, males and females, promiscuously. They were so thick on the floor, that in passing through the room it was necessary to step over them.

'There were three drivers, one of whom staid in the room to watch the drove, and the other two slept in an adjoining room. Each of the latter took a female from the drove to lodge with him, as is the common practice of the drivers generally. There is no doubt about this particular instance, *for they were seen together*. The mud was so thick on the floor where this *drove* slept, that it was necessary to take a shovel, the next morning, and clear it out. Six or eight in this drove were chained; all were for the south.

'In the autumn of the same year I saw a drove of upwards of a hundred, between 40 and 50 of them were fastened to one chain, the links being made of iron rods, as thick in diameter as a man's little finger. This drove was bound westward to the Ohio river, to be shipped to the south. I have seen many droves, and more or less in each, almost without exception, were chained. I never saw but one drove, that went on their way making merry. In that one they were blowing horns, singing, &c., and appeared as if they had been drinking whisky.

'They generally appear extremely dejected. I have seen in the course of five years, on the road near where I reside, 12 or 15 droves at least, passing to the south. They would average 40 in each drove. Near the first of January, 1834, I started about sunrise to go to Lewisburg. It was a bitter cold morning. I met a drove of negroes, 30 or 40 in number, remarkably ragged and destitute of clothing. One little boy particularly excited my sympathy. He was some distance behind the others, not being able to keep up with the rest. Although he was shivering with cold and crying, the driver was pushing him up in a trot to overtake the main gang. All of them looked as if they were half-frozen. There was one remarkable instance of tyranny, exhibited by a boy, not more than eight years old, that came under my observation, in a family by the name of D—n, six miles from Lewisburg. This youngster would swear at the slaves, and exert all the strength he possessed, to flog or beat them, with whatever instrument or weapon he could lay hands on, provided they did not obey him *instantly*. He was encouraged in this by his father, the master of the slaves. The slaves often fled from this young tyrant in terror."

Mr. Hall adds:—

"The following extract is from a letter, to a student in Marietta College, by his friend in Alabama. With the writer, Mr. ISAAC KNAPP, I am perfectly acquainted. He was a student in the above College, for the space of one year, before going to Alabama, was formerly a resident of Dummerston, Vt. He is a professor of religion, and as worthy of belief as any member of the community. Mr. K. has returned from the South, and is now a member of the same college.

'In Jan. (1838) a negro of a widow Phillips, ranaway, was taken up, and confined in Pulaski jail. One Gibbs, overseer for Mrs. P., mounted on horseback, took him from confinement, compelled him to run back to Elkton, a distance of fifteen miles, whipping him all the way. When he reached home, the negro exhausted and worn out, exclaimed 'you have broke my heart,' i. e. you have killed me. For this, Gibbs flew into a violent passion, tied the negro to a stake, and, in the language of a witness, '*cut his back to mince-meat*.' But the fiend was not satisfied with this. He burnt his legs to a blister, with hot embers, and then chained him *naked,* in the open air, weary with running, weak from the loss of blood, and smarting from his burns. It was a cold night—and *in the morning the negro was dead*. Yet this monster escaped without even *the shadow* of a trial. 'The negro,' said the doctor, 'died, by—he knew not what; any how, Gibbs did not kill him.'* A short time since, (the letter is dated, April, 1838), 'Gibbs whipped another negro unmercifully because the horse, with which he was ploughing, broke the reins and ran. He then raised his whip against Mr. Bowers, (son of Mrs. P.) who shot him. Since I came here,' (a period of about six months), 'there have been eight white men and two negroes killed, within 30 miles of me.'

"The following is from Mr. Knapp's own lips, taken down a day or two since.

'Mr. Buster, with whom I boarded, in Limestono Co., Ala., related to me the following incident: 'George, a slave belonging to one of the estates in my neighborhood, was lurking about my residence without a pass. We were making preparations to give him a flogging, but he escaped from us. Not long afterwards, meeting a patrol which had just taken a negro in custody without a pass, I inquired, Who have you there? on learning that it was *George,* well, I rejoined, there is a small matter between him and myself, that needs adjustment, so give me the raw hide, which I accordingly took, and laid 60 strokes on his back, to the utmost of my strength.' I was speaking of this barbarity, afterwards, to Mr. Bradley, an overseer of the Rev. Mr. Donnell, who lives in the vicinity of Moresville, Ala., 'Oh,' replied he, 'we consider *that* a very light whipping here.' Mr. Bradley is a professor of religion, and is esteemed in that vicinity a very pious, exemplary Christian.'"

EXTRACT OF A LETTER FROM REV. C. STEWART RENSHAW, of Quincy, Illinois, dated Jan. 1, 1839.

"I do not feel at liberty to disclose the name of the brother who has furnished the following facts. He is highly esteemed as a man of scrupulous veracity. I will confirm my own testimony by the certificate of Judge Snow and Mr. Keyes, two of the oldest and most respectable settlers in Quincy.

---

* Mr. Knapp, gives me some further verbal particulars about this affair. He says that his informant saw the negro dead the next morning, that his legs were blistered, and that the negroes affirmed that Gibbs compelled them to throw embers upon him. But Gibbs denied it, and said the blistering was the effect of frost, as the negro was much exposed to it before being taken up. Mr. Bowers, a son of Mrs. Phillips by a former husband, attempted to have Gibbs brought to justice, but his mother justified Gibbs, and nothing was therefore done about it. The affair took place in Upper Elkton, Tennessee, near the Alabama line.

Quincy, Dec. 29, 1838.

"Dear Sir,—We have been long acquainted with the Christian brother who has named to you some facts that fell under his observation whilst a resident of slave states. He is a member of a Christian church, in good standing; and is a man of strict integrity of character.

HENRY H. SNOW,
WILLARD KEYES.

Rev. C. Stewart Renshaw."

"My informant spent thirty years of his life in Kentucky and Missouri. Whilst in Kentucky he resided in Hardin co. I noted down his testimony very nearly in his own words, which will account for their *evidence-like* form. On the general condition of the slaves in Kentucky, through Hardin co., he said, their houses were very uncomfortable, generally without floors, other than the earth: many had puncheon floors, but he never remembers to have seen a plank floor. In regard to clothing they were very badly off. In summer they cared little for anything; but in winter they almost froze. Their rags might hide their nakedness from the sun in summer, but would not protect them from the cold in winter. Their bed-clothes were tattered rags, thrown into a corner by day, and drawn before the fire by night. 'The only thing,' said he, 'to which I can compare them, in winter, is *stock without a shelter.*'

"He made the following comparison between the condition of slaves in Kentucky and Missouri. So far as he was able to compare them, he said, that in Missouri the slaves had better *quarters*—but are not so well clad, and are more severely punished than in Kentucky. In both states, the slaves are huddled together, without distinction of sex, into the same quarter, till it is filled, then another is built; often two or three families in a log hovel, twelve feet square.

"It is proper to state, that the sphere of my informant's observation was mainly in the region of Hardin co., Kentucky, and the eastern part of Missouri, and not through those states generally.

"Whilst at St. Louis, a number of years ago, as he was going to work with Mr. Henry Males, and another carpenter, they heard groans from a barn by the road-side: they stopped, and looking through the cracks of the barn, saw a negro bound hand and foot to a post, so that his toes just touched the ground; and his master, Captain Thorpe, was inflicting punishment; he had whipped him till exhausted,—rested himself, and returned again to the punishment. The wretched sufferer was in a most pitiable condition, and the warm blood and dry dust of the barn had formed a mortar up to his instep.

Mr. Males jumped the fence, and remonstrated so effectually with Capt. Thorpe, that he ceased the punishment. It was six weeks before that slave could put on his shirt!

"John Mackey, a rich slaveholder, lived near Clarksville, Pike co., Missouri, some years since. He whipped his slave Billy, a boy fourteen years old, till he was sick and stupid; he then sent him home. Then, for his stupidity, whipped him again, and fractured his skull with an axe-helve. He buried him away in the woods; dark words were whispered, and the body was disinterred. A coroner's inquest was held, and Mr. R. Anderson, the coroner, brought in a verdict of death from fractured skull, occasioned by blows from an axe-handle, inflicted by John Mackey. The case was brought into court, but Mackey was rich, and his murdered victim was his SLAVE; after expending about $500 he walked free.

"One Mrs. Mann, living near ——, in —— co., Missouri, was known to be very cruel to her slaves. She had a bench made purposely to whip them upon; and what she called her "six pound paddle," an instrument of prodigious torture, bored through with holes; this she would wield with both hands as she stood over her prostrate victim.

"She thus punished a hired slave woman named Fanny, belonging to Mr. Charles Trabue, who lives near Palmyra, Marion co., Missouri; on the morning after the punishment Fanny was a corpse; she was silently and quickly buried, but rumor was not so easily stopped. Mr. Trabue heard of it, and commenced suit for his *property*. The murdered slave was disinterred, and an inquest held; her back was a mass of jellied muscle; and the coroner brought in a verdict of death by the 'six pound paddle.' Mrs. Mann fled for a few months, but returned again, and her friends found means to protract the suit.

"This same Mrs. Mann had another hired slave woman living with her, called Patterson's Fanny, she belonged to a Mr. Patterson; she had a young babe with her, just beginning to creep. One day, after washing, whilst a tub of rinsing water yet stood in the kitchen, Mrs. Mann came out in haste, and sent Fanny to do something out of doors. Fanny tried to beg off—she was afraid to leave her babe, lest it should creep to the tub and get hurt—Mrs. M. said she would watch the babe, and sent her off. She went with much reluctance, and heard the child struggle as she went out the door. Fearing lest Mrs. M. should leave the babe alone, she watched the room, and soon saw her pass out of the opposite door. Immediately Fanny hurried in, and looked around for her babe, she could not see it, she looked at the tub—there her babe was floating, a strangled corpse.

The poor woman gave a dreadful scream; and Mrs. M. rushed into the room, with her hands raised, and exclaimed, 'Heavens, Fanny! have you drowned your child?' It was vain for the poor bereaved one to attempt to vindicate herself: in vain she attempted to convince them that the babe had not been alone a moment, and could not have drowned itself; and that she had not been in the house a moment, before she screamed at discovering her drowned babe. All was false! Mrs. Mann declared it was all pretence—that Fanny had drowned her own babe, and now wanted to lay the blame upon her! and Mrs. Mann was a white woman—of course her word was more valuable than the oaths of all the slaves of Missouri. No evidence but that of slaves could be obtained, or Mr. Patterson would have prosecuted for his 'loss of property.' As it was, every one believed Mrs. M. guilty, though the affair was soon hushed up."

Extract of a letter from Col. THOMAS ROGERS, a native of Kentucky, now an elder in the Presbyterian Church at New Petersburg, Highland co., Ohio.

"When a boy, in Bourbon co., Kentucky, my father lived near a slaveholder of the name of Clay, who had a large number of slaves; I remember being often at their quarters; not one of their shanties, or hovels, had any floor but the earth. Their clothing was truly neither fit for covering nor decency. We could distinctly, of a still morning, hear this man whipping his blacks, and hear their screams from my father's farm: this could be heard almost any still morning about the dawn of day. It was said to be his usual custom to repair, about the break of day, to their cabin doors, and, as the blacks passed out, to give them as many strokes of his cowskin as opportunity afforded; and he would proceed in this manner from cabin to cabin until they were all out. Occasionally some of his slaves would abscond, and upon being retaken they were punished severely; and some of them, it is believed, died in consequence of the cruelty of their usage. I saw one of this man's slaves, about seventeen years old, wearing a collar, with long iron horns extending from his shoulders far above his head.

"In the winter of 1828-29 I traveled through part of the states of Maryland and Virginia to Baltimore. At Frost Town, on the national road, I put up for the night. Soon after, there came in a slaver with his drove of slaves; among them were two young men, chained together. The bar room was assigned to them for their place of lodging—those in chains were guarded when they had to go out. I asked the 'owner' why he kept these men chained; he replied, that they were stout young fellows, and should they rebel, he and his son would not be able to manage them. I then left the room, and shortly after heard a *scream,* and when the landlady inquired the cause, the slaver coolly told her not to trouble herself, he was only chastising one of his women. It appeared that three days previously her child had died on the road, and been thrown into a hole or crevice in the mountain, and a few stones thrown over it; and the mother weeping for her child was chastised by her master, and told by him, she 'should have something to cry for.' The name of this man I can give if called for.

"When engaged in this journey I spent about one month with my relations in Virginia. It being shortly after new year, *the time of hiring* was over; but I saw the pounds, and the scaffolds which remained of the pounds, in which the slaves had been penned up."

Mr. GEORGE W. WESTGATE, of Quincy, Illinois, who lived in the southwestern slave states a number of years, has furnished the following statement.

"The great mass of the slaves are under drivers and overseers. I never saw an overseer without a whip; the whip usually carried is a short loaded stock, with a heavy lash from five to six feet long. When they whip a slave they make him pull off his shirt, if he has one, then make him lie down on his face, and taking their stand at the length of the lash, they inflict the punishment. Whippings are so *universal* that a negro that has not been whipped is talked of in all the region as a wonder. By whipping I do not mean a few lashes across the shoulders, but a set flogging, and generally *lying down*.

"On sugar plantations generally, and on some cotton plantations, they have negro drivers, who are in such a degree responsible for their gang, that if they are at fault, the driver is whipped. The result is, the gang are constantly driven by him to the extent of the influence of the lash; and it is uniformly the case that gangs dread a negro driver more than a white overseer.

"I spent a winter on widow Calvert's plantation, near Rodney, Mississippi, but was not in a situation to see extraordinary punishments. Bellows, the overseer, for a trifling offence, took one of the slaves, stripped him, and with a piece of burning wood applied to his posteriors, burned him cruelly; while the poor wretch screamed in the greatest agony. The principal preparation for punishment that Bellows had, was single handcuffs made of iron, with chains, by which the offender could be chained to four stakes on the ground.

These are very common in all the lower country. I noticed one slave on widow Calvert's plantation, who was whipped from twenty-five to fifty lashes every fortnight during the whole winter. The expression 'whipped to death,' as applied to slaves, is common at the south.

"Several years ago I was going below New-Orleans, in what is called the Plaquemine country, and a planter sent down in my boat a runaway he had found in New-Orleans, to his plantation at Orange 5 Points. As we came near the Points he told me, with deep feeling, that he expected to be whipped almost to death: pointing to a graveyard, he said, 'There lie five who were whipped to death.' Overseers generally keep some of the women on the plantation; I scarce know an exception to this. Indeed, their intercourse with them is very much promiscuous,—they show them not much, if any favor. Masters frequently follow the example of their overseers in this thing.

"GEORGE W. WESTGATE."

II. TORTURES, BY IRON COLLARS, CHAINS, FETTERS, HANDCUFFS, &c.

The slaves are often tortured by iron collars, with long prongs or "horns" and sometimes bells attached to them—they are made to wear chains, handcuffs, fetters, iron clogs, bars, rings, and bands of iron upon their limbs, iron masks upon their faces, iron gags in their mouths, &c.

In proof of this, we give the testimony of slaveholders themselves, under their own names; it will be mostly in the form of extracts from their own advertisements, in southern newspapers, in which, describing their runaway slaves, they specify the iron collars, handcuffs, chains, fetters, &c., which they wore upon their necks, wrists, ankles, and other parts of their bodies. To publish the *whole* of each advertisement, would needlessly occupy space and tax the reader; we shall consequently, as heretofore, give merely the name of the advertiser, the name and date of the newspaper containing the advertisement, with the place of publication, and only so much of the advertisement as will give the particular *fact,* proving the truth of the assertion contained in the *general head.*

WITNESSES	TESTIMONY
William Toler, sheriff of Simpson county, Mississippi, in the "Southern Sun," Jackson, Mississippi, September 22, 1838.	"Was committed to jail, a yellow boy named Jim—had on a *large lock chain around his neck.*"
Mr. James R. Green, in the "Beacon," Greensborough, Alabama, August 23, 1838.	Ranaway, a negro man named Squire— had on a *chain locked with a house-lock, around his neck.*"
Mr. Hazlet Loflano, in the "Spectator," Staunton, Virginia, Sept. 27, 1838.	"Ranaway, a negro named David—with some *iron hobbles around each ankle.*"
Mr. T. Enggy, New Orleans, Gallatin street, between Hospital and Barracks, N. O. "Bee," Oct. 27, 1837.	"Ranaway, negress Caroline—had on a *collar with one prong turned down.*"
Mr. John Henderson, Washington county, Mi., in the "Grand Gulf Advertiser," August 29, 1838.	"Ranaway, a black woman, Betsey—had an *iron bar on her right leg.*"
William Dyer, sheriff, Claiborne, Louisiana, in the "Herald," Natchitoches, (La.) July 26, 1837.	"Was committed to jail, a negro named Ambrose—has a *ring of iron around his neck.*"
Mr. Owen Cooke, Mary street, between Common and Jackson streets, New Orleans, in the N. O. "Bee," September 12, 1837.	"Ranaway, my slave Amos, had *a chain* attached to one of his legs."
H. W. Rice, sheriff, Colleton district, South Carolina, in the "Charleston Mercury," September 1, 1838.	"Committed to jail, a negro named Patrick, about forty-five years old, and is *handcuffed.*"

WITNESSES	TESTIMONY
W. P. Reeves, jailor, Shelby county, Tennessee, in the "Memphis Enquirer, June 17, 1837.	"Committed to jail, a negro—had on his right leg an *iron band* with one link of a chain."
Mr. Francis Durett, Lexington, Lauderdale county, Ala., in the "Huntsville Democrat," August 29, 1837.	"Ranaway, a negro man named Charles—had on a *drawing chain,* fastened around his ankle with a house lock."
Mr. A. Murat, Baton Rouge, in the New Orleans "Bee," June 20, 1837.	"Ranaway, the negro Manuel, *much marked with irons.*"
Mr. Jordan Abbott, in the "Huntsville Democrat," Nov. 17, 1838.	"Ranaway, a negro boy named Daniel, about nineteen years old, and was *hand-cuffed.*"
Mr. J. Alacoin, No. 177 Ann street, New Orleans, in the "Bee," August 11, 1838.	"Ranaway, the negress Fanny—had on an *iron band about her neck.*"
Menard Brothers, parish of Bernard, Louisiana, in the N. O. "Bee," August 18, 1838.	"Ranaway, a negro named John—having an *iron around his right foot.*"
Messrs. J. L. and W. H. Bolton, Shelby county, Tennessee, in the "Memphis Enquirer," June 7, 1837.	"Absconded, a colored boy named Peter—had an *iron round his neck* when he went away."
H. Gridly, sheriff of Adams county, Mi., in the "Memphis (Tenn.) Times," September, 1834.	"Was committed to jail, a negro boy—had on a *large neck iron* with a *huge pair of horns* and a *large bar or band of iron* on his left leg."
Mr. Lambre, in the "Natchitoches (La.) Herald," March 29, 1837.	"Ranaway, the negro boy Teams—he had on his neck *an iron collar.*"

WITNESSES	TESTIMONY
Mr. Ferdinand Lemos, New Orleans, in the "Bee," January 29, 1838.	"Ranaway, the negro George—he had on *his neck an iron collar*, the branches of which had been taken off."
Mr. T. J. De Yampert, merchant, Mobile, Alabama, of the firm of De Yampert, King & Co., in the "Mobile Chronicle," June 15, 1838.	"Ranaway, a negro boy about *twelve* years old—had round his neck *a chain dog-collar,* with 'De Yampert' engraved on it."
J. H. Hand, jailor, St. Francisville, La., in the "Louisiana Chronicle," July 26, 1837.	"Committed to jail, slave John—has several scars on his wrists, occasioned, as he says, by *handcuffs.*"
Mr. Charles Curcner, New Orleans, in the "Bee," July 2, 1833.	"Ranaway, the negro, Hown—has a ring of iron on his left foot. Also, Grisee, his *wife,* having a *ring and chain on the left leg.*"
Mr. P. T. Manning, Huntsville, Alabama, in the "Huntsville Advocate," Oct. 23, 1838.	"Ranaway, a negro boy named James— said boy was *ironed* when he left me."
Mr. William L. Lambeth, Lynchburg, Virginia, in the "Moulton [Ala.] Whig," January 30, 1836.	"Ranaway, Jim—had on when he escaped a pair of *chain handcuffs.*"
Mr. D. F. Guex, Secretary of the Steam Cotton Press Company, New Orleans, in the "Commercial Bulletin," May 27, 1837.	"Ranaway, Edmund Coleman—it is supposed he must have *iron shackles on his ankles.*"
Mr. Francis Durett, Lexington, Alabama, in the "Huntsville Democrat," March 8, 1838.	"Ranaway——, a mulatto—had on when he left, a *pair of handcuffs* and a *pair of drawing chains.*"

WITNESSES	TESTIMONY
B. W. Hodges, jailor, Pike county, Alabama, in the "Montgomery Advertiser," Sept. 29, 1837.	"Committed to jail, a man who calls his name John—he has a *clog of iron on his right foot which will weigh four or five pounds.*"
P. Bayhi, captain of police, in the N. O. "Bee," June 9, 1838.	"Detained at the police jail, the negro wench Myra—has several marks of *lashing,* and has *irons on her feet.*"
Mr. Charles Kernin, parish of Jefferson, Louisiana, in the N. O. "Bee," August 11, 1837.	"Ranaway, Betsey—when she left she had on her *neck an iron collar.*"

The foregoing advertisements are sufficient for our purpose, scores of similar ones may be gathered from the newspapers of the slave states every month.

To the preceding testimony of slaveholders, published by themselves, and vouched for by their own signatures, we subjoin the following testimony of other witnesses to the same point.

JOHN M. NELSON, Esq., a native of Virginia, now a highly respected citizen of Highland county, Ohio, and member of the Presbyterian Church in Hillsborough, in a recent letter states the following:—

"In Staunton, Va., at the house of Mr. Robert M'Dowell, a merchant of that place, I once saw a colored woman, of intelligent and dignified appearance, who appeared to be attending to the business of the house, with an *iron collar* around her neck, with horns or prongs extending out on either side, and up, until they met at something like a foot above her head, at which point there was a bell attached. This *yoke,* as they called it, I understood was to prevent her from running away, or to punish her for having done so. I had frequently seen *men* with iron collars, but this was the first instance that I recollect to have seen a *female* thus degraded."

Major HORACE NYE, an elder in the Presbyterian Church at Putnam, Muskingum county, Ohio, in a letter, dated Dec. 5, 1838, makes the following statement:—

"Mr. WM. ARMSTRONG, of this place, who is frequently employed by our citizens as captain and supercargo of descending boats, whose word maybe relied on, has just made to me the following statement:—

"While laying at Alexandria, on Red River, Louisiana, he saw a slave brought to a blacksmith's shop and a collar of iron fastened round his neck, with two pieces rivetted to the sides, meeting some distance above his head. At the top of the arch, thus formed, was attached a large cow-bell, the motion of which, while walking the streets, made it necessary for the slave to hold his hand to one of its sides, to steady it.

"In New Orleans he saw several with iron collars, with horns attached to them. The first he saw had three prongs projecting from the collar ten or twelve inches, with the letter S on the end of each. He says iron collars are quite frequent there."

To the preceding Major Nye adds:—

"When I was about twelve years of age I lived at Marietta, in this state: I knew little of slaves, as there were few or none, at that time, in the part of Virginia opposite that place. But I remember seeing a slave who had run away from some place beyond my knowledge at that time: he had an iron collar round his neck, to which was a strap of iron rivetted to the collar, on each side, passing over the top of the head; and another strap, from the back side to the top of the first—thus inclosing the head on three sides. I looked on while the blacksmith severed the collar with a file, which, I think, took him more than an hour."

Rev. JOHN DUDLEY, Mount Morris, Michigan, resided as a teacher at the missionary station, among the Choctaws, in Mississippi, during the years 1830 and 31. In a letter just received Mr. Dudley says:—

"During the time I was on missionary ground, which was in 1830 and 31, I was frequently at the residence of the agent, who was a slaveholder.—I never knew of his treating his own slaves with cruelty; but the poor fellows who were escaping, and lodged with him when detected, found no clemency. I once saw there a fetter for '*the d—d runaways,*' the weight of which can be judged by its size. It was at least three inches wide, half an inch thick, and something over a foot long. At this time I saw a poor fellow compelled to work in the field, at 'logging,' with such a galling fetter on his ankles. To prevent it from wearing his ankles, a string was tied to the centre, by which the victim suspended it when he walked, with one hand, and with the other carried his burden. Whenever he lifted, the fetter rested on his bare ankles. If he lost his balance and made a misstep, which must very often occur in lifting and rolling logs, the torture of his fetter was severe. Thus he was doomed to work while wearing the torturing iron, day after day, and at night he was confined in the runaways' jail. Some time after this, I saw the same dejected, heart-broken creature obliged to wait on the other hands, who were husking corn. The privilege of sitting with the others was too much for him to enjoy; he was made to hobble from house to barn and barn to house, to carry food and drink for the rest. He passed round the end of the house where I was sitting with the agent: he seemed to take no notice of me, but fixed his eyes on his tormentor till he passed quite by us."

Mr. ALFRED WILKINSON, member of the Baptist Church in Skeneateles, N. Y., and an assessor of that town, testifies as follows:—

"I stayed in New Orleans three weeks: during that time there used to pass by where I stayed a number of slaves, each with an iron band around his ankle, a chain attached to it, and an eighteen pound ball at the end. They were employed in wheeling dirt with a wheelbarrow; they would put the ball into the barrow when they moved.— I recollect one day, that I counted nineteen of them, sometimes there were not as many; they were driven by a slave, with a long lash, as if they were beasts. These, I learned, were runaway slaves from the plantations above New Orleans.

"There was also a negro woman, that used daily to come to the market with milk; she had an iron band around her neck, with three rods projecting from it, about sixteen inches long, crooked at the ends."

For the fact which follows we are indebted to Mr. SAMUEL HALL, a teacher in Marietta College, Ohio. We quote his letter.

"Mr. CURTIS, a journeyman cabinet-maker, of Marietta, relates the following, of which he was an eye witness. Mr. Curtis is every way worthy of credit.

"In September, 1837, at 'Milligan's Bend,' in the Mississippi river, I saw a negro with an iron band around his head, locked behind with a padlock. In the front, where it passed the mouth, there was a projection inward of an inch and a half, which entered the mouth.

"The overseer told me, he was so addicted to running away, it did not do any good to whip him for it. He said he kept this gag constantly on him, and intended to do so as long as he was on the plantation: so that, if he ran away, he could not eat, and would starve to death. The slave asked for drink in my presence; and the overseer made him lie down on his back, and turned water on his face two or three feet high, in order to torment him, as he could not swallow a drop.—The slave then asked permission to go to the river; which being granted, he thrust his face and head entirely under the water, that being the only way he could drink with his gag on. The gag was taken off when he took his food, and then replaced afterwards."

EXTRACT OF A LETTER FROM MRS. SOPHIA LITTLE, of Newport, Rhode Island, daughter of Hon. Asher Robbins, senator in Congress for that state.

"There was lately found, in the hold of a vessel engaged in the southern trade, by a person who was clearing it out, an iron collar, with three horns projecting from it. It seems that a young female slave, on whose slender neck was riveted this fiendish instrument of torture, ran away from her tyrant, and begged the captain to bring her off with him. This the captain refused to do; but unriveted the collar from her neck, and threw it away in the hold of the vessel. The collar is now at the anti-slavery office, Providence. To the truth of these facts Mr. WILLIAM H. REED, a gentleman of the highest moral character, is ready to vouch.

"Mr. Reed is in possession of many facts of cruelty witnessed by persons of veracity; but these witnesses are not willing to give their names. One case in particular he mentioned. Speaking with a certain captain, of the state of the slaves at the south, the captain contended that their punishments were often very *lenient*; and, as an instance of their excellent clemency, mentioned, that in one instance, not wishing to whip a slave, they sent him to a blacksmith, and had an iron band fastened around him, with three long projections reaching above his head; and this he wore some time."

EXTRACT OF A LETTER FROM MR. JONATHAN F. BALDWIN, of Lorain county, Ohio. Mr. B. was formerly a merchant in Massillon, Ohio, and an elder in the Presbyterian Church there.

"DEAR BROTHER,—In conversation with Judge Lyman, of Litchfield county, Connecticut, last June, he stated to me, that several years since he was in Columbia, South Carolina, and observing a colored man lying on the floor of a blacksmith's shop, as he was passing it, his curiosity led him in. He learned the man was a slave and rather unmanageable. Several men were attempting to detach from his ankle an iron which had been bent around it.

"The iron was a piece of a flat bar of the ordinary size from the forge hammer, and bent around the ancle, the ends meeting, and forming a hoop of about the diameter of the leg. There was one or more strings attached to the iron and extending up around his neck, evidently so to suspend it as to prevent its galling by its weight when at work, yet it had galled or gripped till the leg had swollen out beyond the iron and inflamed and suppurated, so that the leg for a considerable distance above and below the iron, was a mass of putrefaction, the most loathsome of any wound he had ever witnessed on any living creature. The slave lay on his back on the floor, with his leg on an anvil which sat also on the floor, one man had a chisel used for splitting iron, and another struck it with a sledge, to drive it between the ends of the hoop and separate it so that it might be taken off. Mr. Lyman said that the man swung the sledge over his shoulders as if splitting iron, and struck many blows before he succeeded in parting the ends of the iron at all, the bar was so large and stubborn—at length they spread it as far as they could without driving the chisel so low as to ruin the leg. The slave, a man of twenty-five years, perhaps, whose countenance was the index of a mind ill adapted to the degradations of slavery, never uttered a word or a groan in all the process, but the copious flow of sweat from every pore, the dreadful contractions and distortions of every muscle in his body, showed clearly the great amount of his sufferings; and all this while, such was the diseased state of the limb, that at every blow, the bloody, corrupted matter gushed out in all directions several feet, in such profusion as literally to cover a large area around the anvil. After various other fruitless attempts to spread the iron, they concluded it was necessary to weaken by filing before it could be got off, which he left them attempting to do."

Mr. WILLIAM DROWN, a well known citizen of Rhode Island, formerly of Providence, who has traveled in nearly all the slave states, thus testifies in a recent letter:

"I recollect seeing large gangs of slaves, generally a considerable number in each gang, being chained, passing westward over the mountains from Maryland, Virginia, &c. to the Ohio. On that river I have frequently seen flat boats loaded with them, and their keepers armed with pistols and dirks to guard them.

"At New Orleans I recollect seeing gangs of slaves that were driven out every day, the Sabbath not excepted, to work on the streets. These had heavy chains to connect two or more together, and some had iron collars and yokes, &c. The noise as they walked, or worked in their chains, was truly dreadful."

Rev. THOMAS SAVAGE, pastor of the Congregational Church at Bedford, New Hampshire, who was for some years a resident of Mississippi and Louisiana, gives the following fact, in a letter dated January 9, 1839.

"In 1819, while employed as an instructor at Second Creek, near Natchez, Mississippi, I resided on a plantation where I witnessed the following circumstance. One of the slaves was in the habit of running away. He had been repeatedly taken, and repeatedly whipped, with great severity, but to no purpose. He would still seize the first opportunity to escape from the plantation. At last his owner declared, I'll fix him, I'll put a stop to his running away. He accordingly took him to a blacksmith, and had an *iron head-frame* made for him, which may be called lock-jaw, from the use that was made of it. It had a lock and key, and was so constructed, that when on the head and locked, the slave could not open his mouth to take food, and the design was to prevent his running away. But the device proved unavailing. He was soon missing, and whether by his own desperate effort, or the aid of others, contrived to sustain himself with food; but he was at last taken, and if my memory serves me, his life was soon terminated by the cruel treatment to which he was subjected."

The Western Luminary, a religious paper published at Lexington, Kentucky, in an editorial article, in the summer of 1833, says:

"A few weeks since we gave an account of a company of men, women and children, part of whom were manacled, passing through our streets. Last week, a number of slaves were driven through the main street of our city, among whom were a number manacled together, two abreast, all connected by, and supporting a *heavy iron chain,* which extended the whole length of the line."

TESTIMONY OF A VIRGINIAN

The *name* of this witness cannot be published, as it would put him in peril; but his *credibility* is vouched for by the Rev. EZRA FISHER,

pastor of the Baptist Church, Quincy, Illinois, and Dr. RICHARD
EELS, of the same place. These gentlemen say of him, "We have great
confidence in his integrity, discretion, and strict Christian principle."
He says—

"About five years ago, I remember to have passed, in *a single day,*
four droves of slaves for the south west; the largest drove had 350
slaves in it, and the smallest upwards of 200. I counted 68 or 70 in
a single *coffle.* The '*coffle chain*' is a chain fastened at one end to the
centre of the bar of a pair of hand cuffs, which are fastened to the
right wrist of one, and the left wrist of another slave, they standing
abreast, and the chain between them. These are the head of the coffle.
The other end is passed through a ring in the bolt of the next handcuffs, and the slaves being manacled thus, two and two together,
walk up, and the coffle chain is passed, and they go up towards the
head of the coffle. Of course they are closer or wider apart in the
coffle, according to the number to be coffled, and to the length of
the chain. *I have seen* HUNDREDS *of droves and chain-coffles of this description,* and every coffle was a scene of misery and wo, of tears and
brokenness of heart."

Mr. SAMUEL HALL, a teacher in Marietta College, Ohio, gives, in
a late letter, the following statement of a fellow student, from Kentucky,
of whom he says, "he is a professor of religion, and worthy of entire
confidence."

"I have seen at least *fifteen* droves of 'human cattle,' passing by us
on their way to the south; and I do not recollect an exception, where
there were not more or less of them *chained* together."

Mr. GEORGE P. C. HUSSEY, of Fayetteville, Franklin county,
Pennsylvania, writes thus:

"I was born and raised in Hagerstown, Washington county,
Maryland, where slavery is perhaps milder than in any other part of
the slave states; and yet I have seen *hundreds* of colored men and
women chained together, two by two, and driven to the south. I have
seen slaves tied up and lashed till the blood ran down to their heels."

Mr. GIDDINGS, member of Congress from Ohio, in his speech in
the House of Representatives, Feb. 13, 1839, made the following
statement:

"On the beautiful avenue in front of the Capitol, members of
Congress, during this session, have been compelled to turn aside from

their path, to permit a coffle of slaves, males and females, *chained to each other by their necks,* to pass on their way to this *national slave market.*"

Testimony of JAMES K. PAULDING, Esq. the present Secretary of the United States' Navy.

In 1817, Mr. Paulding published a work, entitled "Letters from the South, written during an excursion in the summer of 1816." In the first volume of that work, page 128, Mr. P. gives the following description:

"The sun was shining out very hot—and in turning the angle of the road, we encountered the following group: first, a little cart drawn by one horse, in which five or six half naked black children were tumbled like pigs together. The cart had no covering, and they seemed to have been broiled to sleep. Behind the cart marched three black women, with head, neck and breasts uncovered, and without shoes or stockings: next came three men, bare-headed, and *chained together with an ox-chain.* Last of all, came a white man on horse back, carrying his pistols in his belt, and who, as we passed him, had the impudence to look us in the face without blushing. At a house where we stopped a little further on, we learned that he had bought these miserable beings in Maryland, and was marching them in this manner to one of the more southern states. Shame on the State of Maryland! and I say, shame on the State of Virginia! and every state through which this wretched cavalcade was permitted to pass! I do say, that when they (the slaveholders) permit such flagrant and indecent outrages upon humanity as that I have described; when they sanction a villain in thus marching half naked women and men, loaded with chains, without being charged with any crime but that of being *black,* from one section of the United States to another, hundreds of miles in the face of day, they disgrace themselves, and the country to which they belong."*

---

* The fact that Mr. Paulding, in the reprint of these "Letters," in 1835, *struck out this passage* with all others disparaging to slavery and its supporters, does not impair the force of his testimony, however much it may sink the man. Nor will the next generation regard with any more reverence, his character as a *prophet,* because in the edition of 1835, two years after the American Anti-Slavery Society was formed, and when its auxiliaries were numbered by hundreds, he inserted a *prediction,* that such movements would be made at the North, with most disastrous results. "Wot ye not that such a man as I can certainly divine!" Mr. Paulding has already been taught by Judge Jay, that he who aspires to the fame of an oracle, without its inspiration, must resort to

III. BRANDINGS, MAIMINGS, GUN-SHOT WOUNDS, &c

The slaves are often branded with hot irons, pursued with fire arms and *shot,* hunted with dogs and torn by them, shockingly maimed with knives, dirks, &c.; have their ears cut off, their eyes knocked out, their bones dislocated and broken with bludgeons, their fingers and toes cut off, their faces and other parts of their persons disfigured with scars and gashes, *besides* those made with the lash.

We shall adopt, under this head, the same course as that pursued under previous ones,—first give the testimony of the slaveholders themselves, to the mutilations, &c. by copying their own graphic descriptions of them, in advertisements published under their own names, and in newspapers published in the slave states, and, generally, in their own immediate vicinity. We shall, as heretofore, insert only so much of each advertisement as will be necessary to make the point intelligible.

WITNESSES	TESTIMONY
Mr. Micajah Ricks, Nash County, North Carolina, in the Raleigh "Standard," July 18, 1838.	"Ranaway, a negro woman and two children; a few days before she went off, *I burnt her with a hot iron,* on the left side of her face, *I tried to make the letter M.*"
Mr. Asa B. Metcalf, Kingston, Adams Co., Mi., in the "Natchez Courier," June 15, 1832.	"Ranaway, Mary, a black woman, has a *scar* on her back and right arm near the shoulder, *caused by a rifle ball.*"
Mr. William Overstreet, Benton, Yazoo Co., Mi., in the "Lexington (Kentucky) Observer," July 22, 1838.	"Ranaway, a negro man named Henry, *his left eye out,* some scars from a *dirk* on and under his left arm, and *much scarred* with the whip."
Mr. R. P. Carney, Clark Co., Ala., in the "Mobile Register," Dec. 22, 1832.	"One hundred dollars reward for a negro fellow Pompey, 40 years old, he is *branded* on the *left jaw.*"
Mr. J. Guyler, Savannah, Georgia, in the "Republican," April 12, 1837.	"Ranaway, Laman, an old negro man, grey, has *only one eye.*"

other expedients to prevent detection, than the clumsy one of *antedating* his responses.

WITNESSES	TESTIMONY
J. A. Brown, jailor, Charleston, South Carolina, in the "Mercury," Jan. 12, 1837.	"Committed to jail a negro man, has *no toes* on his left foot."
Mr. J. Scrivener, Herring Bay, Anne Arundel Co., Maryland, in the "Annapolis Republican," April 18, 1837.	"Ranaway negro man Elijah, has a scar on his left cheek, apparently occasioned by *a shot.*"
Madame Burvant, corner of Chartres and Toulouse streets, New Orleans, in the "Bee," Dec. 21, 1838.	"Ranaway a negro woman named Rachel, has *lost all her toes* except the large one."
Mr. O. W. Lains, in the "Helena (Ark.) Journal," June 1, 1833.	"Ranaway Sam, he was *shot* a short time since, through the hand, and has *several shots in his left arm and side.*"
Mr. R. W. Sizer, in the "Grand Gulf [Mi.] Advertiser," July 8, 1837.	"Ranaway my negro man Dennis, said negro has been *shot* in the left arm between the shoulders and elbow, which has paralyzed the left hand."
Mr. Nicholas Edmunds, in the "Petersburgh [Va.] Intelligencer," May 22, 1838,	"Ranaway my negro man named Simon, he *has been shot badly* in his back and right arm."
Mr. J. Bishop, Bishopville, Sumpter District, South Carolina, in the "Camden [S. C.] Journal," March 4, 1837.	"Ranaway a negro named Arthur, has a considerable *scar* across his *breast* and *each arm,* made by a knife; loves to talk much of the goodness of God."
Mr. S. Neyle, Little Ogeechee, Georgia, in the "Savannah Republican," July 3, 1837.	"Ranaway George, he has a *sword cut* lately received on his left arm."
Mrs. Sarah Walsh, Mobile, Ala., in the "Georgia Journal," March 27, 1837.	"Twenty five dollars reward for my man Isaac, he has a scar on his forehead caused by a *blow,* and one on his back made by *a shot from a pistol.*"

WITNESSES	TESTIMONY
Mr. J. P. Ashford, Adams Co., Mi., in the "Natchez Courier," August 24, 1838.	"Ranaway a negro girl called Mary, has a small scar over her eye, *a good many teeth missing,* the letter A. *is branded an her cheek and forehead.*"
Mr. Ely Townsend, Pike Co., Ala., in the "Pensacola Gazette," Sep. 16, 1837.	"Ranaway negro Ben, has a scar on his right hand, his thumb and fore finger being injured by being *shot* last fall, a part of *the bone came out,* he has also one or two *large scars* on his back and hips."
S. B. Murphy, jailer, Irvington, Ga., in the "Milledgeville Journal," May 29, 1838.	"Committed a negro man, is *very badly shot in the right side* and right hand."
Mr. A. Luminais, Parish of St. John, Louisiana, in the New Orleans "Bee," March 3, 1838.	"Detained at the jail, a mulatto named Tom, has a *scar* on the right cheek and appears to have been *burned with powder* on the face."
Mr. Isaac Johnson, Pulaski Co., Georgia, in the "Milledgeville Journal," June 19, 1838.	"Ranaway a negro man named Ned, *three of his fingers* are drawn into the palm of his hand by a *cut,* has a *scar* on the back of his neck nearly half round, done by a *knife.*"
Mr. Thomas Hudnall, Madison Co., Mi., in the "Vicksburg Register," September 5, 1838.	"Ranaway a negro named Hambleton, *limps* on his left foot where he was *shot* a few weeks ago, while runaway."
Mr. John McMurrain, Columbus, Ga., in the "Southern Sun," August 7, 1838.	"Ranaway a negro boy named Mose, he has a *wound* in the right shoulder near the back bone, which was occasioned by *a rifle shot.*"
Mr. Moses Orme, Annapolis, Maryland, in the "Annapolis Republican," June 20, 1837.	"Ranaway my negro man Bill, he has a *fresh wound in his head* above his ear."
William Strickland, Jailor, Kershaw District, S. C., in the "Camden [S. C] Courier," July 8, 1837.	"Committed to jail a negro, says his name is Cuffee, he is lame in one knee, occasioned *by a shot.*"

WITNESSES	TESTIMONY
The Editor of the "Grand Gulf Advertiser," Dec. 7, 1838.	"Ranaway Joshua, his thumb is off of his left hand."
Mr. William Bateman, in the "Grand Gulf Advertiser," Dec. 7, 1838.	"Ranaway William, *scar* over his left eye, one between his eye brows, one on his breast, and his right leg has been *broken*."
Mr. B. G. Simmons, in the "Southern Argus," May 30, 1837.	"Ranaway Mark, his left arm has been *broken*, right *leg also*."
Mr. James Artop, in the "Macon [Ga.] Messenger," May 25, 1837.	"Ranaway, Caleb, 50 years old, has an awkward gait occasioned by his being *shot* in the thigh."
J. L. Jolley, Sheriff of Clinton Co, Mi., in the "Clinton Gazette," July 23, 1836.	"Was committed to jail a negro man, says his name is Josiah, his back very much scarred by the whip, and *branded on the thigh and hips, in three or four places,* thus (J. M.) the *rim of his right ear has been bit or cut off.*"
Mr. Thomas Ledwith, Jacksonville East Florida, in the "Charleston [S. C] Courier," Sept. 1, 1838.	"Fifty dollars reward, for my fellow Edward, he has a *scar* on the corner of his mouth, two *cuts* on and under his arm, and the *letter E on his arm.*"
Mr. Joseph James, Sen., Pleasant Ridge, Paulding Co., Ga., in the "Milledgeville Union," Nov. 7, 1837.	"Ranaway, negro boy Ellic, has a *scar* on one of his arms *from the bite of a dog.*"
Mr. W. Riley, Orangeburg District, South Carolina, in the "Columbia [S.C.] Telescope," Nov. 11, 1837.	"Ranaway a negro man, has a *scar* on the ankle produced by a *burn*, and a *mark on his arm* resembling the letter S."
Mr. Samuel Mason, Warren Co, Mi., in the "Vicksburg Register," July 18, 1838.	"Ranaway, a negro man named Allen, he has scar on his breast, also a scar under the left eye, and has *two buck shot in his right arm.*"

WITNESSES	TESTIMONY
Mr. F. L. C. Edwards, in the "Southern Telegraph," Sept. 25, 1837.	"Ranaway from the plantation of James Surgette, the following negroes, Randal, *has one ear cropped;* Bob, *has lost one eye,* Kentucky Tom, *has one jaw broken."*
Mr. Stephen M. Jackson, in the "Vicksburg Register," March 10, 1837.	"Ranaway, Anthony, one of his *ears cut off,* and his left hand cut with an axe."
Philip Honerton, deputy sheriff of Halifax Co., Virginia, Jan. 1837.	"Was committed, a negro man, has a *scar* on his right side by a burn, one on his knee, and one on the calf of his leg *by the bite of a dog."*
Stearns & Co. No. 28, New Levee, New Orleans, in the "Bee," March 22, 1837.	"Absconded, the mulatto boy Tom, his fingers *scarred* on his right hand, and has a *scar* on his right cheek."
Mr. John W. Walton, Greensboro, Ala., in the "Alabama Beacon," Dec. 13, 1838.	"Ranaway my black boy Frazier, with a *scar* below and one above his right ear."
Mr. R. Furman, Charleston, S. C., in the "Charleston Mercury," Jan. 12, 1839.	"Ranaway, Dick, about 19, has lost the small toe of one foot."
Mr. John Tart, Sen. in the "Fayetteville [N. C.] Observer," Dec. 26, 1838.	"Stolen a mulatto boy, *ten* years old, he has a *scar* over his eye which was made by an axe."
Mr. Richard Overstreet, Brook Neal, Campbell Co., Virginia, in the "Danville [Va.] Reporter," Dec. 21, 1838.	"Absconded my negro man Coleman, has a *very large scar* on one of his legs, also one on *each* arm, by a burn, and his heels have been frosted."
The editor of the New Orleans "Bee," in that paper, August 27, 1837.	"Fifty dollars reward, for the negro Jim Blake—has a *piece cut out of each ear,* and the middle finger of the left hand *cut off* to the second joint."

WITNESSES	TESTIMONY
Mr. Bryant Johnson, Fort Valley, Houston county, Georgia, in the Milledgeville "Union," Oct. 2, 1838.	"Ranaway, a negro woman named Maria—has a scar on one side of her cheek, by a *cut*—some scars on her back."
Mr. Lemuel Miles, Steen's Creek, Rankin county, Mi., in the "Southern Sun," Sept. 22, 1838.	"Ranaway, Gabriel—has *two or three scars across his neck* made with a knife."
Mr. Bezou, New Orleans, in the "Bee," May 23, 1838.	"Ranaway, the mulatto wench Mary— has a *cut on the left arm, a scar on the shoulder, and two upper teeth missing.*"
Mr. James Kimborough, Memphis, Tenn., in the "Memphis Enquirer," July 13, 1838.	"Ranaway, a negro boy, named Jerry— has a *scar* on his right cheek two inches long, from the cut of a knife."
Mr. Robert Beasley, Macon, Georgia, in the "Georgia Messenger," July 27, 1837.	"Ranaway, my man Fountain—has *holes in his ears,* a *scar* on the right side of his forehead—has been *shot in the hind parts of his legs*—is marked on the back with the whip."
Mr. B. G. Barrer, St. Louis, Missouri, in the "Republican," Sept. 6, 1837.	"Ranaway, a negro man named Jarrett— *has a scar* on the under part of one of his arms, occasioned by a wound from a knife."
Mr. John D. Turner, near Norfolk, Virginia, in the "Norfolk Herald," June 27, 1838.	"Ranaway, a negro by the name of Joshua—he has a cut across one of his ears, which he will conceal as much as possible— one of his ankles is *enlarged by an ulcer.*"
Mr. William Stansell, Picksville, Ala., in the "Huntsville Democrat," August 29, 1837.	"Ranaway, negro boy Harper—*has a scar* on one of his hips in the form of a G."
Hon. Ambrose H. Sevier, Senator in Congress, from Arkansas, in the "Vicksburg Register," of Oct. 13, 1837.	"Ranaway, Bob, a slave—has a *scar across his breast,* another on the *right side of his head*—his back is *much scarred* with the whip."

WITNESSES	TESTIMONY
Mr. R. A. Greene, Milledgeville, Georgia, in the "Macon Messenger," July 27, 1837.	"Two hundred and fifty dollars reward, for my negro man Jim—he is much marked with *shot* in his right thigh,—the shot entered on the outside, half way between the hip and knee joints."
Benjamin Russel, deputy sheriff, Bibb county, Ga., in the "Macon Telegraph," December 25, 1837.	"Brought to jail, John—*left ear cropt.*"
Hon. H. Hitchcock, Mobile, judge of the Supreme Court, in the "Commercial Register," Oct. 27, 1837.	"Ranaway, the slave Ellis—he has *lost one of his ears.*"
Mrs. Elizabeth L. Carter, near Groveton, Prince William county, Virginia, in the "National Intelligencer," Washington, D. C., June 10, 1837.	"Ranaway, a negro man, Moses—he has *lost a part* of one of his ears."
Mr. William D. Buckels, Natchez, Mi., in the "Natchez Courier," July 28, 1838.	"Taken up, a negro man—is *very much scarred* about the face and body, and has the left *ear bit off.*"
Mr. Walter R. English, Monroe county, Ala., in the "Mobile Chronicle," Sept. 2, 1837.	"Ranaway, my slave Lewis—he has lost a *piece of one ear,* and a *part of one of his fingers,* a *part of one of his toes* is also lost."
Mr. James Saunders, Grany Spring, Hawkins county, Tenn., in the "Knoxville Register," June 6, 1838.	"Ranaway, a black girl named Mary—has a *scar* on her cheek, and the end of one of her toes *cut off.*"
Mr. John Jenkins, St. Joseph's, Florida, captain of the steamboat Ellen, "Apalachicola Gazette," June 7, 1838.	"Ranaway, the negro boy Cæsar—he has *but one eye.*"

WITNESSES	TESTIMONY
Mr. Peter Hanson, Lafayette city, La., in the New Orleans "Bee," July 28, 1838.	"Ranaway, the negress Martha—she has *lost her right eye.*"
Mr. Orren Ellis, Georgeville, Mi., in the "North Alabamian," Sept. 15, 1837.	"Ranaway, George—has had the lower part *of one of his ears bit off.*"
Mr. Zadock Sawyer, Cuthbert, Randolph county, Georgia, in the "Milledgeville Union," Oct. 9, 1838.	"Ranaway, my negro Tom—has a piece *bit off the top of his right ear,* and his little finger is *stiff.*"
Mr. Abraham Gray, Mount Morino, Pike county, Ga., in the "Milledgeville Union," Oct. 9, 1838.	"Ranaway, my mulatto woman Judy—she has had her *right arm broke.*"
S. B. Tuston, jailer, Adams county, Mi., in the "Natchez Courier," June 15, 1833.	"Was committed to jail, a negro man named Bill—has had the *thumb of his left hand split.*"
Mr. Joshua Antrim, Nineveh, Warren county, Virginia, in the "Winchester Virginian," July 11, 1837.	"Ranaway, a mulatto man named Joe—his fingers on the left hand are *partly amputated.*"
J. B. Randall, jailor, Marietta, Cobb county, Ga., in the "Southern Recorder," Nov. 6, 1838.	"Lodged in jail, a negro man named Jupiter—is very *lame in his left hip,* so that he can hardly walk—has lost a joint of the middle finger of his left hand."
Mr. John N. Dillahunty, Woodville, Mi., in the "N. O. Commercial Bulletin," July 21, 1837.	"Ranaway, Bill—has a scar over one eye, also one on his leg, from *the bite of a dog*—has a *burn on his buttock, from a piece of hot iron in shape of a T.*"
William K. Ratcliffe, sheriff, Frankin county, Mi., in the "Natchez Free Trader," August 23, 1838.	"Committed to jail, a negro named Mike—*his left ear off.*"

WITNESSES	TESTIMONY
Mr. Preston Halley, Barnwell, South Carolina, in the "Augusta [Ga.] Chronicle," July 27, 1838.	"Ranaway, my negro man Levi—his left hand has been *burnt,* and I think the end of his fore finger *is off.*"
Mr. Welcome H. Robbins, St. Charles county, Mo., in the "St. Louis Republican," June 30, 1838.	"Ranaway, a negro named Washington—has *lost a part of his middle finger and the end of his little finger.*"
G. Gourdon & Co. druggists, corner of Rampart and Hospital streets, New Orleans, in the "Commercial Bulletin," Sept. 13, 1838.	"Ranaway, a negro named David Drier—has *two toes cut.*"
Mr. William Brown, in the "Grand Gulf Advertiser," August 29, 1838.	"Ranaway, Edmund—has a *scar* on his right temple, and under his right eye, and *holes in both ears.*"
Mr. James McDonnell, Talbot county, Georgia, in the "Columbus Enquirer," Jan. 18, 1838.	"Runaway, a negro boy *twelve or thirteen* years old—has a scar on his left cheek *from the bite of a dog.*"
Mr. John W. Cherry, Marengo county, Ala., in the "Mobile Register," June 15, 1838.	"Fifty dollars reward, for my negro man John—he has a considerable scar on his *throat,* done with a *knife.*"
Mr. Thos. Brown, Roane co., Tenn., in the "Knoxville Register," Sept. 12, 1838.	"Twenty-five dollars reward, for my man John—the *tip* of his nose is *bit off.*"
Messrs. Taylor, Lawton & Co., Charleston, South Carolina, in the "Mercury," Nov. 1838.	"Ranaway, a negro fellow called Hover—has a *cut* above the right eye."
Mr. Louis Schmidt, Taubourg, Sivaudais, La., in the New Orleans "Bee," Sept. 5, 1837.	"Ranaway, the negro man Hardy—has a *scar* on the upper lip, and another made with a *knife* on his neck."

WITNESSES	TESTIMONY
W. M. Whitehead, Natchez, in the "New Orleans Bulletin," July 21, 1837.	"Ranaway, Henry—has half of one *ear bit off*."
Mr. Conrad Salvo, Charleston, South Carolina, in the "Mercury," August 10, 1837.	"Ranaway, my negro man Jacob—he has but *one eye*."
William Baker, jailer, Shelby county, Ala., in the "Montgomery (Ala.) Advertiser," Oct. 5, 1838.	"Committed to jail, Ben—his *left thumb off* at the first joint."
Mr. S. N. Hite, Camp street, New Orleans, in the "Bee," Feb. 19, 1838.	"Twenty-five dollars reward for the negro slave Sally—walks as though *crippled* in the back."
Mr. Stephen M. Richards, Whitesburg, Madison county, Alabama, in the "Huntsville Democrat," Sept. 8, 1838.	"Ranaway, a negro man named Dick—has a *little finger off* the right hand."
Mr. A. Brove, parish of St. Charles, La., in the "New Orleans Bee," Feb. 19, 1838.	"Ranaway, the negro Patrick—has his little finger of the right hand *cut close to the hand*."
Mr. Needham Whitefield, Aberdeen, Mi., in the "Memphis (Tenn.) Enquirer," June 15, 1838.	"Ranaway, Joe Dennis—has a small *notch* in one of his ears."
Col. M. J. Sheith, Charleston, South Carolina, in the "Mercury," Nov. 27, 1837.	"Ranaway, Dick—has *lost the little toe* of one of his feet."
Mr. R. Lancette, Haywood, North Carolina, in the "Raleigh Register," April 30, 1838.	"Escaped, my negro man Eaton—his *little finger* of the right hand has been *broke*."

WITNESSES	TESTIMONY
Mr. G. C. Richardson, Owen Station, Mo., in the St. Louis "Republican," May 5, 1838.	"Ranaway, my negro man named Top—has had one of his *legs broken*."
Mr. E. Han, La Grange, Fayette county, Tenn., in the Gallatin "Union," June 23, 1837.	"Ranaway, negro boy Jack—has a small *crop out of his left ear*."
D. Herring, warden of Baltimore city jail, in the "Marylander," Oct. 6, 1837.	"Was committed to jail, a negro man—has *two scars* on his forehead, and the *top of his left ear cut off*."
Mr. James Marks, near Natchitoches, La., in the "Natchitoches Herald," July 21, 1838.	"Stolen, a negro man named Winter—has a *notch* cut out of the left ear, and the mark *of four or five buck shot* on his legs."
Mr. James Barr, Amelia Court House, Virginia, in the "Norfolk Herald," Sept. 12, 1838.	"Ranaway, a negro man—*scar back of his left eye,* as if from the *cut* of a knife."
Mr. Isaac Michell, Wilkinson county, Georgia, in the "Augusta Chronicle," Sept. 21, 1837.	"Ranaway, negro man Buck—has a very *plain mark* under his ear on his jaw, about the size of a dollar, having been *inflicted by a knife*."
Mr. P. Bayhi, captain of the police, Suburb Washington, third municipality, New Orleans, in the "Bee," Oct. 13, 1837.	"Detained at the jail, the negro boy Hermon—has a scar below his left ear, from the *wound of a knife*."
Mr. Willie Paterson, Clinton, Jones county, Ga., in the "Darien Telegraph," Dec. 5, 1837.	"Ranaway, a negro man by the name of John—he has a *scar* across his cheek, and one on his right arm, apparently done with a *knife*."
Mr. Samuel Ragland, Triana, Madison county, Alabama, in the "Huntsville Advocate," Dec. 23, 1837.	"Ranaway, Isham—has a *scar* upon the breast and upon the under lip, from the *bite of a dog*."

WITNESSES	TESTIMONY
Mr. Moses E. Bush, near Clayton, Ala., in the "Columbus [Ga.] Enquirer," July 5, 1838.	"Ranaway, a negro man—has a *scar* on his hip and on his breast, and *two front teeth out*."
C. W. Wilkins, sheriff, Baldwin Co, Ala., in the "Mobile Advertiser," Sept. 22, 1837.	"Committed to jail, a negro man, he is *crippled* in the right leg."
Mr. James H. Taylor, Charleston, South Carolina, in the "Courier," August 7, 1837.	"Absconded, a colored boy, named Peter, *lame* in the right leg."
N. M. C. Robinson, jailer, Columbus, Georgia, in the "Columbus (Ga.) Enquirer," August 2, 1838.	"Brought to jail, a negro man, his left ankle has been *broke*."
Mr. Littlejohn Rynes, Hinds Co., Mi., in the "Natchez Courier," August 17, 1838.	"Ranaway, a negro man named Jerry, has a small piece *cut out of the top of each ear*."
The Heirs of J. A. Alston, near Georgetown, South Carolina, in the "Georgetown [S. C.] Union," June 17, 1837.	"Absconded a negro named Cuffee, has *lost one finger;* has an *enlarged leg*."
A. S. Ballinger, Sheriff, Johnston Co, North Carolina, in the "Raleigh Standard," Oct. 18, 1838.	"Committed to jail, a negro man; has a *very sore leg*."
Mr. Thomas Crutchfield, Atkins, Tenn., in the "Tennessee Journal," Oct. 17, 1838.	"Ranaway, my mulatto boy Cy, has but *one hand,* all the fingers of his right hand were *burnt* off when young."
J. A. Brown, jailer, Orangeburg, South Carolina, in the "Charleston Mercury," July 18, 1838.	"Was committed to jail, a negro named Bob, appears to be *crippled* in the right leg."

WITNESSES	TESTIMONY
S. B. Turton, jailer, Adams Co., Miss., in the "Natchez Courier," Sept. 28, 1828.	"Was committed to jail, a negro man, has his *left thigh broke*."
Mr. John H. King, High street, Georgetown, in the "National Intelligencer," August 1, 1837.	"Ranaway, my negro man, he has the *end of one* of his fingers *broken*."
Mr. John B. Fox, Vicksburg, Miss., in the "Register," March 29, 1837.	"Ranaway, a yellowish negro boy named Torn, has a *notch* in the back of one of his ears."
Messrs. Fernandez and Whiting, auctioneers, New Orleans, in the "Bee," April 8, 1837.	"Will be sold Martha, aged nineteen, *has one eye out*."
Mr. Marshall Jett, Farrowsville, Fauquier Co., Virginia, in the "National Intelligencer," May 30, 1837.	"Ranaway, negro man Ephraim, has a *mark* over one of his eyes, occasioned by a *blow*."
S. B. Turton, jailer, Adams Co., Miss., in the "Natchez Courier," Oct. 12, 1838.	"Was committed a negro, calls himself Jacob, has been *crippled* in his right leg."
John Ford, sheriff of Mobile County, in the "Mississippian," Jackson, Mi., Dec. 28, 1838.	"Committed to jail, a negro man Cary, a *large scar on his forehead*."
E. W. Morris, sheriff of Warren County, in the "Vicksburg [Mi.] Register," March 28, 1838.	"Committed as a runaway, a negro man Jack, he has *several scars* on his face."
Mr. John P. Holcombe, in the "Charleston Mercury," April 17, 1828.	"Absented himself, his negro man Ben, *has scars* on his throat, occasioned by the *cut of a knife*."

WITNESSES	TESTIMONY
Mr. Willis Patterson, in the "Charleston Mercury," December 11, 1837.	"Ranaway, a negro man, John, a *scar* across his cheek, and one on his right arm, apparently done *with a knife.*"
Wm. Magee, sheriff, Mobile Co., in the "Mobile Register," Dec. 27, 1837.	"Committed to jail, a runaway slave, Alexander, a *scar* on his left cheek."
Mr. Henry M. McGregor, Prince George County, Maryland, in the "Alexandria [D.C.] Gazette," Feb. 6, 1838.	"Ranaway, negro Phil, *scar through the right eye brow,* part of the *middle toe* on the right foot *cut off.*"
Green B. Jourdan, Baldwin County, Ga., in the "Georgia Journal," April 18, 1837.	"Ranaway, John, has a *scar* on one of his hands extending from the wrist joint to the little finger, also a *scar* on one of his legs."
Messrs. Daniel and Goodman, New Orleans, in the "N. O. Bee," Feb. 2, 1838.	"Absconded, mulatto slave Alick, has a *large scar over* one of his cheeks."
Jeremiah Woodward, Goochland Co., Va., in the "Richmond Va. Whig," Jan. 30, 1838.	"200 DOLLARS REWARD for Nelson, has a *scar* on his forehead occasioned by a *burn,* and one on his lower lip and one about the knee."
Samuel Rawlins, Gwinet Co., Ga., in the "Columbus Sentinel," Nov. 29, 1838.	"Ranaway, a negro man and his wife, named Nat and Priscilla, he has a small *scar* on his left cheek, *two stiff fingers* on his right hand with a *running sore* on them; his wife has a *scar* on her left arm, and one *upper tooth out.*"

The reader perceives that we have under this head, as under previous ones, given to the testimony of the slaveholders themselves, under their own names, a precedence over that of all other witnesses. We now ask the reader's attention to the testimonies which follow. They are endorsed by responsible names—men who 'speak what they know, and testify what they have seen'—testimonies which show, that the slaveholders who wrote the preceding advertisements, describing the work of their own hands, in branding with hot irons, maiming, mutilating, cropping, shooting, knocking out the teeth and eyes of their slaves, breaking their bones, &c., have manifested, *as far as they have gone* in the description, a commendable fidelity to truth.

It is probable that some of the scars and maimings in the preceding advertisements were the result of accidents; and some *may be* the result of violence inflicted by the slaves upon each other. Without arguing that point, we say, these are the *facts*; whoever reads and ponders them, will need no argument to convince him, that the proposition which they have been employed to sustain, *cannot be shaken.* That any considerable portion of them were *accidental,* is totally improbable, from the nature of the case; and is in most instances disproved by the advertisements themselves. That they have not been produced by assaults of the slaves upon each other, is manifest from the fact, that injuries of that character inflicted by the slaves upon each other, are, as all who are familiar with the habits and condition of slaves well know, exceedingly rare; and of necessity must be so, from the constant action upon them of the strongest dissuasives from such acts that can operate on human nature.

Advertisements similar to the preceding may at any time be gathered by scores from the daily and weekly newspapers of the slave states. Before presenting the reader with further testimony in proof of the proposition at the head of this part of our subject, we remark, that some of the tortures enumerated under this and the preceding heads, are not in all cases inflicted by slaveholders as *punishments,* but sometimes merely as preventives of escape, for the greater security of their 'property.' Iron collars, chains, &c. are put upon slaves when they are driven or transported from one part of the country to another, in order to keep them from running away. Similar measures are often resorted to upon plantations. When the master or owner suspects a slave of plotting an escape, an iron collar with long 'horns,' or a bar of iron, or a ball and chain, are often fastened upon him, for the double purpose of retarding his flight, should he attempt it, and of serving as an easy means of detection.

Another inhuman method of *marking* slaves, so that they may be easily described and detected when they escape, is called cropping. In the preceding advertisements, the reader will perceive a number of cases, in which the runaway is described as '*cropt,*' or a '*notch cut in the ear, or a part or the whole of the ear cut off,*' &c.

Two years and a half since, the writer of this saw a letter, then just received by Mr. Lewis Tappan, of New York, containing a negro's ear cut off close to the head. The writer of the letter, who signed himself Thomas Aylethorpe, Montgomery, Alabama, sent it to Mr. Tappan as 'a specimen of a negro's ears,' and desired him to add it to his 'collection.'

Another method of *marking* slaves, is by drawing out or breaking off one or two *front teeth*—commonly the upper ones, as the mark would in that case be the more obvious. An instance of this kind the reader will recall in the testimony of Sarah M. Grimké, page 30, and of which she had *personal* knowledge; being well acquainted both with the inhuman master, (a distinguished citizen of South Carolina), by whose order the brutal deed was done, and with the poor young girl whose mouth was thus barbarously mutilated, to furnish a convenient mark by which to describe her in case of her elopement, as she had frequently run away.

The case stated by Miss G. serves to unravel what, to one uninitiated, seems quite a mystery: i. e. the frequency with which, in the advertisements of runaway slaves published in southern papers, they are described as having *one or two front teeth out*. Scores of such advertisements are in southern papers now on our table. We will furnish the reader with a dozen or two.

WITNESSES	TESTIMONY
Jesse Debruhl, sheriff, Richland District, "Columbia (S. C.) Telescope," Feb. 24, 1838.	"Committed to jail, Ned, about 25 years of age, has lost his *two upper front teeth*."
Mr. John Hunt, Black Water Bay, "Pensacola (Ga.) Gazette," October 14, 1837.	"100 DOLLARS REWARD, for Perry, *one under front tooth* missing, aged 23 years."
Mr. John Frederick, Branchville, Orangeburgh District, S. C. "Charleston [S. C.] Courier," June 12, 1837.	"10 DOLLARS REWARD, for Mary, *one* or *two upper teeth* out, about 25 years old."
Mr. Egbert A. Raworth, eight miles west of Nashville on the Charlotte road, "Daily Republican Banner," Nashville, Tennessee, April 30, 1838.	"Ranaway, Myal, 23 years old, one of his *fore teeth out*."

WITNESSES	TESTIMONY
Benjamin Russel, Deputy sheriff, Bibb Co., Ga., "Macon (Ga.) Telegraph," Dec. 25, 1837.	"Brought to jail John, 23 years old, *one fore tooth out*."
F. Wisner, Master of the Work-house, "Charleston (S. C.) Courier," Oct. 17, 1837.	"Committed to the Charleston Work-house, Tom, *two of his upper front teeth out*, about 30 years of age."
Mr. S. Neyle, "Savannah (Ga.) Republican," July 3, 1837.	"Ranaway, Peter, has lost *two front teeth* in the upper jaw."
Mr. John McMurrain, near Columbus, "Georgia Messenger," Aug. 2, 1838.	"Ranaway, a boy named Moses, some of his *front teeth out*."
Mr. John Kennedy, Stewart Co. La. "New Orleans Bee," April 7, 1837.	"Ranaway, Sally, her *fore teeth out*."
Mr. A. J. Hutchings, near Florence, Ala., "North Alabamian," August 25, 1838.	"Ranaway, George Winston, two of his *upper fore teeth out* immediately in front."
Mr. James Purdon, 33 Common street, N. O. "New Orleans Bee," Feb. 13, 1838.	"Ranaway, Jackson, has lost *one of his front teeth*."
Mr. Robert Calvert, in the "Arkansas State Gazette," August 22, 1838.	"Ranaway, Jack, 25 years old, has lost *one of his fore teeth*."
Mr. A. G. A. Beazley, in the "Memphis Gazette," March 18, 1838.	"Ranaway, Abraham, 20 or 22 years of age, *his front teeth out*."
Mr. Samuel Townsend, in the "Huntsville [Ala.] Democrat," May 24, 1837.	"Ranaway, Dick, 18 or 20 years of age, *has one front tooth out*."

WITNESSES	TESTIMONY
Mr. Philip A. Dew, in the "Virginia Herald," of May 24, 1837.	"Ranaway, Washington, about 25 years of age, has *an upper front tooth out*."
Mr. John Frederick, in the "Charleston Mercury," August 10, 1837.	"50 DOLLARS REWARD, for Mary, 25 or 26 years old, *one or two upper teeth out*."
Jesse Debruhl, sheriff of Richland District, in the "Columbia [S. C.] Telegraph," Sept. 2, 1837.	"Committed to jail, Ned, 25 or 26 years old, has lost his *two upper front teeth*."
M. E. W. Gilbert, in the "Columbus [Ga.] Enquirer," Oct. 5, 1837.	"50 DOLLARS REWARD, for Prince, 25 or 26 years old, *one or two teeth out* in front on the upper jaw."
Publisher of the "Charleston Mercury," Aug. 31, 1838.	"Ranaway, Seller Saunders, one *fore tooth out,* about 22 years of age."
Mr. Byrd M. Grace, in the "Macon [Ga.] Telegraph," Oct. 16, 1838.	"Ranaway, Warren, about 25 or 26 years old, has lost *some of his front teeth*."
Mr. George W. Barnes, in the "Milledgeville [Ga.] Journal," May 22, 1837.	"Ranaway, Henry, about 23 years old, has one of his *upper front teeth out*."
D. Herring, Warden of Baltimore Jail, in "Baltimore Chronicle," Oct. 6, 1837.	"Committed to jail Elizabeth Steward, 17 or 18 years old, has *one of her front teeth out*."
Mr. J. L. Colborn, in the "Huntsville [Ala.] Democrat," July 4, 1837.	"Ranaway Liley, 26 years of age, *one fore tooth gone*."
Samuel Harman Jr., in the "New Orleans Bee," Oct. 12, 1838.	"50 DOLLARS REWARD, for Adolphe, 28 years old, *two of his front teeth* are missing."

Were it necessary, we might easily add to the preceding list, *hundreds*. The reader will remark that all the slaves, whose ages are given, are *young*—not one has arrived at middle age; consequently it can hardly be supposed that they have lost their teeth either from age or decay. The probability that their teeth were taken out by force, is increased by the fact of their being *front teeth* in almost every case, and from the fact that the loss of no *other* is mentioned in the advertisements. It is well known that the front teeth are not generally the first to fail. Further, it is notorious that the teeth of the slaves are remarkably sound and serviceable, that they decay far less, and at a much later period of life than the teeth of the whites: owing partly, no doubt, to original constitution; but more probably to their diet, habits, and mode of life.

As an illustration of the horrible mutilations *sometimes* suffered by them in the breaking and tearing out of their teeth, we insert the following, from the New-Orleans Bee of May 31, 1837.

"$10 REWARD.—Ranaway, Friday, May 12, JULIA, a negress, EIGHTEEN OR TWENTY YEARS OLD. SHE HAS LOST HER UPPER TEETH, and the under ones ARE ALL BROKEN. Said reward will be paid to whoever will bring her to her master, No. 172 Barracks-street, or lodge her in the jail."

The following is contained in the same paper.

"Ranaway, NELSON, 27 years old,—ALL HIS TEETH ARE MISSING." This advertisement is signed by "SELFER," Faubourg Marigny.

We now call the attention of the reader to a mass of testimony in support of our general proposition.

GEORGE B. RIPLEY, Esq., of Norwich, Connecticut, has furnished the following statement, in a letter dated Dec. 12, 1838.

"GURDON CHAPMAN, Esq., a respectable merchant of our city, one of our county commissioners,—last spring a member of our state legislature,—and whose character for veracity is above suspicion, about a year since visited the county of Nansemond, Virginia, for the purpose of buying a cargo of corn. He purchased a large quantity from Mr.———, with whose family he spent a week or ten days; after he returned, he related to me and several other citizens the following facts. In order to prepare the corn for market by the time agreed upon, the slaves were worked as hard as they would bear, from daybreak until 9 or 10 o'clock at night. They were called directly from their bunks in the morning to their work, without a morsel of food until noon, when they took their breakfast and dinner, consisting of bacon and corn bread. The quantity of meat was not one tenth of what the same number of northern laborers usually have at a meal. They were allowed but fifteen minutes to take this meal, at the expiration of this time the horn was blown. The rigor with which they enforce punctuality to its call, may be imagined from the fact, that a little boy only nine years old was whipped so severely by the driver, that in many places the whip cut through his clothes (which were of cotton), for tardiness of not over three minutes. They then worked without intermission until 9 or 10 at night; after which they prepared and ate their second meal, as scanty as the first. An aged slave, who was remarkable for his industry and fidelity, was working with all his might on the threshing floor; amidst the clatter of the shelling and winnowing machines the master spoke to him, but he did not hear; he presently gave him several severe cuts with the raw hide, saying, at the same time, 'damn you, if you cannot hear I'll see if you can feel.' One morning the master rose from breakfast and whipped most cruelly, with a raw hide, a nice girl who was waiting on the table, for not opening a *west* window when he had told her to open an east one. The number of slaves was only forty, and yet the lash was in constant use. The bodies of all of them were literally covered with old scars.

"Not one of the slaves attended church on the Sabbath. The social relations were scarcely recognised among them, and they lived in a state of promiscuous concubinage. The master said he took pains to breed from his best stock—the whiter the progeny the higher they would sell for house servants. When asked by Mr. C. if he did not fear his slaves would run away if he whipped them so much, he replied, they know too well what they must suffer if they are taken—and then said, 'I'll tell you how I treat my runaway niggers. I had a big nigger that ran away the second time; as soon as I got track of him I took three good fellows and went in pursuit, and found him in the night, some miles distant, in a corn-house; we took him and ironed him hand and foot, and carted him home. The next morning we tied him to a tree, and whipped him until there was not a sound place on his back. I then tied his ankles and hoisted him up to a *limb*—feet up and head down—we then whipped him, until the damned nigger smoked so that I thought he would take fire and burn up. We then took him down; and to make sure that he should not run away the third time, I run my knife in back of the ankles, and *cut off the large cords,*—and then I ought to have put some lead into the wounds, but I forgot it.'

"The truth of the above is from unquestionable authority; and you may publish or suppress it, as shall best subserve the cause of God and humanity."

EXTRACT OF A LETTER FROM STEPHEN SEWALL, Esq., Winthrop, Maine, dated Jan. 12th, 1839. Mr. S. is a member of the Congregational church in Winthrop, and late agent of the Winthrop Manufacturing company.

"Being somewhat acquainted with slavery, by a residence of about five years in Alabama, and having witnessed many acts of slavehold-ing cruelty, I will mention one or two that came under my eye; and one of excessive cruelty mentioned to me at the time, by the gentle-man (now dead), that interfered in behalf of the slave.

"I was witness to such cruelties by an overseer to a slave, that he twice attempted to drown himself, to get out of his power: this was on a raft of staves, in the Mobile river. I saw an owner take his run-away slave, tie a rope round him, then get on his horse, give the slave and horse a cut with the whip, and run the poor creature barefooted, very fast, over rough ground, where small black jack oaks had been cut up, leaving the sharp stumps, on which the slave would frequently fall; then the master would drag him as long as he could himself hold out; then stop, and whip him up on his feet again—then proceed as before. This continued until he got out of my sight, which was about half a mile. But what further cruelties this wretched man, (whose passion was so excited that he could scarcely utter a word when he took the slave into his own power), inflicted upon his poor victim, the day of judgment will unfold.

"I have seen slaves severely whipped on plantations, but this *is an every day occurrence,* and comes under the head of general treatment.

"I have known the case of a husband compelled to whip his wife. This I did not witness, though not two rods from the cabin at the time.

"I will now mention the case of cruelty before referred to. In 1820 or 21, while the public works were going forward on Dauphin Island, Mobile Bay, a contractor, engaged on the works, beat one of his slaves so severely that the poor creature had no longer power to writhe under his suffering: he then took out his knife, and began to *cut his flesh in strips, from his hips down.* At this moment, the gentleman referred to, who was also a contractor, shocked at such inhumanity, stepped forward, between the wretch and his victim, and exclaimed, 'If you touch that slave again you do it at the peril of your life.' The slaveholder raved at him for interfering between him and his slave; but he was obliged to drop his victim, fearing the arm of my friend—whose stature and physical powers were extraordinary."

EXTRACT OF A LETTER FROM Mrs. MARY COWLES, a member of the Protestant Church at Geneva, Ashtabula county, Ohio, dated 12th mo., 18th, 1838. Mrs. Cowles is a daughter of Mr. James Colwell of Brooke county, West Virginia, near West Liberty.

"In the year 1809, I think, when I was twenty-one years old, a man in the vicinity where I resided, in Brooke co., WV., near West Liberty, by the name of Morgan, had a little slave girl about six years old, who had a habit or rather a natural infirmity common to children of that age. On this account her master and mistress would pinch her ears with hot tongs, and throw hot embers on her legs. Not being able to accomplish their object by these means, they at last resorted to a method too indelicate, and too horrible to describe in detail. Suffice it to say, it soon put an end to her life in the most excruciating manner. If further testimony to authenticate what I have stated is necessary, I refer you to Dr. Robert Mitchel who then resided in the vicinity, but now lives at Indiana, Pennsylvania, above Pittsburgh."

MARY COWLES.

TESTIMONY OF WILLIAM LADD, Esq., now of Minot, Maine, formerly a slaveholder in Florida. Mr. Ladd is now the President of the American Peace Society. In a letter dated November 29, 1838, Mr. Ladd says:

"While I lived in Florida I knew a slaveholder whose name was Hutchinson, he had been a preacher and a member of the Senate of Georgia. He told me that he dared not keep a gun in his house, because he was so passionate; and that he had *been the death of three or four men*. I understood him to mean *slaves*. One of his slaves, a girl, once came to my house. She had run away from him at Indian river. The cords of one of her hands were so much contracted that her hand was useless. It was said that he had thrust her hand into the fire while he was in a fit of passion, and held it there, and this was the effect. My wife had hid the girl when Hutchinson came for her. Out of compassion for the poor slave, I offered him more than she was worth, which he refused. We afterward let the girl escape, and I do not know what became of her, but I believe he never got her again. It was currently reported of Hutchinson, that he once knocked down a *new* negro (one recently from Africa) who was clearing up land, and who complained of the cold, as it was mid-winter. The slave was stunned with the blow. Hutchinson, supposing he had the 'sulks,' applied fire to the side of the slave until it was so roasted that he said the slave was not worth curing, and ordered the other slaves to pile on brush, and he was consumed.

"A murder occurred at the settlement, (Musquito) while I lived there. An overseer from Georgia, who was employed by a Mr. Cormick, in a fit of jealousy shot a slave of Samuel Williams, the owner of the next plantation. He was apprehended, but afterward suffered to escape. This man told me that he had rather whip a negro than sit down to the best dinner. This man had, near his house, a contrivance like that which is used in armies where soldiers are punished with the picket; by this the slave was drawn up from the earth, by a cord passing round his wrists, so that his feet could just touch the ground. It somewhat resembled a New England well sweep, and was used when the slaves were flogged.

"The treatment of slaves at Musquito I consider much milder than that which I have witnessed in the United States. Florida was under the Spanish government while I lived there. There were about fifteen or twenty plantations at Musquito. I have an indistinct recollection of four or five slaves dying of the cold in Amelia Island. They belonged to Mr. Runer of Musquito. The compensation of the overseers was a certain portion of the crop."

GERRIT SMITH, Esq., of Peterboro, in a letter, dated Dec. 15, 1838, says:

"I have just been conversing with an inhabitant of this town, on the subject of the cruelties of slavery. My neighbors inform me that he is a man of veracity. The candid manner of his communication utterly forbade the suspicion that he was attempting to deceive me.

"My informant says that he resided in Louisiana and Alabama during a great part of the years 1819 and 1820:—that he frequently saw slaves whipped, never saw any killed; but often heard of their being killed:—that in several instances he had seen a slave receive, in the space of two hours, five hundred lashes—each stroke drawing blood. He adds that this severe whipping was always followed by the application of strong brine to the lacerated parts.

"My informant further says, that in the spring of 1819, he steered a boat from Louisville to New Orleans. Whilst stopping at a plantation on the east bank of the Mississippi, between Natchez and New Orleans, for the purpose of making sale of some of the articles with which the boat was freighted, he and his fellow boatmen saw a shockingly cruel punishment inflicted on a couple of slaves for the repeated offence of running away. Straw was spread over the whole of their backs, and, after being fastened by a band of the same material, was ignited, and left to burn, until entirely consumed. The agonies and screams of the sufferers he can never forget."

Dr. DAVID NELSON, late president of Marion College, Missouri, a native of Tennessee, and till forty years old a slaveholder, said in an Anti-Slavery address at Northampton, Mass., Jan. 1839—
"I have not attempted to harrow your feelings with stories of cruelty. I will, however, mention one or two among the many incidents that came under my observation as family physician. I was one day dressing a blister, and the mistress of the house sent a little black girl into the kitchen to bring me some warm water. She probably mistook her message; for she returned with a bowl full of boiling water; which her mistress no sooner perceived, than she thrust her hand into it, and held it there till it was half cooked."

Mr. HENRY H. LOOMIS, a member of the Presbyterian Theological Seminary in the city of New York, says, in a recent letter—
"The Rev. Mr. Hart, recently my pastor, in Otsego county, New York, and who has spent some time at the south as a teacher, stated to me that in the neighborhood in which he resided a slave was set to watch a turnip patch near an academy, in order to keep off the boys who occasionally trespassed on it. Attempting to repeat the trespass in presence of the slave, they were told that his 'master forbad it.' At this the boys were enraged, and hurled brickbats at the slave until his face and other parts were much injured and wounded—but nothing was said or done about it as an injury to the slave.

"He also said, that a slave from the same neighborhood was found out in the woods, with his arms and legs burned almost to a cinder, up as far as the elbow and knee joints; and there appeared to be but little more said or thought about it than if he had been a brute. It was supposed that his master was the cause of it—making him an example of punishment to the rest of the gang!"

The following is an extract of a letter dated March 5, 1839, from Mr. JOHN CLARKE, a highly respected citizen of Scriba, Oswego county, New York, and a member of the Presbyterian church.

The 'Mrs. Turner' spoken of in Mr. C.'s letter, is the wife of Hon. Fielding S. Turner, who in 1803 resided at Lexington, Kentucky, and was the attorney for the Commonwealth. Soon after that, he removed to New Orleans, and was for many years Judge of the Criminal Court of that city. Having amassed an immense fortune, he returned to Lexington a few years since, and still resides there. Mr. C. the writer, spent the winter of 1836-7 in Lexington. He says,

"Yours of the 27th ult. is received, and I hasten to state the facts which came to my knowledge while in Lexington, respecting the occurrences about which you inquire. Mrs. Turner was originally a Boston lady. She is from 35 to 40 years of age, and the wife of Judge Turner, formerly of New Orleans, and worth a large fortune in slaves and plantations. I repeatedly heard, while in Lexington, Kentucky, during the winter of 1836-7, of the wanton cruelty practised by this woman upon her slaves, and that she had caused several to be *whipped to death*; but I never heard that she was suspected of being deranged, otherwise than by the indulgence of an ungoverned temper, until I heard that her husband was attempting to incarcerate her in the Lunatic Asylum. The citizens of Lexington, believing the charge to be a false one, rose and prevented the accomplishment for a time, until, lulled by the fair promises of his friends, they left his domicil, and in the dead of night she was taken by force, and conveyed to the asylum. This proceeding being judged illegal by her friends, a suit was instituted to liberate her. I heard the testimony on the trial, which related only to proceedings had in order to getting her admitted into the asylum; and no facts came out relative to her treatment of her slaves, other than of a general character.

"Some days after the above trial, (which by the way did not come to an ultimate decision, as I believe) I was present in my brother's office, when Judge Turner, in a long conversation with my brother on the subject of his trials with his wife, said, '*That woman has been the immediate cause of the death of six of my servants, by her severities.*'

"I was repeatedly told, while I was there, that she drove a colored boy from the second story window, a distance of 15 to 18 feet, on to the pavement, which made him a cripple for a time.

"I heard the trial of a man for the murder of his slave, by whipping, where the evidence was to my mind perfectly conclusive of his guilt; but the jury were two of them for convicting him of man-slaughter, and the rest for acquitting him; and as they could not agree were discharged—and on a subsequent trial, as I learned by the papers, the culprit was acquitted."

Rev. THOMAS SAVAGE, of Bedford, New Hampshire, in a recent letter, states the following fact:

"The following circumstance was related to me last summer, by my brother, now residing as a physician, at Rodney, Mississippi; and who, though a pro-slavery man, spoke of it in terms of reprobation, as an act of capricious, wanton cruelty. The planter who was the actor in it I myself knew; and the whole transaction is so character-istic of the man, that, independent of the strong authority I have, I should entertain but little doubt of its authenticity. He is a wealthy planter, residing near Natchez, eccentric, capricious and intemperate. On one occasion he invited a number of guests to an elegant enter-tainment, prepared in the true style of southern luxury. From some cause, none of the guests appeared. In a moody humor, and under the influence, probably, of mortified pride, he ordered the overseer to call the people (a term by which the field hands are generally designated), on to the piazza. The order was obeyed, and the people came. 'Now,' said he, 'have them seated at the table.' Accordingly they were seated at the well-furnished, glittering table, while he and his overseer waited on them, and helped them to the various dainties of the feast. 'Now,' said he, after a while, raising his voice, 'take these rascals, and give them twenty lashes a piece. I'll show them how to eat at my table.' The overseer, in relating it, said he had to comply, though reluctantly, with this brutal command."

Mr. HENRY P. THOMPSON, a native and still a resident of Nicholasville, Kentucky, made the following statement at a public meeting in Lane Seminary, Ohio, in 1833. He was at that time a slaveholder.

"*Cruelties,*" said he, "*are so common,* I hardly know what to relate. But one fact occurs to me just at this time, that happened in the vil-lage where I live. The circumstances are these. A colored man, a slave, ran away. As he was crossing the Kentucky river, a white man, who suspected him, attempted to stop him. The negro resisted. The white man procured help, and finally succeeded in securing him. He then wreaked his vengeance on him for resisting—flogging him till he was not able to walk. They then put him on a horse, and came on with him ten miles to Nicholasville. When they entered the village, it was noticed that he sat upon his horse like a drunken man. It was a very hot day; and whilst they were taking some refreshment, the negro sat down upon the ground, under the shade. When they ordered him to go, he made several efforts before he could get up; and when he attempted to mount the horse, his strength was entirely insufficient. One of the men struck him, and with an oath ordered him to get on the horse without any more fuss. The negro staggered back a few steps, fell down, and died. I do not know that any notice was ever taken of it."

Rev. COLEMAN S. HODGES, a native and still a resident of Western Virginia, gave the following testimony at the same meeting.

"I have frequently seen the mistress of a family in Virginia, with whom I was well acquainted, beat the woman who performed the kitchen work, with a stick two feet and a half long, and nearly as thick as my wrist; striking her over the head, and across the small of the back, as she was bent over at her work, with as much spite as you would a snake, and for what I should consider no offence at all. There lived in this same family a young man, a slave, who was in the habit of running away. He returned one time after a week's absence. The master took him into the barn, stripped him entirely naked, tied him up by his hands so high that he could not reach the floor, tied his feet together, and put a small rail between his legs, so that he could not avoid the blows, and commenced whipping him. He told me that he gave him five hundred lashes. At any rate, he was covered with wounds from head to foot. Not a place as big as my hand but what was cut. Such things as these are perfectly common all over Virginia; at least so far as I am acquainted. Generally, planters avoid punishing their slaves before strangers."

Mr. CALVIN H. TATE, of Missouri, whose father and brother were slaveholders, related the following at the same meeting. The plantation on which it occurred, was in the immediate neighborhood of his father's.

"A young woman, who was generally very badly treated, after receiving a more severe whipping than usual, ran away. In a few days she came back, and was sent into the field to work. At this time the garment next to her skin was stiff like a scab, from the running of the sores made by the whipping. Towards night, she told her master that she was sick, and wished to go to the house. She went, and as soon as she reached it, laid down on the floor exhausted. The mistress asked her what the matter was? She made no reply. She asked again; but received no answer. 'I'll see,' said she, 'if I can't make you speak.' So taking the tongs, she heated them red hot, and put them upon the bottoms of her feet; then upon her legs and body; and, finally, in a rage, took hold of her throat. This had the desired effect. The poor girl faintly whispered, 'Oh, misse, don't—I am most gone;' and expired."

Extract of a letter from Rev. C. S. RENSHAW, pastor of the Congregational Church, Quincy, Illinois.

"Judge Menzies of Boone county, Kentucky, an elder in the Presbyterian Church, and a slaveholder, told me that *he knew* some overseers in the tobacco growing region of Virginia, who, to make their slaves careful in picking the tobacco, that is taking the worms off, (you know what a loathsome thing the tobacco worm is) would make them *eat* some of the worms, and others who made them eat every worm they missed in picking.

"Mrs. NANCY JUDD, a member of the Nonconformist Church in Osnaburg, Stark county, Ohio, and formerly a resident of Kentucky, testifies that she knew a slaveholder, Mr. Brubecker, who had a number of slaves, among whom was one who would frequently avoid labor by hiding himself; for which he would get severe floggings without the desired effect, and that at last Mr. B. would tie large cats on his naked body and whip them to make them tear his back, in order to break him of his habit of hiding."

Rev. HORACE MOULTON, a minister of the Methodist Episcopal Church in Marlborough, Massachusetts, says:

"Some, when other modes of punishment will not subdue them, *cat-haul* them; that is, take a cat by the nap of the neck and tail, or by its hind legs, and drag the claws across the back until satisfied; this kind of punishment, as I have understood, poisons the flesh much worse than the whip, and is more dreaded by the slave."

Rev. ABEL BROWN, Jr., late pastor of the first Baptist Church, Beaver, Pennsylvania, in a communication to Rev. C. P. Grosvenor, Editor of the Christian Reflector, says:

"I almost daily see the poor heart-broken slave making his way to a land of freedom. A short time since, I saw a noble, pious, distressed, spirit-crushed slave, a member of the Baptist church, escaping from a (professed Christian) bloodhound, to a land where he could enjoy that of which he had been robbed during forty years. His prayers would have made us all feel. I saw a Baptist sister of about the same age, her children had been torn from her, her head was covered with fresh wounds, while her upper lip had scarcely ceased to bleed, in consequence of a blow with the poker, which knocked out her teeth; she too, was going to a land of freedom. Only a very few days since, I saw a girl of about eighteen, with a child as white as myself, aged ten months; a Christian master was raising her child (as well his own perhaps) to sell to a southern market. She had heard of the intention, and at midnight took her only treasure and traveled twenty miles on foot through a land of strangers—she found friends."

Rev. HENRY T. HOPKINS, pastor of the Primitive Methodist Church in New York City, who resided in Virginia from 1821 to 1826, relates the following fact:

"An old colored man, the slave of Mr. Emerson, of Portsmouth, Virginia, being under deep conviction for sin, went into the back part of his master's garden to pour out his soul in prayer to God. For this offence he was whipped thirty-nine lashes."

Extract of a letter from DOCTOR F. JULIUS LE MOYNE, of Washington, Pennsylvania, dated Jan. 9, 1839.

"Lest you should not have seen the statement to which I am going to allude, I subjoin a brief outline of the facts of a transaction which occurred in Western Virginia, adjacent to this county, a number of years ago—a full account of which was published in the "Witness" about two years since by Dr. Mitchell, who now resides in Indiana county, Pennsylvania. A slave boy ran away in cold weather, and during his concealment had his legs frozen; he returned, or was retaken. After some time the flesh decayed and *sloughed*—of course was offensive—he was carried out to a field and left there without bed, or shelter, *deserted to die*. His only companions were the house dogs which he called to him. After several days and nights spent in suffering and exposure, he was visited by Drs. McKitchen and Mitchell in the field, of their own accord, having heard by report of his lamentable condition; they remonstrated with the master; brought the boy to the house, amputated both legs, and he finally recovered."

Hon. JAMES K. PAULDING, the Secretary of the Navy of the United States, in his "Letters from the South" published in 1817, relates the following:

"At one of the taverns along the road we were set down in the same room with an elderly man and a youth who seemed to be well acquainted with him, for they conversed familiarly and with true republican independence—for they did not mind who heard them. From the tenor of his conversation I was induced to look particularly at the elder. He was telling the youth something like the following detested tale. He was going, it seems, to Richmond, to inquire about a draft for seven thousand dollars, which he had sent by mail, but which, not having been acknowledged by his correspondent, he was afraid had been stolen, and the money received by the thief. 'I should not like to lose it,' said he, 'for I worked hard for it, and sold many a poor d——l of a black to Carolina and Georgia, to scrape it together.' He then went on to tell many a perfidious tale. All along the road it seems he made it his business to inquire where lived a man who might be tempted to become a party in this accursed traffic, and when he had got some half dozen of these poor creatures, *he tied their hands behind their backs,* and drove them three or four hundred miles or more, bareheaded and half naked through the burning southern sun. Fearful that *even southern humanity* would revolt at such an exhibition of human misery and human barbarity, he gave out that they were runaway slaves he was carrying home to their masters. On one occasion a poor black woman exposed this fallacy, and told the story of her *being kidnapped,* and when he got her into a wood out of hearing, he beat her, to use his own expression, 'till her back was white.' It seems he married all the men and women he bought, himself, because they would sell better for being man and wife! But, said the youth, were you not afraid, in traveling through the wild country and sleeping in lone houses, these slaves would rise and kill you? 'To be sure I was,' said the other, 'but I always fastened my door, put a chair on a table before it, so that it might wake me in falling, and slept with a loaded pistol in each hand. It was a bad life, and I left it off as soon as I could live without it; for many is the time I have separated wives from husbands, and husbands from wives, and parents from children, but then I made them amends by marrying them again as soon as I had a chance, that is to say, I made them call each other man and wife, and sleep together, which is quite enough for negroes. I made one bad purchase though,' continued he. 'I bought a young mulatto girl, a lively creature, a great bargain. She had been the favorite of her master, who had lately married. The difficulty was to get her to go, for the poor creature loved her master. However, I swore most bitterly I was only going to take her to her mother's at —— and she went with me, though she seemed to doubt me very much. But when she discovered, at last, that we were out of the state, I thought she would go mad, and in fact, the next night she drowned herself in the river close by. I lost a good five hundred dollars by this foolish trick.'" Vol. I. p. 121.

Mr. —— SPILLMAN, a native, and till recently, a resident of Virginia, now a member of the Presbyterian church in Delhi, Hamilton co., Ohio, has furnished the two following facts, of which he had personal knowledge.

"David Stallard, of Shenandoah co., Virginia, had a slave, who run away; he was taken up and lodged in Woodstock jail. Stallard went with another man and took him out of the jail—tied him to their horses—and started for home. The day was excessively hot, and they rode so fast, dragging the man by the rope behind them, that he became perfectly exhausted—fainted—dropped down, and died.

"Henry Jones, of Culpepper co., Virginia, owned a slave, who ran away. Jones caught him, tied him up, and for two days, at intervals, continued to flog him, and rub salt into his mangled flesh, until his back was literally cut up. The slave sunk under the torture; and for some days it was supposed he must die. He, however, slowly recovered; though it was some weeks before he could walk."

Mr. NATHAN COLE, of St. Louis, Missouri, in a letter to Mr. Arthur Tappan, of New-York, dated July 2, 1834, says,—

"You will find inclosed an account of the proceedings of an inquest lately held in this city upon the body of a slave, the details of which, if published, not one in ten could be induced to believe true.* It appears that the master or mistress, or both, suspected the unfortunate wretch of hiding a bunch of keys which were missing; and to extort some explanation, which, it is more than probable, the slave was as unable to do as her mistress, or any other person, her master, Major Harney, an officer of our army, had whipped her for three successive days, and it is supposed by some, that she was kept tied during the time, until her flesh was so lacerated and torn that it was impossible for the jury to say whether it had been done with a whip or hot iron;

---

* The following is the newspaper notice referred to:—

An inquest was held at the dwelling house of Major Harney, in this city, on the 27th inst. by the coroner, on the body of Hannah, a slave. The jury, on their oaths, and after hearing the testimony of physicians and several other witnesses, found, that said slave "came to her death by wounds inflicted by William S. Harney."

some think both—but she was tortured to death. It appears also that the husband of the said slave had become suspected of telling some neighbor of what was going on, for which Major Harney commenced torturing him, until the man broke from him, and ran into the Mississippi and drowned himself. The man was a pious and very industrious slave, perhaps not surpassed by any in this place. The woman has been in the family of John Shackford, Esq., the present doorkeeper of the Senate of the United States, for many years; was considered an excellent servant—was the mother of a number of children—and I believe was sold into the family where she met her fate, as matter of conscience, to keep her from being sent below."

Mr. EZEKIEL BIRDSEYE, a highly respected citizen of Cornwall, Litchfield co., Connecticut, who resided for many years at the south, furnished to the Rev. E. R. Tyler, editor of the Connecticut Observer, the following personal testimony.

"While I lived in Limestone co., Alabama, in 1826-7, a tavern-keeper of the village of Moresville discovered a negro carrying away a piece of old carpet. It was during the Christmas holidays, when the slaves are allowed to visit their friends. The negro stated that one of the servants of the tavern owed him some twelve and a half or twenty-five cents, and that he had taken the carpet in payment. This the servant denied. The innkeeper took the negro to a field near by, and whipped him cruelly. He then struck him with a stake, and punched him in the face and mouth, knocking out some of his teeth. After this, he took him back to the house, and committed him to the care of his son, who had just then come home with another young man. This was at evening. They whipped him by turns, with heavy cowskins, and made the *dogs shake him.* A Mr. Phillips, who lodged at the house, heard the cruelty during the night. On getting up he found the negro in the bar-room, terribly mangled with the whip, and his flesh so torn by the dogs, that the cords were bare. He remarked to the landlord that he was dangerously hurt, and needed care. The landlord replied that he deserved none. Mr. Phillips went to a neighboring magistrate, who took the slave home with him, where he soon died. The father and son were both tried, and acquitted!! A suit was brought, however, for damages in behalf of the owner of the slave, a young lady by the name of Agnes Jones. *I was on the jury when these facts were stated on oath.* Two men testified, one that he would have given $1000 for him, the other $900 or $950. The jury found the latter sum.

"At Union Court House, S. C., a tavern-keeper, by the name of Samuel Davis, procured the conviction and execution of his own slave, for stealing a cake of gingerbread from a grog shop. The slave raised the latch of the back door, and took the cake, doing no other injury. The shop keeper, whose name was Charles Gordon, was willing to forgive him, but his master procured his conviction and execution by hanging. The slave had but one arm; and an order on the state treasury by the court that tried him, which also assessed his value, brought him more money than he could have obtained for the slave in market."

Mr.——, an elder of the Presbyterian Church in one of the slave states, lately wrote a letter to an agent of the Anti-Slavery Society, in which he states the following fact. The name of the writer is with the Executive Committee of the American Anti-Slavery Society.

"I was passing through a piece of timbered land, and on a sudden I heard a sound as of murder; I rode in that direction, and at some distance discovered a naked black man, hung to the limb of a tree by his hands, his feet chained together, and a pine rail laid with one end on the chain between his legs, and the other upon the ground, to steady him; and in this condition the overseer gave him *four hundred lashes*. The miserably lacerated slave was then taken down, and put to the care of a physician. And what do you suppose was the offence for which all this was done? Simply this: his owner, observing that he laid off corn rows too crooked, he replied, 'Massa, much corn grow on crooked row as on straight one.' This was it—this was enough. His overseer, boasting of his skill in managing a *nigger,* he was submitted to him, and treated as above."

DAVID L. CHILD, Esq., of Northampton, Massachusetts, Secretary of the United States minister at the Court of Lisbon during the administration of President Monroe, stated the following fact in an oration delivered by him in Boston, in 1834. (See Child's "Despotism of Freedom," p. 30.

"An honorable friend, who stands high in the state and in the nation,* was *present at the* burial of a female slave in Mississippi, who *had been whipped to death* at the stake by her master, because she was gone longer of an errand to the neighboring town than her master

---

* "The narrator of this fact is now absent from the United States, and I do not feel at liberty to mention his name."

thought necessary. Under the lash she protested that she was ill, and was obliged to rest in the fields. To complete the climax of horror, she was delivered of a dead infant while undergoing the punishment."

The same fact is stated by Mrs. CHILD in her "Appeal." In answer to a recent letter, inquiring of Mr. and Mrs. Child if they were now at liberty to disclose the name of their informant, Mr. C. says,—

"The witness who stated to us the fact was John James Appleton, Esq., of Cambridge, Mass. He is now in Europe, and it is not without some hesitation that I give his name. He, however, has openly embraced our cause, and taken a conspicuous part in some anti-slavery public meetings since the time that I felt a scruple at publishing his name. Mr. Appleton is a gentleman of high talents and accomplishments. He has been Secretary of Legation at Rio Janeiro, Madrid, and The Hague; Commissioner at Naples, and Charge d'Affaires at Stockholm."

The two following facts are stated upon the authority of the Rev. JOSEPH G. WILSON, pastor of the Presbyterian Church in Salem, Washington co., Indiana.

"In Bath co., Kentucky, Mr. L., in the year '32 or '33, while intoxicated, in a fit of rage whipped a female slave until she fainted and fell on the floor. Then he whipped her to get up; then with red hot tongs he burned off her ears, and whipped her again! but all in vain. He then ordered his negro men to carry her to the cabin. There she was found dead next morning.

"One Wall, in Chester district, S. C., owned a slave, whom he hired to his brother-in-law, Wm. Beckman, for whom the slave worked eighteen months, and worked well. Two weeks after returning to his master he ran away on account of bad treatment. To induce him to return, the master sold him *nominally* to his neighbor, to whom the slave gave himself up, and by whom he was returned to his master:—Punishment, *stripes*. To prevent escape a bar of iron was fastened with three bands, at the waist, knee, and ankle. That night he broke the bands and bar, and escaped. Next day he was taken and whipped to death, by three men, the master, Thorn, and the overseer. First, he was whipped and driven towards home; on the way he attempted to escape, and was shot at by the master,—caught, and knocked down with the butt of the gun by Thorn. In attempting to cross a ditch he fell, with his feet down, and face on the bank; they whipped in vain to get him up—he died. His soul ascended to God, to be a swift witness against his oppressors. This took place at 12 o'clock. Next evening an inquest was held. Of thirteen jurors, summoned by the coroner, nine said it was murder; two said it was manslaughter, and two said it was JUSTIFIABLE! He was bound over to court, tried, and acquitted—not even fined!"

The following fact is stated on the authority of Mr. WM. WILLIS, of Green Plains, Clark co., Ohio; formerly of Caroline co. on the eastern shore of Maryland.

"Mr. W. knew a slave called Peter White, who was sold to be taken to Georgia; he escaped, and lived a long time in the woods—was finally taken. When he found himself surrounded, he surrendered himself quietly. When his pursuers had him in their possession, they shot him in the leg, and broke it, out of mere wantonness. The next day a Methodist minister set his leg, and bound it up with splints. The man who took him, then went into his place of confinement, wantonly jumped upon his leg and crushed it. His name was William Sparks."

Most of our readers are familiar with the horrible atrocities perpetrated in New Orleans, in 1834, by a certain Madame La Laurie, upon her slaves. They were published extensively in northern newspapers at the time. The following are extracts from the accounts as published in the New Orleans papers immediately after the occurrence. The New Orleans Bee says:—

"Upon entering one of the apartments, the most appalling spectacle met their eyes. Seven slaves, more or less horribly mutilated, were seen suspended by the neck, with their limbs apparently stretched and torn, from one extremity to the other. They had been confined for several months in the situation from which they had thus providentially been rescued; and had been merely kept in existence to prolong their sufferings, and to make them taste all that a most refined cruelty could inflict."

The New Orleans Mercantile Advertiser says:

"A negro woman was found chained, covered with bruises and wounds from severe flogging.—All the apartments were then forced open. In a room on the ground floor, two more were found chained, and in a deplorable condition. Up stairs and in the garret, four more were found chained; some so weak as to be unable to walk, and all covered with wounds and sores. One mulatto boy declares himself to

have been chained for five months, being fed daily with only a handful of meal, and receiving every morning the most cruel treatment."

The New Orleans Courier says:—
"We saw one of these miserable beings.—He had a large hole in
his head—his body, from head to foot, was covered with scars and
filled with worms."

The New Orleans Mercantile Advertiser says:
"Seven poor unfortunate slaves were found—some chained to the
floor, others with chains around their necks, fastened to the ceiling;
and one poor old man, upwards of sixty years of age, chained hand
and foot, and made fast to the floor, in a *kneeling position*. His head
bore the appearance of having been beaten until it was broken, and
the worms were actually to be seen making a feast of his brains!! A
woman had her back literally cooked (if the expression may be used)
with the lash; *the very bones might be seen projecting through the skin!*"

The New York Sun, of Feb. 21, 1837, contains the following:—
"Two negroes, runaways from Virginia, were overtaken a few
days since near Johnstown, Columbia co., N. Y., when the persons
in pursuit called out for them to stop or they would shoot them.—
One of the negroes turned around and said, he would die before he
would be taken, and at the moment received a rifle ball through his
knee: the other started to run, but was brought to the ground by a
ball being shot in his back. After receiving the above wounds they
made battle with their pursuers, but were captured and brought into
Johnstown. It is said that the young men who shot them had orders
to take them dead or alive."

Mr. M. M. SHAFTER, of Townsend, Vermont, recently a graduate
of the Wesleyan University at Middletown, Connecticut, makes the
following statement:
"Some of the events of the Southampton, Va. insurrection were
narrated to me by Mr. Benjamin W. Britt, from Riddicksville,
N. C. Mr. Britt claimed the honor of having shot a black on that
occasion, for the crime of disobeying Mr. Britt's imperative 'Stop!'
And Mr. Ashurst, of Edenton, Georgia, told me that a neighbor of
his 'fired at a likely negro boy of his mother,' because the said boy
encroached upon his premises."

Mr. DAVID HAWLEY, a class leader in the Methodist Episcopal Church at St. Albans, Licking county, Ohio, who moved from Kentucky to Ohio in 1831, certifies as follows:—

"About the year 1825, a slave had escaped for Canada, but was arrested in Hardin county. On his return, I saw him in Hart county—his wrists tied together before, his arms tied close to his body, the rope then passing behind his body, thence to the neck of a horse on which rode the master, with a club about three feet long, and of the size of a hoe handle; which, by the appearance of the slave, had been used on his head, so as to wear off the hair and skin in several places, and the blood was running freely from his mouth and nose; his heels very much bruised by the horse's feet, as his master had rode on him because he *would* not go fast enough. Such was the slave's appearance when passing through where I resided. Such cases were not unfrequent."

The following is furnished by Mr. F. A. HART, of Middletown, Connecticut, a manufacturer, and an influential member of the Methodist Episcopal Church. It occurred in 1824, about twenty-five miles this side of Baltimore, Maryland.—

"I had spent the night with a Methodist brother; and while at breakfast, a person came in and called for help. We went out and found a crowd collected around a carriage. Upon approaching we discovered that a slave-trader was endeavoring to force a woman into his carriage. He had already put in three children, the youngest apparently about eight years of age. The woman was strong, and whenever he brought her to the side of the carriage, she resisted so effectually with her feet that he could not get her in. The woman becoming exhausted, at length, by her frantic efforts, he thrust her in with great violence, *stamped her down upon the bottom with his feet*! shouted to the driver to go on; and away they rolled, the miserable captives moaning and shrieking, until their voices were lost in the distance."

Mr. SAMUEL HALL, a teacher in Marietta College, Ohio, writes as follows:—

"Mr. ISAAC C. FULLER is a member of the Methodist Episcopal Church in Marietta. He was a fellow student of mine while in college, and now resides in this place. He says:—In 1832, as I was descending the Ohio with a flat boat, near the 'French Islands,' so called, below Cincinnati, I saw two negroes on horseback. The horses apparently took fright at something and ran. Both jumped over a rail fence; and one of the horses, in so doing, broke one of his fore-legs, falling at the same time and throwing the negro who was upon his back. A white man came out of a house not over two hundred yards distant, and came to the spot. Seizing a stake from the fence, he knocked the negro down five or six times in succession.

"In the same year I worked for a Mr. Nowland, eleven miles above Baton Rouge, La. at a place called 'Thomas' Bend.' He had an overseer who was accustomed to flog more or less of the slaves every morning. I heard the blows and screams as regularly as we used to hear the college bell that summoned us to any duty when we went to school. This overseer was a nephew of Nowland, and there were about fifty slaves on his plantation. Nowland himself related the following to me. One of his slaves ran away, and came to the Homo Chitto river, where he found no means of crossing. Here he fell in with a white man who knew his master, being on a journey from that vicinity. He induced the slave to return to Baton Rouge, under the promise of giving him a pass, by which he might escape, but, in reality, to betray him to his master. This he did, instead of fulfilling his promise. Nowland said that he took the slave and inflicted five hundred lashes upon him, cutting his back all to pieces, and then threw on hot embers. The slave was on the plantation at the time, and told me the same story. He also rolled up his sleeves, and showed me the scars on his arms, which, in consequence, appeared in places to be callous to the bone. I was with Nowland between five and six months."

Rev. JOHN RANKIN, formerly of Tennessee, now pastor of the Presbyterian Church of Ripley, Ohio, has furnished the following statement:—

"The Rev. LUDWELL G. GAINES, now pastor of the Presbyterian Church of Goshen, Clermont county, Ohio, stated to me, that while a resident of a slave state, he was summoned to assist in taking a man who had made his black woman work naked several days, and afterwards murdered her. The murderer armed himself, and threatened to shoot the officer who went to take him; and although there was ample assistance at hand, the officer declined further interference."

Mr. RANKIN adds the following:—

"A Presbyterian preacher, now resident in a slave state, and there-fore it is not expedient to give his name, stated, that he saw on board of a steamboat at Louisville, Kentucky, a woman who had been forced on board, to be carried off from all she counted dear on earth. She ran across the boat and threw herself into the river, in order to end a life of intolerable sorrows. She was drawn back to the boat and taken up. The brutal driver beat her severely, and she immediately threw herself again into the river. She was hooked up again, chained, and carried off."

Testimony of Mr. WILLIAM HANSBOROUGH, of Culpepper county, Virginia, the "owner" of sixty slaves.

"I saw a slave taken out of prison by his master, on a hot summer's day, and driven, by said master, on the road before him, till he dropped down dead."

The above statement was made by Mr. Hansborough to Lindley Coates, of Lancaster county, Pa., a distinguished member of the Society of Friends, and a member of the late Convention in Pa. for altering the State Constitution. The letter from Mr. C. containing this testimony of Mr. H. is now before us.

Mr. TOBIAS BOUDINOT, a member of the Methodist Church in St. Albans, Licking county, Ohio, says:

"In Nicholasville, Ky. in the year 1823, he saw a slave fleeing before the patrol, but he was overtaken near where he stood, and a man with a knotted cane, as large as his wrist, struck the slave a number of times on his head, until the club was broken and he made tame; the blood was thrown in every direction by the violence of the blows."

The Rev. WILLIAM DICKEY, of Bloomingburg, Fayette county, Ohio, wrote a letter to the Rev. John Rankin, of Ripley, Ohio, thirteen years since, containing a description of the *cutting up of a slave* with a broad axe; beginning at the feet and gradually cutting the legs, arms, and body into pieces! This diabolical atrocity was committed in the state of Kentucky, in the year 1807. The perpetrators of the deed were two brothers, Lilburn and Isham Lewis, NEPHEWS OF PRESIDENT JEFFERSON. The writer of this having been informed by Mr. Dickey, that some of the facts connected with this murder were not contained in his letter published by Mr. Rankin, requested him to write the account *anew,* and furnish the additional facts. This he did, and the letter containing it was published in the "Human Rights" for August, 1837. We insert it here, slightly abridged, with the introductory remarks which appeared in that paper.

"Mr. Dickey's first letter has been scattered all over the country, south and north; and though multitudes have affected to disbelieve its statements, *Kentuckians* know the truth of them quite too well to call them in question. The story is fiction or fact—if *fiction,* why has it not been nailed to the wall? Hundreds of people around the mouth of Cumberland River are personally knowing to these facts. *There* are the records of the court that tried the wretches.—*There* their acquaintances and kindred still live. All over that region of country, the brutal butchery of George is a matter of public notoriety. It is quite needless, perhaps, to add, that the Rev. Wm. Dickey is a Presbyterian clergyman, one of the oldest members of the Chilicothe Presbytery, and greatly respected and beloved by the churches in Southern Ohio. He was born in South Carolina, and was for many years pastor of a church in Kentucky.

REV. WM. DICKEY'S LETTER

"In the county of Livingston, Ky., near the mouth of the Cumberland River, lived Lilburn Lewis, a sister's son of the celebrated Jefferson. He was the wealthy owner of a considerable gang of negroes, whom he drove constantly, fed sparingly, and lashed severely. The consequence was, that they would run away. Among the rest was an ill-thrived boy of about seventeen, who, having just returned from a skulking spell, was sent to the spring for water, and in returning let fall an elegant pitcher: it was dashed to shivers upon the rocks. This was made the occasion for reckoning with him. It was night, and the slaves were all at home. The master had them all collected in the most roomy negro-house, and a rousing fire put on. When the door was secured, that none might escape, either through *fear of him* or *sympathy with George,* he opened to them the design of the interview, namely, that they might be effectually advised to *stay at home and obey his orders.* All things now in train, he called up George, who approached his master with unreserved submission. He bound him with cords; and by the assistance of Isham Lewis, his youngest brother, laid him on a broad bench, the *meatblock.* He then proceeded to *hack off George at the ankles!* It was with the *broad axe!* In vain did the unhappy victim *scream and roar!* for he was completely in his master's power; not a hand among so many durst interfere: casting the feet into the fire, he lectured them at some length.—He next *chopped him off below the knees!* George *roaring out* and praying his master to begin at the *other end!* He admonished them again, throwing the legs into the fire—then, above the knees, tossing the joints into the fire—the next stroke severed the thighs from the body; these were also committed to the flames—and so it may be said of the arms, head, and trunk, until all was in the fire! He threatened any of them with similar punishment who should in future disobey, run away, or disclose the proceedings of that evening. Nothing now remained but to consume the flesh and bones; and for this purpose the fire was brightly stirred until two hours after midnight; when a coarse and heavy back-wall, composed of rock and clay, covered the fire and the remains of George. It was the Sabbath—this put an end to the *amusements* of the evening. The negroes were now permitted to disperse, with charges to keep this matter among themselves, and never to whisper it in the neighborhood, under the penalty of a like punishment.

"When he returned home and retired, his wife exclaimed, 'Why, Mr. Lewis, where have you been, and what were you doing?' She had heard a strange *pounding* and dreadful *screams,* and had smelled something like fresh meat *burning.* The answer he returned was, that he had never enjoyed himself at a ball so well as he had enjoyed himself that night.

"Next morning he ordered the hands to rebuild the back-wall, and he himself superintended the work, throwing the pieces of flesh that still remained, with the bones, behind, as it went up—thus hoping to conceal the matter. But it *could not be hid*—much as the negroes seemed to hazard, they did *whisper the horrid deed*. The neighbors came, and in his presence tore down the wall; and finding the *remains* of the boy, they apprehended Lewis and his brother, and testified against them. They were committed to jail, that they might answer at the coming court for this shocking outrage; but finding security for their appearance at court, THEY WERE ADMITTED TO BAIL!

"In the interim, other articles of evidence leaked out. That of Mrs. Lewis hearing a pounding, and screaming, and her smelling fresh meat burning, for not till now had this come out. He was offended with her for disclosing these things, alleging that they might have some weight against him at the pending trial.

"In connection with this is another item, full of horror. Mrs. Lewis, or her girl, in making her bed one morning after this, found, under her bolster, *a keen* BUTCHER KNIFE! The appalling discovery forced from her the confession that she considered her life in jeopardy. Messrs. Rice and Philips, whose wives were her sisters, went to see her and to bring her away if she wished it. Mr. Lewis received them with all the expressions of *Virginia hospitality*. As soon as they were seated they said, 'Well, Letitia, we supposed that you might be unhappy here, and afraid for your life; and we have come to-day to take you to your father's, if you desire it.' She said, 'Thank you, kind brothers, I am indeed afraid for my life.'—We need not interrupt the story to tell how much surprised he affected to be with this strange procedure of his brothers-in-law, and with this declaration of his wife. But all his professions of fondness for her, to the contrary notwithstanding, they rode off with her before his eyes.—He followed and overtook, and went with them to her father's; but she was locked up from him, with her own consent, and he returned home.

"Now he saw that his character was gone, his respectable friends believed that he had massacred George; but, worst of all, he saw that they considered the life of the harmless Letitia was in danger from his perfidious hands. It was too much for his chivalry to sustain. The proud Virginian sunk under the accumulated load of public odium. He proposed to his brother Isham, who had been his accomplice in the George affair, that they should finish the play of life with a still deeper tragedy. The plan was, that they should shoot one another. Having made the hot-brained bargain, they repaired with their guns to the graveyard, which was on an eminence in the midst of his plantation. It was inclosed with a railing, say thirty feet square. One was to stand at one railing, and the other over against him at the other. They were to make ready, take aim, and count deliberately 1, 2, 3, and then fire. Lilburn's will was written, and thrown down open beside him. They cocked their guns and raised them to their faces; but the peradventure occurring that one of the guns might miss fire, Isham was sent for a rod, and when it was brought, Lilburn cut it off at about the length of two feet, and was showing his brother how the survivor might do, provided one of the guns should fail; (for they were determined upon going together;) but forgetting, perhaps, in the perturbation of the moment that the gun was cocked, when he touched the trigger with the rod the gun fired, and he fell, and died in a few minutes—and was with George in the eternal world, where *the slave is free from his master*. But poor Isham was so terrified with this unexpected occurrence and so confounded by the awful contortions of his brother's face, that he had not nerve enough to follow up the play, and finish the plan as was intended, but suffered Lilburn to go alone. The negroes came running to see what it meant that a gun should be fired in the grave-yard. There lay their master, dead! They ran for the neighbors. Isham still remained on the spot. The neighbors at the first charged him with the murder of his brother. But he, though as if he had lost more than half his mind, told the whole story; and the course or range of the ball in the dead man's body agreeing with his statement, Isham was not farther charged with Lilburn's death.

"The Court sat—Isham was judged to be guilty of a capital crime in the affair of George. He was to be hanged at Salem. The day was set. My good old father visited him in the prison—two or three times talked and prayed with him; I visited him once myself. We fondly hoped that he was a sincere penitent. Before the day of execution came, by some means, I never knew what, Isham was *missing*. About two years after, we learned that he had gone down to Natchez, and had married a lady of some refinement and piety. I saw her letters to his sisters, who were worthy members of the church of which I was pastor. The last letter told of his death. He was in Jackson's army, and fell in the famous battle of New Orleans.

"I am, sir, your friend,
"WM. DICKEY."

PERSONAL NARRATIVES

NARRATIVE AND TESTIMONY OF
REV. FRANCIS HAWLEY

Mr. HAWLEY is the pastor of the Baptist Church in Colebrook, Litchfield county, Connecticut. He has resided fourteen years in the slave states, North and South Carolina. His character and standing with his own denomination at the south, may be inferred from the fact, that the Baptist State Convention of North Carolina appointed him, a few years since, their general agent to visit the Baptist churches within their bounds, and to secure their co-operation in the objects of the Convention. Mr. H. accepted the appointment, and for some time traveled in that capacity.

"I rejoice that the Executive Committee of the American Anti-Slavery Society have resolved to publish a volume of facts and testimony relative to the character and workings of American slavery. Having resided fourteen years at the south, I cheerfully comply with your request, to give the result of my observation and experience. And I would here remark, that one may reside at the south for years, and not witness extreme cruelties; a northern man, and one who is not a slaveholder, would be the last to have an opportunity of witnessing the infliction of cruel punishments.

PLANTATIONS

"A majority of the large plantations are on the banks of rivers, far from the public eye. A great deal of low marshy ground lies in the vicinity of most of the rivers at the south; consequently the main roads are several miles from the rivers, and generally no *public* road passes the plantations. A stranger traveling on the *ridge,* would think himself in a miserably poor country; but every two or three miles he will see a road turning off, and leading into the swamp; taking one of those roads, and traveling from two to six miles, he will come to a large gate; passing which, he will find himself in a clearing of several hundred acres of the first quality of land; passing on, he will see 30, or 40, or more slaves—men, women, boys and girls, at their task, every one with a hoe; or, if in cotton picking season, with their baskets. The overseer, with his whip, either riding or standing about among them; or if the weather is hot, sitting under a shade. At a distance, on a little rising ground, if such there be, he will see a cluster of huts, with a tolerable house in the midst, for the overseer. Those huts are from ten to fifteen feet square, built of logs, and covered, not with shingles, but with boards, about four feet long, split out of pine timber with a '*frow.*' The floors are very commonly made in this way. Clay is first worked until it is soft; it is then spread upon the ground, about four or five inches thick; when it dries, it becomes nearly as hard as a brick. The crevices between the logs are sometimes filled with the same. These huts generally cost the master nothing—they are commonly built by the negroes at night, and on Sundays. When a slave of a neighboring plantation takes a wife, or to use the phrase common at the south, 'takes up' with one of the women, he builds a hut, and it is called her house. Upon entering these huts, (not as comfortable in many instances as the horse stable), generally, you will find no chairs, but benches and stools; no table, no bedstead, and no bed, except a blanket or two, and a few rags or moss; in some instances a knife or two, but very rarely a fork. You may also find a pot or skillet, and generally a number of gourds, which serve them instead of bowls and plates. The cruelties practiced on those secluded plantations, the judgment day alone can reveal. Oh, brother, could I summon ten slaves from ten plantations that I could name, and have them give but one year's history of their bondage, it would thrill the land with horror. Those overseers who follow the business of overseeing for a livelihood, are generally the most unprincipled and abandoned of men. Their wages are regulated according to their skill in extorting labor. The one who can make the most bags of cotton, with a given number of hands, is the one generally sought after; and there is a competition among them to see who shall make the largest crop, according to the hands he works. I ask, what must be the condition of the poor slaves, under the unlimited power of such men, in whom, by the long-continued practice of the most heart-rending cruelties, every feeling of humanity has been obliterated? But it may be asked, cannot the slaves have redress by appealing to their masters? In many instances it is impossible, as their masters live hundreds of miles off. There are perhaps thousands in the northern slave states, [and many in the free states,] who own plantations in the southern slave states, and many more spend their summers at the north, or at the various watering places. But what would the slaves gain, if they should appeal to the master? He has placed the overseer over them, with the understanding that he will make as large a crop as possible, and that he is to have entire control, and manage them according to his own judgment. Now, suppose that in the midst of the season, the slaves make complaint of cruel treatment. The master cannot get along without an overseer—it is perhaps very sickly on the plantation—he dare not risk his own life there. Overseers are all engaged at that season, and if he takes part with his slaves against the overseer, he would destroy his authority, and very likely provoke him to leave his service—which would of course be a very great injury to him. Thus, in nineteen cases out of twenty, self-interest would prevent the master from paying any attention to the complaints of his slaves. And, if any should complain, it

would of course come to the ears of the overseer, and the complain-
ant would be inhumanly punished for it.

CLOTHING

"The rule, where slaves are hired out, is two suits of clothes per year,
one pair of shoes, and one blanket; but as it relates to the great body
of the slaves, this cannot be called a general rule. On many plantations, the children under ten or twelve years old, go *entirely naked*—
or, if clothed at all, they have nothing more than a shirt. The cloth
is of the coarsest kind, far from being durable or warm; and their
shoes frequently come to pieces in a few weeks. I have never known
any provision made, or time allowed for the washing of clothes. If
they wish to wash, as they have generally but one suit, they go after
their day's toil to some stream, build a fire, pull off their clothes and
wash them in the stream, and dry them by the fire; and in some
instances they wear their clothes until they are worn off, without
washing. I have never known an instance of a slaveholder putting
himself to any expense, that his slaves might have decent clothes for
the Sabbath. If, by making baskets, brooms, mats, &c. at night or on
Sundays, the slaves can get money enough to buy a Sunday suit, very
well. I have never known an instance of a slaveholder furnishing his
slaves with stockings or mittens. I *know* that the slaves suffer much,
and no doubt many die in consequence of not being well clothed.

FOOD

"In the grain-growing part of the south, the slaves, as it relates to
food, fare tolerably well; but in the cotton, and rice-growing, and
sugar-making portion, some of them fare badly. I have been on
plantations where, from the appearance of the slaves, I should judge
they were half-starved. They receive their allowance very commonly
on Sunday morning. They are left to cook it as they please, and when
they please. Many slaveholders rarely give their slaves meat, and very
few give them more food than will keep them in a working condition. They rarely ever have a *change* of food. I have never known an
instance of slaves on plantations being furnished either with sugar,
butter, cheese, or milk.

WORK

"If the slaves on plantations were well fed and clothed, and had the stimulus of wages, they could perhaps in general perform their tasks without injury. The horn is blown soon after the dawn of day, when all the hands destined for the field must be 'on the march.' If the field is far from their huts, they take their breakfast with them. They toil till about ten o'clock, when they eat it. They then continue their toil till the sun is set.

"A neighbor of mine, who has been an overseer in Alabama, informs me, that there they ascertain how much labor a slave can perform in a day, in the following manner. When they commence a new cotton field, the overseer takes his watch, and marks how long it takes them to hoe one row, and then lays off the task accordingly. My neighbor also informs me, that the slaves in Alabama are worked very hard; that the lash is almost universally applied at the close of the day, if they fail to perform their task in the cotton-picking season. You will see them, with their baskets of cotton, slowly bending their way to the cotton house, where each one's basket is weighed. They have no means of knowing accurately, in the course of the day, how they make progress; so that they are in suspense, until their basket is weighed. Here comes the mother, with her children; she does not know whether herself, or children, or all of them, must take the lash; they cannot weigh the cotton themselves—the whole must be trusted to the overseer. While the weighing goes on, all is still. So many pounds short, cries the overseer, and takes up his whip, exclaiming, 'Step this way, you d—n lazy scoundrel,' or 'bitch.' The poor slave begs, and promises, but to no purpose. The lash is applied until the overseer is satisfied. Sometimes the whipping is deferred until the weighing is all over. I have said that all must be *trusted* to the overseer. If he owes any one a grudge, or wishes to enjoy the fiendish pleasure of whipping a little, (for some overseers really delight in it), they have only to tell a falsehood relative to the weight of their basket; they can then have a pretext to gratify their diabolical disposition; and from the character of overseers, I have no doubt that it is frequently done. On all plantations, the male and female slaves fare pretty much alike; those who are with child are driven to their task till within a few days of the time of their delivery; and when the child is a few weeks old, the mother must again go to the field. If it is far from her hut, she must take her babe with her, and leave it in the care of some of the children—perhaps of one not more than four or five years old. If the child cries, she cannot go to its relief; the eye of the overseer is upon her; and if, when she goes to nurse it, she stays a little longer than the overseer thinks necessary, he commands her back to her task, and perhaps a husband and father must hear and witness it all. Brother, you cannot begin to know what the poor slave mothers suffer, on thousands of plantations at the south.

"I will now give a few facts, showing the workings of the system. Some years since, a Presbyterian minister moved from North Carolina to Georgia. He had a negro man of an uncommon mind. For some cause, I know not what, this minister whipped him most unmercifully. He next nearly *drowned* him; he then put him *in the fence*; this is done by lifting up the corner of a 'worm' fence, and then putting the feet through; the rails serve as *stocks*. He kept him there some time, how long I was not informed, but the poor slave *died* in a few days; and, if I was rightly informed, nothing was done about it, either in church or state. After some time, he moved back to North Carolina, and is now a member of——Presbytery. I have heard him preach, and have been in the pulpit with him. May God forgive me!

"At Laurel Hill, Richmond county, North Carolina, it was reported that a runaway slave was in the neighborhood. A number of young men took their guns, and went in pursuit. Some of them took their station near the stage road, and kept on the look-out. It was early in the evening—the poor slave came along, when the ambush rushed upon him, and ordered him to surrender. He refused, and kept them off with his club. They still pressed upon him with their guns presented to his breast. Without seeming to be daunted, he caught hold of the muzzle of one of the guns, and came near getting possession of it. At length, retreating to a fence on one side of the road, he sprang over into a corn-field, and started to run in one of the rows. One of the young men stepped to the fence, fired, and lodged the whole charge between his shoulders; he fell, and died in a short time. He died without telling who his master was, or whether he had any, or what his own name was, or where he was from. A hole was dug by the side of the road his body tumbled into it, and thus ended the whole matter.

"The Rev. Mr. C. a Methodist minister, held as his slave a negro man, who was a member of his own church. The slave was considered a very pious man, had the confidence of his master, and all who knew him, and if I recollect right, he sometimes attempted to preach. Just before the Nat Turner insurrection, in Southampton county,

Virginia, by which the whole south was thrown into a panic, this worthy slave obtained permission to visit his relatives, who resided either in Southampton, or the county adjoining. This was the only instance that ever came to my knowledge, of a slave being permitted to go so far to visit his relatives. He went and returned according to agreement. A few weeks after his return, the insurrection took place, and the whole country was deeply agitated. Suspicion soon fixed on this slave. Nat Turner was a Baptist minister, and the south became exceedingly jealous of all negro preachers. It seemed as if the whole community were impressed with the belief that he knew all about it; that he and Nat Turner had concerted an extensive insurrection; and so confident were they in this belief, that they took the poor slave, tried him, and hung him. It was all done in a few days. He protested his innocence to the last. After the excitement was over, many were ready to acknowledge that they believed him innocent. He was hung upon *suspicion*!

"In R—— county, North Carolina, lived a Mr. B. who had the name of being a cruel master. Three or four winters since, his slaves were engaged in clearing a piece of new land. He had a negro girl, about 14 years old, whom he had severely whipped a few days before, for not performing her task. She again failed. The hands left the field for home; she went with them a part of the way, and fell behind; but the negroes thought she would soon be along; the evening passed away, and she did not come. They finally concluded that she had gone back to the new ground, to lie by the log heaps that were on fire. But they were mistaken: she had sat down by the foot of a large pine. She was thinly clad—the night was cold and rainy. In the morning the poor girl was found, but she was speechless and died in a short time.

"One of my neighbors sold to a speculator a negro boy, about 14 years old. It was more than his poor mother could bear. Her reason fled, and she became a perfect *maniac,* and had to be kept in close confinement. She would occasionally get out and run off to the neighbors. On one of these occasions she came to my house. She was indeed a pitiable object. With tears rolling down her cheeks, and her frame shaking with agony, she would cry out, '*don't you hear him—they are whipping him now, and he is calling for me!*' This neighbor of mine, who tore the boy away from his poor mother, and thus broke her heart, was a *member of the Presbyterian church*.

"Mr. S——, of Marion District, South Carolina, informed me that a boy was killed by the overseer on Mr. P——'s plantation. The boy was engaged in driving the horses in a cotton gin. The driver generally sits on the end of the sweep. Not driving to suit the overseer, he knocked him off with the butt of his whip. His skull was fractured. He died in a short time.

"A man of my acquaintance in South Carolina, and of considerable wealth, had an only son, whom he educated for the bar; but not succeeding in his profession, he soon returned home. His father having a small plantation three or four miles off, placed his son on it as an overseer. Following the example of his father, as I have good reason to believe, he took the wife of one of the negro men. The poor slave felt himself greatly injured, and expostulated with him. The wretch took his gun, and deliberately shot him. Providentially he only wounded him badly. When the father came, and undertook to remonstrate with his son about his conduct, he threatened to shoot him also! and finally, took the negro woman, and went to Alabama, where he still resided when I left the south.

"An elder in the Presbyterian church related to me the following.— 'A speculator with his drove of negroes was passing my house, and I bought a little girl, nine or ten years old. After a few months, I concluded that I would rather have a plough-boy. Another speculator was passing, and I sold the girl. She was much distressed, and was very unwilling to leave.'—She had been with him long enough to become attached to his own and his negro children, and he concluded by saying, that in view of the little girl's tears and cries, he had determined never to do the like again. I would not trust him, for I know him to be a very avaricious man.

"While traveling in Anson county, North Carolina, I put up for a night at a private house. The man of the house was not at home when I stopped, but came in the course of the evening, and was noisy and profane, and nearly drunk. I retired to rest, but not to sleep; his cursing and swearing were enough to keep a regiment awake. About midnight he went to his kitchen, and called out his two slaves, a man and woman. His object, he said, was to whip them. They both begged and promised, but to no purpose. The whipping began, and continued for some time. Their cries might have been heard at a distance.

"I was acquainted with a very wealthy planter, on the Pedee river, in South Carolina, who has since died in consequence of intemperance. It was said that he had occasioned the death of twelve of his slaves, by compelling them to work in water, opening a ditch in the midst of winter. The disease with which they died was a pleurisy.

"In crossing Pedee river, at Cashway Ferry, I observed that the ferryman had no hair on either side of his head. I asked him the cause. He informed me that it was caused by his master's cane. I said, you have a very bad master. 'Yes, a very bad master.' I understood that he was once a member of Congress from South Carolina.

"While traveling as agent for the North Carolina Baptist State Convention, I attended a three days' meeting in Gates county. Friday, the first day, passed off. Saturday morning came, and the pastor of the church, who lived a few miles off, did not make his appearance. The day passed off, and no news from the pastor. On Sabbath morning, he came hobbling along, having but little use of one foot. He soon explained: said he had a hired negro man, who, on Saturday morning, gave him a 'little *slack jaw*.' Not having a stick at hand, he fell upon him with his fist and foot, and in *kicking* him, he injured his foot so seriously, that he could not attend meeting on Saturday.

"Some of the slaveholding ministers at the south, put their slaves under overseers, or hire them out, and then take the pastoral care of churches. The Rev. Mr. B——, formerly of Pennsylvania, had a plantation in Marlborough District, South Carolina, and was the pastor of a church in Darlington District. The Rev. Mr. T——, of Johnson county, North Carolina, has a plantation in Alabama.

"I was present, and saw the Rev. J—— W——, of Mecklenburg county, North Carolina, hire out four slaves to work in the gold mines in Burke county. The Rev. H—— M——, of Orange county, sold for $900, a negro man to a speculator, on a Monday of a camp meeting.

"Runaway slaves are frequently hunted with guns and dogs. *I was once out on such an excursion, with my rifle and two dogs*. I trust the Lord has forgiven me this heinous wickedness! We did not take the runaways.

"Slaves are sometimes most unmercifully punished for trifling offences, or mere mistakes.

"As it relates to amalgamation, I can say, that I have been in respectable families, (so called), where I could distinguish the family resemblance in the slaves who waited upon the table. I once hired a slave who belonged to his own *uncle*. It is so common for the female slaves to have white children, that little or nothing is ever said about it. Very few inquiries are made as to who the father is.

"Thus, brother ——, I have given you very briefly, the result, in part, of my observations and experience relative to slavery. You can make what disposition of it you please. I am willing that my name should go to the world with what I have now written.

"Yours affectionately, for the oppressed,
"FRANCIS HAWLEY."
Colebrook, Connecticut, March 18, 1839.

TESTIMONY OF REUBEN G. MACY AND RICHARD MACY

The following is an extract of a letter recently received from CHARLES MARRIOTT of Hudson, New York. Mr. Marriott is an elder in the Religious Society of Friends, and is extensively known and respected.

"The two following brief statements, are furnished by Richard Macy and Reuben G. Macy, brothers, both of Hudson, New York. They are head carpenters by trade, and have been well known to me for more than thirty years, as esteemed members of the Religious Society of Friends. They inform me that during their stay in South Carolina, a number more similar cases to those here related, came under their notice, which to avoid repetition they omit.

C. MARRIOTT.

TESTIMONY OF REUBEN G. MACY

"During the winter of 1818 and 19, I resided on an island near the mouth of the Savannah river, on the South Carolina side. Most of the slaves that came under my particular notice, belonged to a widow and her daughter, in whose family I lived. No white man belonged to the plantation. Her slaves were under the care of an overseer who came once a week to give orders, and settled the score laid up against such as their mistress thought deserved punishment, which was from twenty-five to thirty lashes on their naked backs, with a whip which the overseer generally brought with him. This whip had a stout handle about two feet long, and a lash about four and a half feet. From two to four received the above, I believe nearly every week during the winter, sometimes in my presence, and always in my hearing. I examined the backs and shoulders of a number of the men, which were mostly naked while they were about their labor, and found them covered with hard ridges in every direction. One day, while busy in the cotton house, hearing a noise, I ran to the door and saw a colored woman pleading with the overseer, who paid no attention to her cries, but tied her hands together, and passed the rope over a beam, over head, where was a platform for spreading cotton, he then drew the rope as tight as he could, so as to let her toes touch the ground; then stripped her body naked to the waist, and went deliberately to work with his whip, and put on twenty-five or thirty lashes, she pleading in vain all the time. I inquired, the cause of such treatment, and was informed it was for answering her mistress rather 'short.'

"A woman from a neighboring plantation came where I was, on a visit; she came in a boat rowed by six slaves, who, according to the common practice, were left to take care of themselves, and having laid them down in the boat and fallen asleep, the tide fell, and the water filling the stern of the boat, wet their mistresses trunk of clothes. When she discovered it, she called them up near where I was, and compelled them to whip each other, till they all had received a severe flogging. She standing by with a whip in her hand to see that they did not spare each other. Their usual allowance of food was one peck of corn per week, which was dealt out to them every first day of the week, and such as were not there to receive their portion at the appointed time, had to live as they could during the coming week. Each one had the privilege of planting a small piece of ground, and raising poultry for their own use which they generally sold, that is, such as did improve the privilege which were but few. They had nothing allowed them besides the corn, except one quarter of beef at Christmas which a slave brought three miles on his head. They were allowed three days rest at Christmas. Their clothing consisted of a pair of trowsers and jacket, made of whitish woollen cloth called negro cloth. The women had nothing but a petticoat, and a very short short-gown, made of the same kind of cloth. Some of the women had an old pair of shoes, but they generally went *barefoot*. The houses for the field slaves were about fourteen feet square, built in the coarsest manner, having but one room, without any chimney, or flooring, with a hole at the roof at one end to let the smoke out.

"Each one was allowed one blanket in which they rolled themselves up. I examined their houses but could not discover any thing like a bed. I was informed that when they had a sufficiency of potatoes the slaves were allowed some; but the season that I was there they did not raise more than were wanted for seed. All their corn was ground in one hand-mill, every night just as much as was necessary for the family, then each one his daily portion, which took considerable time in the night. I often awoke and heard the sound of the mill. Grinding the corn in the night, and in the dark, after their day's labor, and the want of other food, were great hardships.

"The traveling in those parts, among the islands, was altogether with boats, rowed by from four to ten slaves, which often stopped at our plantation, and staid through the night, when the slaves, after rowing through the day, were left to shift for themselves; and when they went to Savannah with a load of cotton they were obliged to sleep in the open boats, as the law did not allow a colored person to be out after eight o'clock in the evening, without a pass from his master."

TESTIMONY OF RICHARD MACY

"The above account is from my brother. I was at work on Hilton Head about twenty miles north of my brother, during the same winter. The same allowance of one peck of corn for a week, the same kind of houses to live in, and the same method of grinding their corn, and always in the night, and in the dark, was practiced there.

"A number of instances of severe whipping came under my notice. The first was this:—two men were sent out to saw some blocks out of large live oak timber on which to raise my building. Their saw was in poor order, and they sawed them badly, for which their master stripped them naked and flogged them.

"The next instance was a boy about sixteen years of age. He had crept into the coach to sleep; after two or three nights he was caught by the coach driver, a *northern man,* and stripped *entirely naked,* and whipped without mercy, his master looking on.

"Another instance. The overseer, a young white man, had ordered several negroes, a boat's crew, to be on the spot at a given time. One man did not appear until the boat had gone. The overseer was very angry and told him to strip and be flogged; he being slow, was told if he did not instantly strip off his jacket, he, the overseer, would whip it off, which he did in shreds, whipping him cruelly.

"The man ran into the barrens and it was about a month before they caught him. He was nearly starved, and at last stole a turkey; then another, and was caught.

"Having occasion to pass a plantation very early one foggy morning, in a boat, we heard the sound of the whip, before we could see, but as we drew up in front of the plantation, we could see the negroes at work in the field. The overseer was going from one to the other causing them to lay down their hoe, strip off their garment, hold up their hands and receive their number of lashes. Thus he went on from one to the other until we were out of sight. In the course of the winter a family came where I was, on a visit from a neighboring island; of course, in a boat with negroes to row them—one of these a barber, told me that he ran away about two years before, and joined a company of negroes who had fled to the swamps. He said they suffered a great deal—were at last discovered by a party of hunters, who fired among them, and caused them to scatter. Himself and one more fled to the coast, took a boat and put off to sea, a storm came on and swamped or upset them, and his partner was drowned, he was taken up by a passing vessel and returned to his master.

RICHARD MACY."

Hudson, 12 *mo*. 29*th*, 1838.

TESTIMONY OF MR. ELEAZAR POWELL

EXTRACT OF A LETTER FROM Mr. WILLIAM SCOTT, a highly respectable citizen of Beaver co., Pennsylvania, dated Jan. 7, 1839.

Chippewa Township, Beaver co., Pa. ⎫
Jan. 7, 1839. ⎭

"I send you the statement of Mr. Eleazar Powell, who was born, and has mostly resided in this township from his birth. His character for sobriety and truth stands above impeachment.

With sentiments of esteem,

I am your friend,

WILLIAM SCOTT.

"In the month of December, 1836, I went to the State of Mississippi to work at my trade, (masonry and bricklaying), and continued to work in the counties of Adams and Jefferson, between four and five months. In following my business I had an opportunity of seeing the treatment of slaves in several places.

"In Adams county I built a chimney for a man named Joseph Gwatney; he had forty-five field hands of both sexes. The field in which they worked at that time, lay about two miles from the house; the hands had to cook and eat their breakfast, prepare their dinner, and be in the field at daylight, and continue there till dark. In the evening the cotton they had picked was weighed, and if they fell short of their task they were whipped. One night I attended the weighing—two women fell short of their task, and the master ordered the black driver to take them to the quarters and flog them; one of them was to receive twenty-five lashes and pick a peck of cotton seed. I have been with the overseer several times through the negro quarters. The huts are generally built of split timber, some larger than rails, twelve and a half feet wide and fourteen feet long—some with and some without chimneys, and generally without floors; they were generally without daubing, and mostly had split clapboards nailed on the cracks on the outside, though some were without even that: in some there was a kind of rough bedstead, made from rails, polished with the axe, and put together in a very rough manner, the bottom covered with clapboards, and over that a bundle of worn out clothes. In some huts there was no bedstead at all. The above description applies to the places generally with which I was acquainted, and they were mostly *old settlements*.

"In the east part of Jefferson county I built a chimney for a man named —— M'Coy; he had forty-seven laboring hands. Near where I was at work, M'Coy had ordered one of his slaves to set a post for a gate. When he came to look at it, he said the slave had not set it in the right place; and ordered him to strip, and lie down on his face; telling him that if he struggled, or attempted to get up, two men, who had been called to the spot, should seize and hold him fast. The slave agreed to be quiet, and M'Coy commenced flogging him on the bare back, with the wagon whip. After some time the sufferer attempted to get up; one of the slaves standing by, seized him by the feet and held him fast; upon which he yielded, and M'Coy continued to flog him ten or fifteen minutes. When he was up, and had put on his trowsers, the blood came through them.

"About half a mile from M'Coy's was a plantation owned by his step-daughter. The overseer's name was James Farr, of whom it appears Mrs. M'Coy's waiting woman was enamoured. One night, while I lived there, M'Coy came from Natchez, about 10 o'clock at night. He said that Dinah was gone, and wished his overseer to go with him to Farr's lodgings. They went accordingly, one to each door, and caught Dinah as she ran out, she was partly dressed in her mistress's clothes; M'Coy whipped her unmercifully, and she afterwards made her escape. On the next day, (Sabbath), M'Coy came to the overseer's, where I lodged, and requested him and me to look for her, as he was afraid that she had hanged herself. He then gave me the particulars of the flogging. He stated that near Farr's he had made her strip and lie down, and had flogged her until he was tired; that before he reached home he had a second time made her strip, and again flogged her until he was tired; that when he reached home he had tied her to a peach-tree, and after getting a drink had flogged her until he was thirsty again; and while he went to get a drink the woman made her escape. He stated that he knew, from the whipping he had given her, there must be in her back cuts an inch deep. He showed the place where she had been tied to the tree; there appeared to be as much blood as if a hog had been stuck there. The woman was found on Sabbath evening, near the spring, and had to be carried into the house.

"While I lived there I heard M'Coy say, if the slaves did not raise him three hundred bales of cotton the ensuing season, he would kill every negro he had.

"Another case of flogging came under my notice:—Philip O. Hughes, sheriff of Jefferson county, had hired a slave to a man, whose name I do not recollect. On a Sabbath day the slave had drank somewhat freely; he was ordered by the tavern keeper, (where his present master had left his horse and the negro), to stay in the kitchen; the negro wished to be out. In persisting to go out he was knocked down three times; and afterwards flogged until another young man and myself ran about half a mile, having been drawn by the cries of the negro and the sound of the whip. When we came up, a number of men that had been about the tavern, were whipping him, and at intervals would ask him if he would take off his clothes. At seeing them drive down the stakes for a regular flogging he yielded, and took them off. They then flogged him until satisfied. On the next morning I saw him, and his pantaloons were all in a gore of blood.

"During my stay in Jefferson county, Philip O. Hughes was out one day with his gun—he saw a negro at some distance, with a club in one hand and an ear of corn in the other—Hughes stepped behind a tree, and waited his approach; he supposed the negro to be a runaway, who had escaped about nine months before from his master, living not very far distant. The negro discovered Hughes before he came up, and started to run; he refusing to stop, Hughes fired, and shot him through the arm. Through loss of blood the negro was soon taken and put in jail. I saw his wound twice dressed, and heard Hughes make the above statement.

"When in Jefferson county I boarded six weeks in Fayette, the county town, with a tavern keeper named James Truly. He had a slave named Lucy, who occupied the station of chambermaid and table waiter. One day, just after dinner, Mrs. Truly took Lucy and bound her arms round a pine sapling behind the house, and commenced flogging her with a riding-whip; and when tired would take her chair and rest. She continued thus, alternately flogging and resting, for at least an hour and a half. I afterwards learned from the bar-keeper, and others, that the woman's offence was that she had bought two candles to set on the table the evening before, not knowing there were yet some in the box. I did not see the act of flogging above related; but it was commenced before I left the house after dinner; and my work not being more than twenty rods from the house, I distinctly heard the cries of the woman all the time, and the manner of tying I had from those who did see it.

"While I boarded at Truly's, an overseer shot a negro about two miles northwest of Fayette, belonging to a man named Hinds Stuart. I heard Stuart himself state the particulars. It appeared that the negro's wife fell under the overseer's displeasure, and he went to whip her. The negro said she should not be whipped. The overseer then let her go, and ordered him to be seized. The negro, having been a driver, rolled the lash of his whip round his hand, and said he would not be whipped at that time. The overseer repeated his orders. The negro took up a hoe, and none dared to take hold of him. The overseer then went to his coat, that he had laid off to whip the negro's wife, and took out his pistol and shot him dead. His master ordered him to be buried in a hole without a coffin. Stuart stated that he would not have taken two thousand dollars for him. No punishment was inflicted on the overseer.

ELEAZAR POWELL, Jr."

TESTIMONY ON THE AUTHORITY OF
REV. WILLIAM SCALES, LYNDON, VT.

The following is an extract of a letter from two professional gentlemen and their wives, who have lived for some years in a small village in one of the slave states. They are all persons of the highest respectability, and are well known in at least one of the New England states. Their names are with the Executive Committee of the American Anti-Slavery Society; but as the individuals would doubtless be murdered by the slaveholders, if they were published, the Committee feel sacredly bound to withhold them. The letter was addressed to a respected clergyman in New England. The writers say:

"A man near us owned a valuable slave—his best—most faithful servant. In a gust of passion, he struck him dead with a lever, or stick of wood.

"During the years '36 and '37, the following transpired. A slave in our neighborhood ran away and went to a place about thirty miles distant. There he was found by his pursuers on horseback, and compelled by the whip to *run* the distance of thirty miles. It was an exceedingly hot day—and within a few hours after he arrived at the end of his journey the slave was dead.

"Another slave ran away, but concluded to return. He had proceeded some distance on his return, when he was met by a company of two or three drivers, who raced, whipped and abused him until he fell down and expired. This took place on the Sabbath." The writers after speaking of another murder of a slave in the neighborhood, without giving the circumstances, say—"There is a powerful New England influence at"—the village where they reside—"We may therefore suppose that there would be as little of barbarian cruelty practiced there as any where;—at least we might suppose that the average amount of cruelty in that vicinity would be sufficiently favorable to the side of slavery.—Describe a circle, the centre of which shall be ——, the residence of the writers, and the radius fifteen miles, and in about one year three, and I think four slaves have been *murdered,* within that circle, under circumstances of horrid cruelty.—What must have been the amount of murder in the whole slave territory? The whole south is rife with the crime of separating husbands and wives, parents and children."

TESTIMONY OF JOSEPH IDE, ESQ.

Mr. IDE is a respected member of the Baptist Church in Sheffield, Caledonia county, Vt.; and recently the Postmaster in that town. He spent a few months at the south in the years 1837 and 8. In a letter to the Rev. Wm. Scales of Lyndon, Vt., written a few weeks since, Mr. Ide writes as follows.

"In answering the proposed inquiries, I will say first, that although there are various other modes resorted to, whipping with the cowskin is the usual mode of inflicting punishment on the poor slave. I have never actually witnessed a whipping scene, for they are usually taken into some back place for that purpose; but I have often heard their groans and screams while writhing under the lash; and have seen the blood flow from their torn and lacerated skins after the vengeance of the inhuman master or mistress had been glutted. You ask if the woman where I boarded whipped a slave to death. I can give you the particulars of the transaction as they were related to me. My informant was a gentleman—a member of the Presbyterian church in Massachusetts—who the winter before boarded where I did. He said that Mrs. T—— had a female slave whom she used to whip unmercifully, and on one occasion, she whipped her as long as she had strength, and after the poor creature was suffered to go, she crawled off into a cellar. As she did not immediately return, search was made, and she was found dead in the cellar, and the horrid deed was kept a secret in the family, and it was reported that she died of sickness. This wretch at the same time was a member of a Presbyterian church. Towards her slaves she was certainly the most cruel wretch of any woman with whom I was ever acquainted—yet she was nothing more than a slaveholder. She would deplore slavery as much as I did, and often told me she was as much of an abolitionist as I was. She was constant in the declaration that her kind treatment to her slaves was proverbial. Thought I, then the Lord have mercy on the rest. She has often told me of the cruel treatment of the slaves on a plantation adjoining her father's in the low country of South Carolina. She says she has often seen them driven to the necessity of eating frogs and lizards to sustain life. As to the mode of living generally, my information is rather limited, being with few exceptions confined to the different families where I have boarded. My stopping places at the south have mostly been in cities. In them the slaves are better fed and clothed than on plantations. The house servants are fed on what the families leave. But they are kept short, and I think are oftener whipped for stealing something to eat than any other crime. On plantations their food is principally hommony, as the southerners call it. It is simply cracked corn boiled. This probably constitutes seven-eights of their living. The house-servants in cities are generally decently clothed, and some favorite ones are richly dressed, but those on the plantations, especially in their dress, if it can be called dress, exhibit the most haggard and squalid appearance. I have frequently seen those of both sexes more than two-thirds naked. I have seen from forty to sixty, male and female, at work in a field, many of both sexes with their bodies entirely naked—who did not exhibit signs of shame more than cattle. As I did not go among them much on the plantations, I have had but few opportunities for examining the backs of slaves—but have frequently passed where they were at work, and been occasionally present with them, and in almost every case there were marks of violence on some parts of them—every age, sex and condition being liable to the whip. A son of the gentleman with whom I boarded, a young man about twenty-one years of age, had a plantation and eight or ten slaves. He used to boast almost every night of whipping some of them. One day he related to me a case of whipping an old negro—I should judge sixty years of age. He said he called him up to flog him for some real or supposed offence, and the poor old man, being pious, asked the privilege of praying before he received his punishment. He said he granted him the favor, and to use his own expression, 'The old nigger knelt down and prayed for me, and then got up and took his whipping.' In relation to negro huts, I will say that planters usually own large tracts of land. They have extensive clearings and a beautiful mansion house—and generally some forty or fifty rods from the dwelling are situated the negro cabins, or huts, built of logs in the rudest manner. Some consist of poles rolled up together and covered with mud or clay—many of them not as comfortable as northern pig-sties."

TESTIMONY OF REV. PHINEAS SMITH

MR. SMITH is now pastor of the Presbyterian Church in Centreville, Allegany county, N. Y. He has recently returned from a residence in the slave states, and the American slave holding settlements in Texas. The following is an extract of a letter lately received from him.

"You inquire respecting instances of cruelty that have come within my knowledge. I reply. Avarice and cruelty constitute the very gist of the whole slave system. Many of the enormities committed upon the plantations will not be described till God brings to light the hidden things of darkness, then the tears and groans and blood of innocent men, women and children will be revealed, and the oppressor's spirit must confront that of his victim.

"I will relate a case of *torture* which occurred on the Brassos while I resided a few miles distant upon the Chocolate Bayou. The case should be remembered as a true illustration of the nature of slavery, as it exists at the south. The facts are these. An overseer by the name of Alexander, notorious for his cruelty, was found dead in the timbered lands of the Brassos. It was supposed that he was murdered, but who perpetrated the act was unknown. Two black men were however seized, taken into the Prairie and put to the torture. A physician by the name of Parrott from Tennessee, and another from New England by the name of Anson Jones, were present on this occasion. The latter gentleman is now the Texan minister plenipotentiary to the United States, and resides at Washington. The unfortunate slaves being stripped, and all things arranged, the torture commenced by whipping upon their bare backs. Six athletic men were employed in this scene of inhumanity, the names of some of whom I well remember. There was one of the name of Brown, and one or two of the name of Patton. Those six executioners were successively employed in cutting up the bodies of these defenceless slaves, who persisted to the last in the avowal of their innocence. The bloody whip was however kept in motion till savage barbarity itself was glutted. When this was accomplished, the bleeding victims were re-conveyed to the inclosure of the mansion house where they were deposited for a few moments. '*The dying groans however incommoding the ladies, they were taken to a back shed where one of them soon expired.*'* The life of the other slave was for a time despaired of, but after hang-

---

* The words of Dr. Parrott, a witness on the trial hereafter referred to.

ing over the grave for months, he at length so far recovered as to walk about and labor at light work. These facts *cannot be controverted.* They were disclosed under the solemnity of an oath, at Columbia, in a court of justice. I was present, and shall never forget them. The testimony of Drs. Parrott and Jones was most appalling. I seem to hear the death-groans of that murdered man. His cries for mercy and protestations of innocence fell upon adamantine hearts. The facts above stated, and others in relation to this scene of cruelty came to light in the following manner. The master of the murdered man commenced legal process against the actors in this tragedy for the *recovery of the value of the chattel,* as one would institute a suit for a horse or an ox that had been unlawfully killed. It was a suit for the recovery of *damages* merely. No *indictment* was even dreamed of. Among the witnesses brought upon the stand in the progress of this cause were the physicians, Parrott and Jones above named. The part which they were called to act in this affair was, it is said, to examine the pulse of the victims during the process of *torture.* But they were mistaken as to the quantum of torture which a human being can undergo and not die under it. Can it be believed that one of these physicians was born and educated in the land of the pilgrims? Yes, in my own native New England. It is even so! The stone-like apathy manifested at the trial of the above cause, and the screams and the death-groans of an innocent man, as developed by the testimony of the witnesses, can never be obliterated from my memory. They form an era in my life, a point to which I look back with horror.

"Another case of cruelty occurred on the San Bernard near Chance Prairie, where I resided for some time. The facts were these. A slave man fled from his master, (Mr. Sweeny) and being closely *pursued* by the overseer and a son of the owner, he stepped a few yards in the Bernard and placed himself upon a root, from which there was no possibility of his escape, for he could not swim. In this situation he was fired upon with a blunderbuss loaded heavily with ball and grape shot. The overseer who shot the gun was at a distance of a few feet only. The charge entered the body of the negro near the groin. He was conveyed to the plantation, lingered in inexpressible agony a few days and expired. A physician was called, but medical and surgical skill was unavailing. No notice whatever was taken of this murder by the public authorities, and the murderer was not discharged from the service of his employer.

"When slaves flee, as they not unfrequently do, to the timbered lands of Texas, they are hunted with guns and dogs.

"The sufferings of the slave not unfrequently drive him to despair and suicide. At a plantation on the San Bernard, where there were but five slaves, two during the same year committed suicide by drowning."

TESTIMONY OF PHILEMON BLISS, ESQ.

Mr. Bliss is a highly respectable member of the bar, in Elyria, Lorain Co., Ohio, and member of the Presbyterian church, in that place. He resided in Florida, during the years 1834 and 5.

The following extracts are from letters, written by Mr. B. in 1835, while residing on a plantation near Tallahassee, and published soon after in the Ohio Atlas; also from letters written in 1836, and published in the New York Evangelist.

"In speaking of slavery as it is, I hardly know where to begin. The physical condition of the slave is far from being accurately known at the north. Gentlemen *traveling* in the south can know nothing of it. They must make the south their residence; they must live on plantations, before they can have any opportunity of judging of the slave. I resided in Augustine five months, and had I not made *particular* inquiries, which most northern visitors very seldom or never do, I should have left there with the impression that the slaves were generally very *well* treated, and were a happy people. Such is the report of many northern travelers who have no more opportunity of knowing their real condition than if they had remained at home. What confidence could we place in the reports of the traveler, relative to the condition of the Irish peasantry, who formed his opinion from the appearance of the waiters at a Dublin hotel, or the household servants of a country gentleman? And it is not often on plantations even, that *strangers* can witness the punishment of the slave. I was conversing the other day with a neighboring planter, upon the brutal treatment of the slaves which I had witnessed: he remarked, that had I been with him I should not have seen this. 'When I whip niggers, I take them out of sight and hearing.' Such being the difficulties in the way of a stranger's ascertaining the treatment of the slaves, it is not to be wondered at that gentlemen, of undoubted veracity, should give directly false statements relative to it. But facts cannot lie, and in giving these I confine myself to what has come under my own personal observation.

"The negroes commence labor by daylight in the morning, and, excepting the plowboys, who must feed and rest their horses, do not leave the field till dark in the evening. There is a good deal of contention among planters, who shall make the most cotton to the hand, or, who shall drive their negroes the hardest; and I have heard bets made and staked upon the issue of the crops. Col. W. was boasting of his large crops, and swore that 'he made for his force, the largest crops in the country.' He was disputed of course. On riding home in company with Mr. C. the conversation turned upon Col. W. My companion remarked, that though Col. W. had the reputation of making a large crop, yet he could beat him himself, and did do it the last year. I remarked that I considered it no honor to *Col. W.* to drive his slaves to death to make a large crop. I have heard no more about large crops from him since. Drivers or overseers usually drive the slaves worse than masters.—Their reputation for good overseers depends in a great measure upon the crops they make, and the death of a slave is no loss to them.

"Of the extent and cruelty of the punishment of the slave, the northern public know nothing. From the nature of the case they can know little, as I have before mentioned.

"I *have seen* a woman, a mother, compelled, in the presence of her master and mistress, *to hold up her clothes,* and endure the whip of the driver on the naked body for more than *twenty minutes,* and while her cries would have rent the heart of any one, who had not hardened himself to human suffering, her master and mistress were conversing with apparent indifference. What was her crime? She had a task given her of sewing which she *must finish* that day. Late at night she finished it; but *the stitches were too long,* and she must be whipped. The same was repeated three or four nights for the same offence. *I have seen* a man tied to a tree, hands and feet, and receive 305 blows with the paddle* on the fleshy parts of the body. Two others received the same kind of punishment at the time, though I did not count the blows. One received 230 lashes. Their crime was stealing mutton. I have *frequently* heard the shrieks of the slaves, male and female, accompanied by the strokes of the paddle or whip, when I have not gone near the scene of horror. I knew not their crimes, excepting of one

---

* A piece of oak timber two and a half feet long, flat and wide at one end.

woman, which was stealing *four potatoes* to eat with her bread! The more common number of lashes inflicted was fifty or eighty; and this I saw not once or twice, but so frequently that I can not tell the number of times I have seen it. So frequently, that my own heart was becoming so hardened that I could witness with comparative indifference, the female writhe under the lash, and her shrieks and cries for mercy ceased to pierce my heart with that keenness, or give me that anguish which they first caused. It was not always that I could learn their crimes; but of those I did learn, the most common was non-performance of tasks. I have seen men strip and receive from one to three hundred strokes of the whip and paddle. My studies and meditations were almost nightly interrupted by the cries of the victims of cruelty and avarice. Tom, a slave of Col. N. obtained permission of his overseer on Sunday, to visit his son, on a neighboring plantation, belonging in part to his master, but neglected to take a "pass." Upon its being demanded by the other overseer, he replied that he had permission to come, and that his having a mule was sufficient evidence of it, and if he did not consider it as such, he could, take him up. The overseer replied he would take him up; giving him at the same time a blow on the arm with a stick he held in his hand, sufficient to lame it for some time. The negro collared him, and threw him; and on the overseer's commanding him to submit to be tied and whipped, he said he would not be whipped by *him* but would leave it to massa J. They came to massa J.'s. I was there. After the overseer had related the case as above, he was blamed for not shooting or stabbing him at once.—After dinner the negro was tied, and the whip given to the overseer, and he used it with a severity that was shocking. I know not how many lashes were given, but from his shoulders to his heels there was not a spot unridged! and at almost every stroke the blood flowed. He could not have received less than 300, *well laid on*. But his offence was great, almost the greatest known, laying hands on a *white* man! Had he struck the overseer, under any provocation, he would have been in some way disfigured, perhaps by the loss of his ears, in addition to a whipping: or he might have been hung. The most common cause of punishments is, not finishing tasks.

"But it would be tedious mentioning further particulars. The negro has no other inducement to work but the *lash*; and as man never acts without motive, the lash must be used so long as all other motives are withheld. Hence corporeal punishment is a necessary part of slavery.

"Punishments for runaways are usually severe. Once whipping is not sufficient. I have known runaways to be whipped for six or seven nights in succession for one offence. I have known others who, with pinioned hands, and a chain extending from an iron collar on their neck, to the saddle of their master's horse, have been driven at a smart trot, one or two hundred miles, being compelled to ford water courses, their drivers, according to their own confession, not abating a whit in the rapidity of their journey for the ease of the slave. One tied a kettle of sand to his slave to render his journey more arduous.

"Various are the instruments of torture devised to keep the slave in subjection. The stocks are sometimes used. Sometimes blocks are filled with pegs and nails, and the slave compelled to stand upon them.

"While stopping on the plantation of a Mr. C. I saw a whip with a knotted lash lying on the table, and inquired of my companion, who was also an acquaintance of Mr. C.'s, if he used that to whip his negroes? 'Oh,' says he, 'Mr. C. is not severe with his hands. He never whips very hard. The *knots in the lash are so large* that he does not usually draw blood in whipping them.'

"It was principally from hearing the conversation of southern men on the subject, that I judge of the cruelty that is generally practiced toward slaves. They will deny that slaves are generally ill treated: but ask them if they are not whipped for certain offences, which either a freeman would have no temptation to commit, or which would not be an offence in any but a slave, and for non-performance of tasks, they will answer promptly in the affirmative. And frequently have I heard them excuse their cruelty by citing Mr. A. or Mr. B. who is a Christian, or Mr. C. a preacher, or Mr. D. from the *north,* who 'drives his hands tighter, and whips them harder, than we ever do.' Driving negroes to the utmost extent of their ability, with occasionally a hundred lashes or more, and a few switchings in the field if they hang back in the driving seasons, viz: in the hoeing and picking months, is perfectly consistent with good treatment!

"While traveling across the Peninsula in a stage, in company with a northern gentleman, and southern lady, of great worth and piety, a dispute arose respecting the general treatment of slaves, the gentleman contending that their treatment was generally good—'Oh, no!' interrupted the lady, 'you can know nothing of the treatment they receive on the plantations. People here do whip the poor negroes most cruelly and many half starve them. You have neither of you had opportunity to know scarcely any thing of the cruelties that are practiced in this country,' and more to the same effect. I met with several others, besides this lady, who appeared to feel for the sins of the land, but they are few and scattered, and not usually of sufficiently stern mould to withstand the popular wave.

"Masters are not forward to publish their 'domestic regulations,' and as neighbors are usually several miles apart, one's observation must be limited. Hence the few instances of cruelty which break out can be but a fraction of what is practised. A planter, a professor of religion, in conversation upon the universality of whipping, remarked that a planter in G——, who had whipped a great deal, at length got tired of it, and invented the following *excellent* method of punishment, which I saw practised while I was paying him a visit. The negro was placed in a sitting position, with his hands made fast above his head, and feet in the stocks, so that he could not move any part of the body.

"The master retired, intending to leave him till morning, but we were awakened in the night by the groans of the negro, which were so doleful that we feared he was dying. We went to him, and found him covered with a cold sweat, and almost gone. He could not have lived an hour longer. Mr. —— found the 'stocks' such an effective punishment, that it almost superseded the whip.

"'How much do you give your niggers for a task while hoeing cotton?'" inquired Mr. C.—— of his neighbor Mr. H.——.

H: "'I give my men an acre and a quarter, and my women an acre.'*

C: "'Well, that is a fair task. Niggers do a heap better if they are drove pretty tight.'

H: "'Oh yes, I have driven mine into complete subordination. When I first bought them they were discontented and wished me to sell them, but I soon whipped *that* out of them; and they now work very contentedly!'

C: "'Does Mary keep up with the rest?'

H: "'No, she doesn't often finish the task alone, she has to get Sam to help her out after he has done his, *to save her a whipping.* There's no other way but to be severe with them.'

C: "'No other, sir, if you favor a nigger you spoil him.'

"The whip is considered as necessary on a plantation as the plough; and its use is almost as common. The negro whip is the common

---

* Cotton is planted in drills about three feet apart, and is hilled like corn.

teamster's whip with a black leather stock, and a short, fine, knotted lash. The paddle is also frequently used, sometimes with holes bored in the flattened end. The ladies (!) in chastising their domestic servants, generally use the cowhide. I have known some use shovel and tongs. It is, however, more common to commit them to the driver to be whipped. The manner of whipping is as follows: The negro is tied by his hands, and sometimes feet, to a post or tree, and stripped to the skin. The female slave is not always tied. The number of lashes depends upon the character for severity of the master or overseer.

"Another instrument of torture is sometimes used, how extensively I know not. The negro, or, in the case which came to my knowledge, the negress was compelled to stand barefoot upon a block filled with sharp pegs and nails for two or three hours. In case of sickness, if the master or overseer thinks them seriously ill, they are taken care of, but their complaints are usually not much heeded. A physician told me that he was employed by a planter last winter to go to a plantation of his in the country, as many of the negroes were sick. Says he—'I found them in a most miserable condition. The weather was cold, and the negroes were barefoot, with hardly enough of *cotton* clothing to cover their nakedness. Those who had huts to shelter them were obliged to build them nights and Sundays. Many were sick and some had died. I had the sick taken to an older plantation of their masters, where they could be made comfortable, and they recovered. I directed that they should not go to work till after sunrise, and should not work in the rain till their health became established. But the overseer refusing to permit it, I declined attending on them farther. I was called,' continued he, 'by the overseer of another plantation to see one of the men. I found him lying by the side of a log in great pain. I asked him how he did, "Oh," says he, "I'm most dead, can live but little longer." "How long have you been sick?" "I've felt for more than six weeks as though I could hardly stir." "Why didn't you tell your master, you was sick?" "I couldn't see my master, and the overseer always whips us when we complain. I could not stand a whipping." 'I did all I could for the poor fellow, but his *lungs were rotten*. He died in three days from the time he left off work.' The cruelty of that overseer is such that the negroes almost tremble at his name. Yet he gets a high salary, for he makes the largest crop of any other man in the neighborhood, though none but the hardiest negroes can stand it under him. 'That man,' says the Doctor, 'would be hung in my country.' He was a German."

TESTIMONY OF REV. WILLIAM A. CHAPIN

Rev. WILLIAM SCALES, of Lyndon, Vermont, has furnished the following testimony, under date of Dec. 15, 1838.

"I send you an extract from a letter that I have just received, which you may use *ad libitum*. The letter is from Rev. Wm. A. Chapin, Greensborough, Vermont. To one who is acquainted with Mr. C. his opinion and statements must carry conviction even to the most obstinate and incredulous. He observes, 'I resided, as a teacher, nearly two years in the family of Carroll Webb, Esq., of Hampstead, New Kent co. about twenty miles from Richmond, Virginia. Mr. Webb had three or four plantations, and was considered one of the two wealthiest men in the county: it was supposed he owned about two hundred slaves. He was a member of the Presbyterian Church, and was elected an elder while I was with him. He was a native of Virginia, but a graduate of a New England college.'

" 'The slaves were called in the morning before daylight, I believe at all seasons of the year, that they might prepare their food, and be ready to go to work as soon as it was light enough to see. I know that at the season of husking corn, October and November, they were usually compelled to work late—till 12 or 1 o'clock at night. I know this fact because they accompanied their work with a loud singing of their own sort. I usually retired to rest between 11 and 12 o'clock, and generally heard them at their work as long as I was awake. The slaves lived in wretched log cabins, of one room each, without floors or windows. I believe the slaves sometimes suffer for want of food. One evening, as I was sitting in the parlor with Mr. W. one of the most resolute of the slaves came to the door, and said, "Master, I am willing to work for you, but I want something to eat." The only reply was, "Clear yourself." I learned that the slaves had been without food all day, because the man who was sent to mill could not obtain his grinding. He went again the next day, and obtained his grist, and the slaves had no food till he returned. He had to go about five miles.'*

---

* To this, Rev. Mr. Scales adds, "In familiar language, and in more detail, as I have learned it in conversation with Mr. Chapin, the fact is as follows:—

"Mr. W. kept, what he called a 'boy,' i. e. a *man*, to go to mill. It was his custom not to give his slaves anything to eat while he was gone to mill—let him have been gone longer or shorter—for this reason, if he was lazy, and delayed, the slaves would become hungry; hence indignant, and abuse him—this was his punishment. On that occasion he went to mill in the morning.

"'I know the slaves were sometimes severely whipped. I saw the backs of several which had numerous scars, evidently caused by long and deep lacerations of the whip; and I have good reason to believe that the slaves were generally in that condition; for I never saw the back of one exposed that was not thus marked,—and from their tattered and scanty clothing their backs were often exposed.'"

TESTIMONY OF MESSRS.
T. D. M. AND F. C. MACY

This testimony is communicated in a letter from Mr. Cyrus Pierce, a respectable and well known citizen of Nantucket, Mass. Of the witnesses, Messrs. T. D. M. and F. C. Macy, Mr. Pierce says, "They are both inhabitants of this island, and have resided at the south; they are both worthy men, for whose integrity and intelligence I can vouch unqualifiedly; the former has furnished me with the following statement.

"During the winter of 1832–3, I resided on the island of St. Simon, Glynn county, Georgia. There are several extensive cotton plantations on the island. The overseer of the plantation on that part of the island where I resided was a Georgian—a man of stern character, and at times *cruelly abusive* to his slaves. I have often been witness of the *abuse* of his power. In South Carolina and Georgia, on the low lands, the cultivation is chiefly of rice. The land where it is raised is often inundated, and the labor of preparing it, and raising a crop, is very arduous. Men and women are in the field from earliest dawn to dark—often *without hats,* and up to their arm-pits in mud and water. At St. Simon's, cotton was the staple article. Ocra, the driver, usually waited on the overseer to receive orders for the succeeding day. If any slave was

---

The slaves came up at noon, and returned to work without food. At night, after having worked hard all day, without food, went to bed without supper. About 10 o'clock the next day, they came up in a company, to their master's door, (that master an elder in the church), and deputed one more resolute than the rest to address him. This he did in the most respectful tones and terms. 'We are willing to work for you, master, but we can't work without food; we want something to eat.' 'Clear yourself,' was the answer. The slaves retired; and in the morning were driven away to work without food. At noon, I think, or somewhat after, they were fed."

insolent, or negligent, the driver was authorized to punish him with the whip, with as many blows as the magnitude of the crime justified. He was frequently cautioned, upon the peril of his skin, to see that all the negroes were off to the field in the morning. 'Ocra,' said the overseer, one evening, to the driver, 'if any pretend to be sick, send me word—allow no lazy wench or fellow to skulk in the negro house.' Next morning, a few minutes after the departure of the hands to the field, Ocra was seen hastening to the house of the overseer. He was soon in his presence. 'Well, Ocra, what now?' 'Nothing, sir, only Rachel says she sick—can't go to de field to-day.' 'Ah, sick, is she? I'll see to her; you may be off. She shall see if I am longer to be fooled with in this way. Here, Christmas, mix these salts—bring them to me at the negro house.' And seizing his whip, he made off to the negro settlement. Having a strong desire to see what would be the result, I followed him. As I approached the negro house, I heard high words. Rachel was stating her complaint—children were crying from fright— and the overseer threatening. Rachel.—'I can't work to-day—I'm sick.' Overseer.—'But you shall work, if you die for it. Here, take these salts. Now move off—quick—let me see your face again before night, and, by G—d, you shall smart for it. Be off—no begging—not a word;'—and he dragged her from the house, and followed her 20 or 30 rods, threatening. The woman did not reach the field. Overcome by the exertion of walking, and by agitation, she sunk down exhausted by the road side—was taken up, and carried back to the house, where an *abortion* occurred, and her life was greatly jeoparded.

"It was *no uncommon* sight to see a whole family, father, mother, and from two to five children, collected together around their piggin of hommony, or pail of potatoes, watched by the overseer. One meal was always eaten in the field. No time was allowed for relaxation.

"It was not unusual for a child of five or six years to perform the office of nurse—because the mother worked in a remote part of the field, and was not allowed to leave her employment to take care of her infant. Want of proper nutriment induces sickness of the worst type.

"No matter what the nature of the service, a peck of corn, dealt out on Sunday, must supply the demands of nature for a week.

"The Sabbath, on a southern plantation, is a mere nominal holiday. The slaves are liable to be called upon at all times, by those who have authority over them.

"When it rained, the slaves were allowed to collect under a tree until the shower had passed. Seldom, on a week day, were they permitted to go to their huts during rain; and even had this privilege been granted, many of those miserable habitations were in so dilapidated a condition, that they would afford little or no protection. Negro huts are built of logs, covered with boards or thatch, having *no flooring,* and but one apartment, serving all the purposes of sleeping, cooking, &c. Some are furnished with a temporary loft. I have seen a whole family herded together in a loft ten feet by twelve. In cold weather, they gather around the fire, spread their blankets *on the ground,* and keep as comfortable as they can. Their supply of clothing is scanty—each slave being allowed a Holland coat and pantaloons, of the coarsest manufacture, and one pair of cowhide shoes. The women, enough of the same kind of cloth for one frock. They have also one pair of shoes. Shoes are given to the slaves in the winter only. In summer, their clothing is composed of osnaburgs. Slaves on different plantations are not allowed without a written permission, to visit their fellow bondsmen, under penalty of severe chastisement. I witnessed the chastisement of a young male slave, who was found lurking about the plantation, and could give no other account of himself, than that he wanted to visit some of his acquaintance. Fifty lashes was the penalty for this offence. I could not endure the dreadful shrieks of the tortured slave, and rushed away from the scene."

The remainder of this testimony is furnished by Mr. F. C. MACY. "I went to Savannah in 1820. Sailing up the river, I had my first view of slavery. A large number of men and women, with *a piece of board on their heads, carrying mud,* for the purpose of dyking, near the river. After tarrying a while in Savannah, I went down to the sea islands of De Fuskee and Hilton Head, where I spent six months. Negro houses are small, built of rough materials, *and no floor.* Their clothing, (one suit), coarse; which they received on Christmas day. Their food was three pecks of potatoes per week, in the potato season, and one peck of corn the remainder of the year. The slaves carried with them into the field their meal, and a gourd of water. They cooked their hommony in the field, and ate it with a wooden paddle. Their treatment was little better than that of brutes. *Whipping* was nearly an every-day practice. On Mr. M——'s plantation, at the island De Fuskee, I saw an old man whipped; he was about 60. He had no clothing on, except a shirt. The man that inflicted the blows was Flim, a tall and stout man. The whipping was *very severe.* I inquired into the cause. Some vegetables had been stolen from his master's garden, of which he could give no account. I saw several women whipped, some of whom were in very *delicate* circumstances. The case of one I will relate. She had been purchased in Charleston, and separated from her husband. On her passage to Savannah, or rather to the island, she was delivered of a child; and in about three weeks after this, she appeared to be deranged. She would leave her work, go into the woods, and sing. Her master sent for her, and ordered the driver to whip her. I was near enough to hear the strokes.

"I have known negro boys, partly by persuasion. and partly by force, made to strip off their clothing and fight for *the amusement of their masters*. They would fight until both got to crying.

"One of the planters told me that his boat had been used without permission. A number of his negroes were called up, and put in a building that was lathed and shingled. The covering could be easily removed from the inside. He called one out for examination. While examining this one, he discovered another negro, coming out of the roof. He ordered him back: he obeyed. In a few moments he attempted it again. The master took deliberate aim at his head, but his gun missed fire. He told me he should probably have killed him, had his gun gone off. The negro jumped and run. The master took aim again, and fired; but he was so far distant, that he received only a few shots in the calf of his leg. After several days he returned, and received a severe whipping.

"Mr. B——, planter at Hilton Head, freely confessed, that he kept one of his slaves as a mistress. She slept in the same room with him. This, I think, is a very common practice."

TESTIMONY OF A CLERGYMAN

The following letter was written to Mr. ARTHUR TAPPAN, of New York, in the summer of 1833. As the name of the writer cannot be published with safety to himself, it is withheld.

The following testimonials, from Mr. TAPPAN, Professor WRIGHT, and THOMAS RITTER, M. D. of New York, establish the trustworthiness and high respectability of the writer.

"I received the following letters from the south during the year 1833. They were written by a gentleman who had then resided some years in the slave states. Not being at liberty to give the writer's name,

I cheerfully certify that he is a gentleman of established character, a graduate of Yale College, and a respected minister of the gospel.

"ARTHUR TAPPAN."

"My acquaintance with the writer of the following letter commenced, I believe, in 1823, from which time we were fellow students in Yale College till 1826. I have occasionally seen him since. His character, so far as it has come within my knowledge, has been that of an upright and remarkably *candid* man. I place great confidence both in his habits of careful and unprejudiced observation and his veracity.

"E. WRIGHT, jun.
"New York, April 13, 1839."

"I have been acquainted with the writer of the following letter about twelve years, and know him to be a gentleman of high respectability, integrity, and piety. We were fellow students in Yale College, and my opportunities for judging of his character, both at that time and since our graduation, have been such, that I feel myself fully warranted in making the above unequivocal declaration.

"THOMAS RITTER.
"104, Cherry-street, New York."

"NATCHEZ, 1833.

"It has been almost four years since I came to the south-west; and although I have been told, from month to month, that I should soon wear off my northern prejudices, and probably have slaves of my own, yet my judgment in regard to oppression, or my prejudices, if they are pleased so to call them, remain with me still. I judge still from those principles which were fixed in my mind at the north; and a residence at the south has not enabled me so to pervert truth, as to make injustice appear justice.

"I have studied the state of things here, now for years, coolly and deliberately, with the eye of an uninterested looker on; and hence I may not be altogether unprepared to state to you some facts, and to draw conclusions from them.

"Permit me then to relate what I have seen; and do not imagine that these are all exceptions to the general treatment, but rather believe that thousands of cruelties are practised in this Christian land, every year, which no eye that ever shed a tear of pity could look upon.

"Soon after my arrival I made an excursion into the country, to the distance of some twenty miles. And as I was passing by a cotton field, where about fifty negroes were at work, I was inclined to stop by the road side to view a scene which was then new to me. While I was, in my mind, comparing this mode of labor with that of my own native place, I heard the driver, with a rough oath, order one that was near him, who seemed to be laboring to the extent of his power, to "lie down." In a moment he was obeyed; and he commenced whipping the offender upon his naked back, and continued, to the amount of about twenty lashes, with a heavy raw-hide whip, the crack of which might have been heard more than half a mile. Nor did the females escape; for although I stopped scarcely fifteen minutes, no less than three were whipped in the same manner, and that so severely, I was strongly inclined to interfere.

"You may be assured, sir, that I remained not unmoved: I could no longer look on such cruelty, but turned away and rode on, while the echoes of the lash were reverberating in the woods around me. Such scenes have long since become familiar to me. But then the full effect was not lost; and I shall never forget, to my latest day, the mingled feelings of pity, horror, and indignation that took possession of my mind. I involuntarily exclaimed, O God of my fathers, how dost thou permit such things to defile our land! Be merciful to us! and visit us not in justice, for all our iniquities and the iniquities of our fathers!

"As I passed on I soon found that I had escaped from one horrible scene only to witness another. A planter with whom I was well acquanted, had caught a negro without a pass. And at the moment I was passing by, he was in the act of fastening his feet and hands to the trees, having previously made him take off all his clothing except his trowsers. When he had sufficiently secured this poor creature, he beat him for several minutes with a green switch more than six feet long; while he was writhing with anguish, endeavoring in vain to break the cords with which he was bound, and incessantly crying out, 'Lord, master! do pardon me this time! do, master, have mercy!' These expressions have recurred to me a thousand times since; and although they came from one that is not considered among the sons of men, yet I think they are well worthy of remembrance, as they might lead a wise man to consider whether such shall receive mercy from the righteous Judge, as never showed mercy to their fellow men.

"At length I arrived at the dwelling of a planter of my acquaintance, with whom I passed the night. At about eight o'clock in the evening I heard the barking of several dogs, mingled with the most agonizing cries that I ever heard from any human being. Soon after the gentleman came in, and began to apologize, by saying that two of his runaway slaves had just been brought home; and as he had previously tried every species of punishment upon them without effect, he knew not what else to add, except to set his blood hounds upon them. 'And,' continued he, 'one of them has been so badly bitten that he has been trying to die. I am only sorry that he did not; for then I should not have been further troubled with him. If he lives I intend to send him to Natchez or to New Orleans, to work with the ball and chain.'

"From this last remark I understood that private individuals have the right of thus subjecting their unmanageable slaves. I have since seen numbers of these 'ball and chain' men, both in Natchez and New Orleans, but I do not know whether there were any among them except the state convicts.

"As the summer was drawing towards a close, and the yellow fever beginning to prevail in town, I went to reside some months in the country. This was the cotton picking season, during which, the planters say, there is a greater necessity for flogging than at any other time. And I can assure you, that as I have sat in my window night after night, while the cotton was being weighed, I have heard the crack of the whip, without much intermission, for a whole hour, from no less than three plantations, some of which were a full mile distant.

"I found that the slaves were kept in the field from daylight until dark; and then, if they had not gathered what the master or overseer thought sufficient, they were subjected to the lash.

"Many by such treatment are induced to run away and take up their lodging in the woods. I do not say that all who run away are thus closely pressed, but I do know that many are; and I have known no less than a dozen desert at a time from the same plantation, in consequence of the overseer's forcing them to work to the extent of their power, and then whipping them for not having done more.

"But suppose that they run away—what is to become of them in the forest? If they cannot steal they must perish of hunger—if the nights are cold, their feet will be frozen; for if they make a fire they may be discovered, and be shot at. If they attempt to leave the country, their chance of success is about nothing. They must return, be whipped—if old offenders, wear the collar, perhaps be branded, and fare worse than before.

"Do you believe it, sir, not six months since, I saw a number of my *Christian* neighbors packing up provisions, as I supposed for a deer hunt; but as I was about offering myself to the party, I learned that their powder and balls were destined to a very different purpose: it was, in short, the design of the party to bring home a number of runaway slaves, or to shoot them if they should not be able to get possession of them in any other way.

"You will ask, Is not this murder? Call it, sir, by what name you please, such are the facts:—many are shot every year, and that too while the masters say they treat their slaves well.

"But let me turn your attention to another species of cruelty. About a year since I knew a certain slave who had deserted his master, to be caught, and for the first time fastened to the stocks. In those same stocks, from which at midnight I have heard cries of distress, while the master slept, and was dreaming, perhaps, of drinking wine and of discussing the price of cotton. On the next morning he was chained in an immovable posture, and branded in both cheeks with red hot stamps of iron. Such are the tender mercies of men who love wealth, and are determined to obtain it at any price.

"Suffer me to add another to the list of enormities, and I will not offend you with more.

"There was, some time since, brought to trial in this town a planter residing about fifteen miles distant, for whipping his slave to death. You will suppose, of course, that he was punished. No, sir, he was acquitted, although there could be no doubt of the fact. I heard the tale of murder from a man who was acquainted with all the circumstances. 'I was,' said he, 'passing along the road near the burying-ground of the plantation, about nine o'clock at night, when I saw several lights gleaming through the woods; and as I approached, in order to see what was doing, I beheld the coroner of Natchez, with a number of men, standing around the body of a young female, which by the torches seemed almost perfectly white. On inquiry I learned that the master had so unmercifully beaten this girl that she died under the operation: and that also he had so severely punished another of his slaves that he was but just alive.'"

We here rest the case for the present, so far as respects the presentation of facts showing the condition of the slaves, and proceed to consider the main objections which are usually employed to weaken such testimony, or wholly to set it aside. But before we enter upon the examination of specific objections, and introductory to them, we remark,—

1. That the system of slavery must be a system of horrible cruelty, follows of necessity, from the fact that two millions seven hundred thousand human beings *are held by force,* and used as articles of property. Nothing but a heavy yoke, and an iron one, could possibly keep so many necks in the dust. That must be a constant and mighty pressure which holds so still such a vast army; nothing could do it but the daily experience of severities, and the ceaseless dread and certainty of the most terrible inflictions if they should dare to toss in their chains.

2. Were there nothing else to prove it a system of monstrous cruelty, the fact that FEAR is the only motive with which the slave is plied during his whole existence, would be sufficient to brand it with execration as the grand tormentor of man. The slave's *susceptibility of pain* is the sole fulcrum on which slavery works the lever that moves him. In this it plants all its stings; here it sinks its hot irons; cuts its deep gashes; flings its burning embers, and dashes its boiling brine and liquid fire: into this it strikes its cold flesh hooks, grappling irons, and instruments of nameless torture; and by it drags him shrieking to the end of his pilgrimage. The fact that the master inflicts pain upon the slave not merely as an *end* to gratify passion, but constantly as a *means* of extorting labor, is enough of itself to show that the system of slavery is unmixed cruelty.

3. That the slaves must suffer frequent and terrible inflictions, follows inevitably from the *character of those who direct their labor.* Whatever may be the character of the slaveholders themselves, all agree that the overseers are, as a class, most abandoned, brutal, and desperate men. This is so well known and believed that any testimony to prove it seems needless. The testimony of Mr. WIRT, late Attorney General of the United States, a Virginian and a slaveholder, is as follows. In his life of Patrick Henry, p. 36, speaking of the different classes of society in Virginia, he says,—"Last and lowest a feculum, of beings called 'overseers'—*the most abject, degraded, unprincipled race,* always cap in hand to the dons who employ them, and furnishing materials for the exercise of their *pride, insolence, and spirit of domination.*"

Rev. PHINEAS SMITH, of Centreville, New York, who has resided some years at the south, says of overseers—

"It need hardly be added that overseers are in general ignorant, *unprincipled and cruel,* and in such low repute that they are not permitted to come to the tables of their employers; yet they have the constant control of all the human cattle that belong to the master.

"These men are continually advancing from their low station to the higher one of masters. These changes bring into the possession of power a class of men of whose mental and moral qualities I have already spoken."

Rev. HORACE MOULTON, of Marlborough, Massachusetts, who lived in Georgia several years, says of them,—

"The overseers are *generally loose in their morals*; it is the object of masters to employ those whom they think will get the most work out of their hands,—hence those who *whip and torment the slaves the most* are in many instances called the best overseers. The masters think those whom the slaves fear the most are the best. Quite a portion of the masters employ their own slaves as overseers, or rather they are called drivers; these are more subject to the will of the masters than the white overseers are; some of them are as lordly as an Austrian prince, and sometimes more cruel even than the whites."

That the overseers are, as a body, sensual, brutal, and violent men is *proverbial*. The tender mercies of such men *must be cruel*.

4. The *ownership* of human beings necessarily presupposes an utter disregard of their happiness. He who assumes it monopolizes their *whole capital,* leaves them no stock on which to trade, and out of which to *make* happiness. Whatever is the master's gain is the slave's loss, a loss wrested from him by the master, for the express purpose of making it *his own gain*; this is the master's constant employment—forcing the slave to toil—violently wringing from him all he has and all he gets, and using it as his own;—like the vile bird that never builds its nest from materials of its own gathering, but either drives other birds from theirs and takes possession of them, or tears them in pieces to get the means of constructing their own. This daily practice of forcibly robbing others, and habitually living on the plunder, cannot but beget in the mind the *habit* of regarding the interests and happiness of those whom it robs, as of no sort of consequence in comparison with its own; consequently whenever those interests and this happiness are in the way of its own gratification, they will be sacrificed without scruple. He who cannot see this would be unable to *feel* it, if it were seen.